Children, Democracy, and Education

Children, Democracy, and Education

A Deliberative Reconsideration

KEI NISHIYAMA

SUNY
PRESS

EU GPSR Authorised Representative:
Logos Europe, 9 rue Nicolas Poussin, 17000, La Rochelle, France
contact@logoseurope.eu

For information, contact State University of New York Press, Albany, NY
www.sunypress.edu

Library of Congress Cataloging-in-Publication Data

Name: Nishiyama, Kei, 1990– author.
Title: Children, democracy, and education : a deliberative reconsideration / Kei Nishiyama.
Description: Albany, New York : State University of New York Press, [2025] | Includes bibliographical references and index.
Identifiers: LCCN 2024039366 | ISBN 9798855801583 (hardcover : alk. paper) | ISBN 9798855801606 (ebook) | ISBN 9798855801590 (pbk. : alk. paper)
Subjects: LCSH: Democracy and education. | Deliberative democracy—Philosophy. | Children—Political activity. | Education and state.
Classification: LCC LC71 .N56 2025 | DDC 379—dc23/eng/20241114
LC record available at https://lccn.loc.gov/2024039366

For Eri and Yuka

Contents

List of Illustrations   ix

Preface   xi

Acknowledgements   xv

Introduction   1

Part I. Theory

1. Children in Deliberative Democracy   25

2. Theorizing Deliberative Democratic Learning   51

Part II. Classroom

3. Reason-Giving in the Classroom   91

4. Listening in the Classroom   117

5. Ethics of Facilitation   139

Part III. Beyond the Classroom

6. The Democratic School as a Mediating Space   165

7. Deliberative Activism 191

Conclusion 223

Appendix 231

Notes 235

Works Cited 251

Index 269

Illustrations

Figures

2.1. Vygotsky's socioculturally mediated act model.   75

2.2. Engeström's expansive model of Vygotsky's triangle.   77

2.3. A revolutionary process of deliberative meaning-making.   83

3.1. Fake Morrison in a climate protest in Sydney, December 8, 2018.   102

3.2. Students' own good communication guidelines: DELIBERATE.   110

3.3. Democratic school as a fun space.   115

4.1. Students' deliberative norm-making.   133

5.1. Disagreement worksheet.   158

6.1. School as a mediating space.   176

7.1. Standing.   192

7.2. M's placard.   199

7.3. Various types of cardboard placard.   203

7.4. Two-person climate protest march and a banner with handprint images.   207

Tables

2.1. Examples of normatively required deliberative
      competencies.   53–54

3.1. When reason-giving turns into a (non- or anti-)deliberative
      practice: Examples.   103

Preface

This book is about children in contemporary democracies and education. I began working on this theme when I was a first-year graduate student in 2012—a year after the great tsunami and nuclear power plant disaster in Japan. At that time, thousands of protestors regularly gathered in front the of the prime minister's residence to criticize the government's decision to reactivate some nuclear power plants. One day, after class, I dropped by to see how the anti-nuclear protest was going. The crowd beat drums and shouted various slogans to express their anger and anxiety. I immediately noticed that there were many shouts and slogans that said "for our children's future!" We adults often use this phrase in various occasions when the world or society becomes more chaotic, notable recent examples being global wars, pandemics, the climate crisis, and (anti-)racism. I do not think that using this phrase is wrong in its own right. When I saw the protests, however, I felt something was wrong with the phrase "for our children's future." Upon closer inspection, only adults were present at the protest, and I couldn't find the presence and voice of real children. If we adults claim and decide "our children's future" without the participation of said children, can we really say that what we are doing is democratic?

The world human population has been climbing for the past couple of decades, with more than a quarter of the population being children. However, I often feel that neither politics nor education have genuinely listened to the voices of this growing population. Both politics and education are cornerstones of democracy, but has it been discussed, theorized, and implemented democratically? Perhaps, and unfortunately, the answer is "no," because both have excluded the marginalized voices of children. Democratic politics is based on the idea that everyone subjected to collective decisions should have a say in those decisions, but in those supposedly democratic governments voices of children are rarely heard. Education is necessary in order to realize and sustain a healthy democracy, but children normally are given no ownership to theorize, design, and implement what, how, and for what purpose they should learn in order to help realize and sustain their democracy.

Democracy has long been discussed as an adult's domain—that is, politicians, educators, parents, and researchers have exclusively discussed it from their adult point of view, and what is expected for children is whether and to what degree they can learn and then fit into the norm and practice of democracy predetermined by those adults. But, if democracy (and the education and politics that underpin it) were to take children's experiences, viewpoints, and voices into account, how would it do so? This does not mean that we have to uncritically accept everything children propose. My question is more about finding a fairer way of weighing both the opinions of children and adults. In other words, I wondered how we adults who have long dominated the process of theorization, design, and implementation of democratic education and democratic politics can share a key part of our privilege in a way that empowers children.

Against this backdrop, I started writing this book. But the biggest challenge I was confronted with was the fact that *I am an adult* (and now university teacher and father of my daughter). When I tried to theorize democracy with respect to politics and education *for our children*, my writing was sometimes interrupted by my inner adultness and my internalized (or socialized) adult viewpoints. Some of these viewpoints were useful for my writing because these are underpinned by widely justified beliefs. However, some of these viewpoints caused me to falsely represent the "voices of children" by writing something paternalistic and one-sided. This is why I devoted most of my time not to writing alone in my office but to doing fieldwork (in classrooms, schools, and on the streets) in order to be with children. To understand children in relation to democracy, politics, and education, I tried to see and listen to children as much as possible. What I observed and heard was brought back to my office, and I (re)started doing my theoretical work. Then, I went back to the field again. By going back and forth between my office and the field, I refined my research and book. Of course, my inner adultness did not disappear altogether even after my fieldwork. Nonetheless, my series of field experiences hopefully helped neutralize my inner adultness to a greater extent, thereby allowing me to theorize the value of children in democracy, education, and politics—*with the participation of children.*

As readers might immediately notice, this book's main field can be categorized as philosophy of education in a broader sense. But *philosophy* here is not just speculative. It is also practical and significantly anchored by my praxis. I dedicate this book not only to philosophers of education but also to theorists and practitioners who (are planning to or want to) practice education, politics, and democracy with children.

Acknowledgments

I started this book at the end of 2019, and many significant events happened around the same time. I got my PhD at the University of Canberra, the COVID-19 pandemic occurred, and, most importantly, I became a dad. I did most of the work on this book during my time at Doshisha University (Kyoto, Japan) as an assistant professor. It was a nontenure contract, but the university provided me with valuable opportunities to proceed with the research and writing for this book even during the pandemic. Thanks to the great support from Doshisha University, I got a couple of research grants that enabled me to collect data and focus on writing this book.

But, as many readers would probably know, concepts and ideas of an academic book do not suddenly appear out of thin air. I slowly, and yet thoroughly, developed the original idea of the book when I was a PhD student and post-PhD researcher at the Centre for Deliberative Democracy and Global Governance at the University of Canberra. Its monthly reading group, regular seminar series, weekly morning tea, everyday conversations with staff (sometimes with drinks) always gave me intellectual inspiration and joy. I especially extend deep thanks to John Dryzek. When I was a master's student in 2012, I read one of his books, *Deliberative Democracy and Beyond* (2000), and dreamed to work with John. His wisdom and encouragement always gave me a perfect direction when I got lost in the academic jungle. John's advice, support, and trust are my source of encouragement—even after obtaining my PhD.

I would also love to express my deep gratitude to my former colleagues and friends at the University of Canberra whose critical and creative suggestions, support, and openness to my work were crucial to its realization. In particular, this book greatly benefited from creative and intellectual dialogue with Selen Ercan, Nicole Curato, Jonathan Pickering, Jensen Sass, Simon Niemeyer, Jean-Paul Gagnon, Emerson Sanchez,

Quinlan Bowman, Hans Asenbaum, Jane Alver, Wendy Conway-Lamb, Wendy Russell, Roger Davis, Mohammad Abdul-Hwas, Nardine Alnemar, and Pierrick Chalaye. In addition, this book project would not have been possible without the trust, collaboration, and encouragement of Tetsuki Tamura, André Bächtiger, John Parkinson, Lucy Parry, Carolyn Hendriks, Dannica Fleuß, Cordula Brand, Javier Romero, Gilbert Burgh, Susan Gardner, Yohsuke Tsuchiya, Tetsuya Kono, Tomoyuki Murase, Taiji Ogawa, Godo Wakako, Ryusuke Matsuo, Shinji Nishiyama, and Keiichiro Ishimoto. One of the most challenging moments was dealing with anonymous reviewers' constructive, professional, critical, and insightful comments, but their critical view definitely helped me to be self-critical and improve the quality of my argument. I thus express my gratitude to four anonymous reviewers for their professional engagement with the earlier version of the manuscript. The editorial and marketing team of the SUNY Press, in particular Michael Rinella (the commissioning editor), also gave me tremendous support throughout the publication process. Finally, my book project would not have been possible without the children and young people who were involved in my research. I cannot write their names here for ethical reasons, but let me express my sincere gratitude to them.

Institutional and organizational support was also essential for this book. This book project was funded by DAAD (2015–2016), IAP2 Pitch for Funds (2018–2019), the Uehiro Foundation on Ethics and Education (2019–2020), Doshisha University and University of Tübingen Researcher-Exchange Program (2022), JSPS (Japan Society for the Promotion of Science) Grant-in-Aid for Research Activity Start-Up (2020–2023; 20K22197), JSPS Grant-in-Aid for Early Career Researchers (2023– ; 23K12720). An earlier draft of this book and its chapters were presented in special seminars at the University of Canberra, the Australian National University, Stuttgart University, University of Tübingen, Autonomous University of Madrid, Doshisha University, Rikkyo University, Childism Institute, and in many online/offline conferences. I thank all participants and commentators who provided critical and valuable input to my presentations.

Lastly, my parents, Kiyoshi and Yumi, my wife, Eri, and my daughter, Yuka, have always been the source of my inspiration, motivation, and curiosity. After Yuka went to bed, Eri and I enjoyed wine and deliberated key issues and concepts presented in my book. Our everyday deliberation sometimes became super heated, but Eri was always my best critical reader. Yuka also gave me a lot of inspiration. For her, everything, including what I am doing, is a subject of curiosity. Why do you study? What do you write? I don't know what you are doing. Such questions from her often enabled me to be reflective, checking whether I am on the right path. Thanks to such a deliberative, democratic family, my big dream (publishing this book) has come true.

Parts of chapter 1 have been taken, with great revisions, from a paper that appeared under the title "Deliberators Not Future Citizens: Children in Democracy," in *Journal of Public Deliberation* [now renamed *Journal of Deliberative Democracy*] 13, no. 1 (2017). This article was published under a CC BY license.

Introduction

Children are one of the last frontiers of democratic inclusion, both in theory and practice. In principle, democracy is a normative project in pursuit of the value of inclusion, listening, recognition, opinion uptake, and equal opportunity of voice. However, democracy thinkers have long viewed children as "neither seen nor heard," with some even justifying their political exclusion with "evidence" of biological immaturity (i.e., children are too young to understand the complexity of politics) or with a paternalistic account (i.e., children do not know politics and democracy, so we adults guide them). This trend has been (re)produced and reinforced by the history of Western political philosophy. Plato and Aristotle alike proposed a classic vision of the ideal political community that completely ignores the presence of children. Immanuel Kant's vision of cosmopolitan citizens allowed quite little room for considering children because they were deemed as "irrational" beings. More recently, even John Rawls fell into a similar trap. Brennen and Noggle criticized Rawls's theory of justice, especially his idea of the original position, arguing that "in his view, the parties in the original position know they will be adults when the veil is lifted" (Brennen and Noggle 2000, 54). In the past several decades, people have become aware of the place and role of women, people with disability, indigenous people, and nonhumans in the political landscape; nonetheless, only a few people have questioned the exclusion or marginalization of children, and a majority of people depicted children merely as less capable beings or, at best, *future* citizens—not citizens of today. It is true that adult citizens should be responsible for maximizing children's well-being and protecting their basic human rights (including their right to participate). The problem, however, is that such claim on adults' responsibility has perpetuated the adult-centric discourse on democratic politics at the expense of children's current democratic agency.

1

The United Nations Convention on the Rights of the Child (UNCRC), established in 1989, was considered a game changer that contributes to the radical improvement of our conventional recognition of children's democratic potential. Indeed, the UNCRC has provided a foundation for shifting our understanding of children away from apolitical beings and toward agents with basic human rights of protection and participation. Starting with Roger Hart's influential work on children's participation in environmental governance and community-making, many human-rights-based approaches to children's participatory practice have been implemented worldwide (see Invernizzi and Williams 2008; Percy-Smith and Thomas 2010).

The UNCRC has dramatically changed the manner in which we cast our gaze at children, but the question remains whether such change was for the better. Today, studies on children's democratic participation are not a novel research field. Sufficient practical, empirical, and theoretical evidence shows that children are important political agents. The presence of children is increasingly seen and recognized in the contemporary political landscape, which, in its own right, is good news. However, whether children are sufficiently heard and whether these studies and evidence properly capture their democratic agency remain unclear. These questions must be considered precisely because not a few cases of children's participation still fail to avoid what John Wall (2019) calls the adultism pitfall. Regardless of the UNCRC's contributions, I believe that ways to interpret, approach, frame, design, and implement children's participation have still been informed by a certain perspective that privileges adults.

For example, while many studies have illustrated how children work for democracy, the mainstream way scholars have argued this topic has mostly been framed in terms of how children fit into existing political systems where adults' voice and presence are privileged. In such an adult sphere, children are recognized only when they act in the same or a similar way to adults, and, as Nikolas Mattheis (2020) indicates, children with a political engagement different from that of adults do tend to be framed as "unruly." Surprisingly, only a few studies have examined *children's* own lived experiences of democracy, unveiled their unique strategies for the democratization of society, or understood the complex way in which they become capable of taking ownership of defining what democratic society ought to be. Children are sometimes invited to an adult-centric sphere, and adults may welcome such children with open arms and listen to their voice. However, adults are often reluctant to listen to children who try to question and challenge the oppressive or exclusive nature of the adult sphere or critically examine the legitimacy of political and moral norms created by adults. Children are certainly seen but not heard seriously.

The question then points to what would be the key to envisioning a society in which children can truly fulfil their potential and act as democratic agents rather than in a tokenistic manner. To consider this, this book focuses on *democratic education* as key for two reasons. The first reason is ironic: it is existing democratic education that reinforces and reproduces the adult-centric understanding and practice of democracy. The second reason is more ambitious in that democratic education, rightly retheorized and reformulated, empowers children in a way that improves their current political status.

The claim that democratic education is causing children's marginalization may sound paradoxical. Educators and mentors influenced by John Dewey believe that democratic education provides the best opportunity for children to experience authentic democracy while positioning it as an important tool for addressing democracy's various pathologies (e.g., political apathy, polarization, citizens' mutual disrespect). Nonetheless, it is important to note that the words we frequently see in democratic education literature are *preparation* and *future*.[1] There are four underlying assumptions about the frequent use of these two words. First, children are understood as not yet full-fledged citizens because they are preparers. It is assumed that they will become citizens only after they have successfully completed the educational program prepared by adults. Hence, what is important here is not to educate citizens but rather to "create" them (Callan 1997). Second, and relatedly, while children's active participation is an important core of democratic education (Gutmann 1999; Molnar-Main 2017), children are allowed to be active only within the framework set by adults precisely because they are preparers for the future. Here adults know goals and what democracy is, while children are expected to practice democracy within such a framework. Third, the relative fixation on the goal to be reached in the future makes it easy to lose sight of the creativity of learning, as children are expected to achieve the set goal rather than question the goal itself or create their own. Finally, the loss of such creativity tends to neglect children's intrinsic motivation. Motives for democratic education are often brought in externally, unilaterally from adults. Children have little opportunity to ask how it relates to their current context where they act, and it is difficult for them to see the inherent importance of democratic education that is outside their control. Thus far, much of the discussion surrounding children and democratic education has focused on answering the question "Why is democratic education important for children?" while little discussion has been devoted to the larger question "What is the relationship between children, democracy, and education?"

All of these assumptions are rooted in the view that children are subordinate to adults. However, when we shift our attention from children's future to their present democratic agency and accept the fact that they, under the right conditions, can play a powerful role in democracy, our treatment of children in education must also be altered by placing them in a central, rather than peripheral, role. This book, as the title *Children, Democracy, and Education* suggests, offers a more inclusive, child-centric and comprehensive account of the relation between children, democracy, and education, with the intention to retheorize an authentic democratic society that encourages children's genuine democratic participation, recognition, and empowerment.

As its subtitle shows, the book seeks to (re)connect children with education and democracy from the perspective of *deliberative democracy*. Today, deliberative democracy is known as the most vibrant research field in political studies, and its insights have transcended communication studies, psychology, international relations, philosophy, environmental politics, and many more (see Bächtiger et al. 2018; O'Flynn 2021). Minimally defined, deliberation refers to citizens' mutual communication for a rationally motivated consensus about their common concern through reason-giving and listening. Deliberative democracy aims to enable people with different beliefs, perspectives, and preferences to understand with respect through negotiation and justification rather than coercion. Deliberation can be facilitated so it may produce a well-examined collective view that is a key source of democratic legitimacy.

Deliberative democracy is often seen as a theory for democratic decision-making, but it is also a democratic theory of inclusion, highlighting marginalized voices and legitimizing their democratic values and contributions (Bohman 1996)—this is why the book uses deliberative democracy as a key theoretical anchor. The deliberative turn requires us to shift our attention, from the traditional vote-centric idea of democracy, where children are inevitably excluded, toward a voice-centric one, requiring a more communication-oriented theory, design, and practice of democracy. In deliberative democracy, citizens do not always refer to voters. Citizens are rather contextually defined, because the deliberative principle requires all individuals affected by a decision to have sufficient opportunities to express their opinions as deliberators (Gutmann and Thompson 2004). Even if children cannot access and play a meaningful role in representative institutions, electoral processes, or legal systems, deliberative theory suggests appreciating their democratic agency and contributions by drawing attention to their communicative engagements. While democracy and education presuppose the old conceptualization of children as future citizens, deliberative theory demands that such a view be updated.

Let me here emphasize that I am not claiming that children should be educated to be able to deliberate like adults. This sort of argument runs the risk of leading to an overromanticization of adults and disrespect for children. As will be discussed in chapter 2, even adults rarely possess all of the competencies outlined by commonly accepted deliberative norms. If the possession of certain competencies constitutes the criterion for a person to be recognized as a deliberator, and if this justifies the exclusion of children, then the same criterion would equally exclude a large portion of the adult population. Instead of seeking for realizing ideal and perfect deliberation, therefore, the book reveals that the meaning of "required delib- erative competencies" should be redefined in a context-responsive fashion. This implies that, regardless of age, maturity, and level of competency, both adults and children have the potential to act as deliberators in any given context, and yet the way in which they deliberate does not always have to be identical. Instead of starting from the assumption that the goal is to educate children who lack the ability to deliberate, the inquiry of the book starts from the fact that children and adults deliberate differently across different contexts and that such differences can contribute to enhancing the deliberative democratic quality of our society.

If we take the position that children, like adults, can be delibera- tors, the theory and practice of democratic education must abandon its persistent adultism and stop seeing its purpose as consisting of ticking a box whenever children acquire paternalistically defined competencies. Instead, we should consider alternative pathways through which dem- ocratic education can be reconceptualized and redesigned to recognize and welcome the exercising of children's current deliberative democratic agency. But what kind of education is that exactly? Are adults the ene- mies or supporters of children's participation? Alternatively, is this kind of enemy-supporter dichotomy a relevant framework in the first place? Which democratic competencies should be the focus of this education? Or is it wrong to assume that competency is a kind of prerequisite for a deliberative democratic practice? Should we consider competency as a means or as an end? Are classrooms and schools the only places where children can learn deliberative democracy? Existing studies on democratic education, such as those on education for deliberative democracy, rarely address these questions. Questions such as "What do children learn from deliberation?" "Which competencies should children learn?" or "What do children deliberate about?" have been sufficiently explored, but questions such as "What does it mean for children to learn about deliberative democracy?" and "When does this learning occur?" remain unanswered. The key task of the book is to answer these questions by offering an integrated account of how democratic education, deliberative democracy, and children's democratic agency work together meaningfully and consistently.

Conceptual Clarity

Before outlining the book's key argument, three key terms, *children*, *democracy*, and *education*, shall be clarified. These terms constitute the main title of the book, and there exist a variety of interpretations about what they mean and how they are connected. Here, I do not intend to provide a universal account of these terms. Instead, I will offer definitions and explanations to clarify what these terms will mean within the context of the book.

CHILDREN

Children are "familiar to us and yet strange" (Alanen 1988, 56). We are or were all children at a certain stage of our life, yet what it exactly means to be a child is contested because of its discursive nature. Sometimes children and childhood are defined in spatial and geographical terms (e.g., street children, American kids, school pupils) (Blundel 2016). Some argue that childhood is discursively constructed from a cultural and historical perspective. In *Centuries of Childhood*, for example, the French historian Philippe Ariés (1996) analyzed old paintings and revealed that medieval Europe had no concept of children and childhood; children were mostly described as "small adults." Meanwhile, educationalists and psychologists inspired by Jean Piaget's developmental psychology usually defined children and childhood in terms of biological growth (Kohlberg 1984). Since different discursive practices construct different outlooks of children, what we must do is not to seek a universally applicable concept of children but rather to identify which discourses constitute the dominant understanding of children. I believe there are at least three dominant and interrelated discourses constructed based on age, biological and social status, and developmental stage that constitute the dominant view of children in both democracy and education.

Perhaps age often comes to mind when we define children and childhood in political and educational contexts. The age-based distinction of children from adults is widely shared and institutionally justified, most famously described in UNCRC's article 1.[2] For many of us, age is difficult to ignore not only because of its persuasiveness linked to the widely shared biologically informed understanding about children but also because of its wide applicability that can encapsulate related or similar concepts in different fields (e.g., kids, school pupils, juveniles, teenagers, young people). The age-based definition widely ranges from institutionalized settings to everyday lives, including schooling, juvenile law, voting entitlement, and censorship of X-rated content.

Despite its wide range of applicability, relying solely on the age-based definition risks the negligence of other key discourses. The status-related discourse is one example. Since the time of Jean-Jacques Rousseau, who philosophically formulated the uniqueness of childhood in terms of children's immaturity and development potential, one's physically and biologically immature status has been considered a key element in understanding the difference between children and adults. Scholars who adopted this position normally emphasized the need for intimate, affective, and economic care and protection from others, namely parents/guardians (Kittay 1999). This biologically defined discourse is deeply intertwined with the Piagetian developmental discourse, which paints the image of children as "vulnerable, immature, and in need of education" (Kjøholt 2007, 30).

In addition, some researchers have argued that children's social agency should be considered because children living and acting under the right conditions can form their own views and make important and responsible decisions about their own lives (Jans 2004; Prout and James 2015).[3] Hauver's empirical research shows that young children who are given adequate opportunities to express their opinion and listen to others can analyze structural civic problems and envision engaging in collective action. Although their engagement is sometimes authoritative or subversive, Jennifer Hauver argues that her research discovered the existence of many kids who "intended to work toward genuine compromise through active listening to others, considering various sides of the problem, and collectively making a decision that reflected shared thinking" (Hauver 2019, 104). However, other researchers indicate that ensuring and achieving children's participation rights remains a work in progress. As Mattheis (2020) criticizes, children are rather seen as "pure" and "apolitical" agents[4] with a limited access to the dominant representative and election-based democracy to express their voice.

Each of these discourses separately provides an insufficient foundation for understanding children, and they have been subject to intense criticism (Jans 2004; Kjøholt 2007; Hartung 2017a). A particular significance of the book reflects the fact that the persuasiveness, usefulness, and applicability of these discourses have long determined our dominant image of children, at least in the field of democracy and education. The book does not rely solely on one of these discourses and even engages in a critical examination of their relevance and legitimacy (particularly in chapters 1 and 2). However, key elements of the above discourses offer a good starting point to formulate a broader and tentative definition of children, that is, individuals aged around 19 and younger who are politically and legally less advantaged than older individuals in that they are not officially allowed to participate in the representative political processes such as voting on the ground that they are usually considered physically and mentally more immature and less capable than older individuals. However, under the right circumstances, children use their social capacity of expressing opinions in different ways and participating in the decision-making that affects their lives.[5]

DEMOCRACY AND EDUCATION

In a number of his works, such as *Democracy and Education* and *The Public and Its Problems*, John Dewey made a conceptual distinction between democracy as a political and as a social system. The former concerns governmental institutions and processes, which today broadly refers to political activities related to electoral systems and parliaments. Dewey believed that political democracy of this sort did not appear in our society from the outset, but was provisionally positioned in our society through a historic process of citizens' experimentation in which earlier institutions and systems were proposed, reexamined, and reconstructed. In this sense, there is no "true" and "completed" democracy—the best one can hope for is a continuing, citizen-centered experimental process devoted to the constant renewing of democracy.

Such experimental practice resonates with what Dewey calls social democracy. In pragmatism, experimentation refers to a continuous (re)iteration of problem-identification and problem-solving within an open and shared community of inquiry. Pragmatists believe that such experimental practice should be open and shared, because monological inquiry can only provide a limited and short-sighted knowledge. When problem-identification and problem-solving are practiced in a multiper-spectival fashion, "it seeks to take into account the positive and negative dimensions of current social conditions as well as to incorporate the various perspectives of relevant social actors in attempting to solve a problem" (Bohman 2004, 24). Dewey's social democracy is anchored by such an open and shared experimental practice where citizens continuously reconstruct and renew social conditions to live better lives and to seek out the meaning of their lives. This is a form of an "associated way of life" (Dewey [1916] 2004), which Dewey considers a precondition for political democracy.[6]

My intention here is not to decide which kind of democracy is more important. It is, however, important to clarify which democracy should be set as a starting point for our argument, given that these two democracies presuppose different understandings of the relationship between children, democracy, and education. On the one hand, political democracy calls for education that trains learners to be able to contribute to existing political institutions, systems, and processes in the future. On the other hand, social democracy envisages education as a practice for building habits for open and shared inquiry.[7]

Political democracy and the form of education it implies regard future political institutions, systems, and processes as the proper field of democracy, which are normally less accessible for many learners (e.g., many children cannot vote). Because of their limited accessibility to the field of political democracy, learners are expected to wait until they become well-trained citizens to fully exercise their democratic agency. From Dewey's point of view, however, educational activities geared toward preparation for the future simply lack urgency and miss the fact that "children pro-verbially live in the present" (Dewey [1916] 2004, 52). Dewey contends that uncoupling children's future from the present and making their future the mainspring for effort exerted in the present separate children from democracy. Dewey acknowledges the value of combining education with political democracy (Dewey 1927), but he is critical of taking political democracy as the *starting point* for democratic education.

Democratic education that designates social democracy as its starting point also values the significance of the future, but Dewey argues that "this should not be mistaken for attaching importance to preparation for future need" (Dewey [1916] 2004, 53). For Dewey, because social democracy should facilitate people's dialogical and experimental ways of living, democratic education should also facilitate a process of *continuous growth* in which children's "every energy should be bent to making the present experience as rich and significant as possible" (Dewey [1916] 2004, 53). Dewey believes that present and future mediated by continuous growth are insensibly merged, and thus a form of democratic education that situates children's present activity should be designed and implemented in a way that enriches both their present and future lives.

Moreover, within this process of continuous growth, children gradually develop a *democratic habit* that helps them (re)examine and (re)construct their social lives. When we hear the term "habit," we tend to image some kind of mechanically repetitive practice. For pragmatists such as Charles Sanders Peirce and Dewey, however, habit is a more dynamic, reflective, and open practice that involves collectively examining the validity of one's own actions and ways of thinking. These actions and ways of thinking can, if needed, be collectively modified in order to make life better for oneself and those around one. In other words, habit is an inseparable process of reflection on the past, creation of the future, and enrichment of the present. For Dewey, building democratic habits through education involves a process of experimentation and learning whereby learners engage in open and shared inquiry to renew their practices and ways of thinking. Within this process, education and democracy are not clearly distinguished, but rather seen as different sides of the same coin. In this understanding, children are not expected to learn about democracy from the perspective of future citizens, but instead are encouraged to practice social democracy in the present, as agents of change. Compared with a version of democratic education that emphasizes the need for preparation, democratic education that Dewey envisioned is grounded in children's reflective, creative, and associated ways of living that merges their past, present, and future in an organic way. Democratic education, as I envisage in this book, is an extension of this Deweyan view.

Deliberative Democratic Learning—What It Is (Not)

Since the rise of the idea of deliberation in democratic theory in the 1990s, education thinkers and practitioners have attempted to introduce deliberation into democratic education. Around the beginning of the 2000s, the term *education for deliberative democracy* began to appear in scholarly publications (Gutmann 1999; Englund 2000), and it is now practiced and theorized in various ways (Hess 2009; Samuelsson 2016; Molnar-Main 2017). As we shall see below, the core features of education for deliberative democracy can be summarized by its five elements: it is an evolutional, reproductive, universal, individual-transformative, and discrete form of practice. The highlighting of these features is informative, but this book is somewhat critical of it insofar as these features are derived from a conception of democratic education anchored on the political form of democracy as discussed in the previous section, which therefore tends to characterize children as future citizens.

Inspired by deliberative theory and the Deweyan idea of democratic education, the author has conducted fieldwork in classrooms and schools and on the streets in order to seek an alternative/counter understanding of democratic education, which in turn leads to an idea of *deliberative democratic learning* that is characterized by five contrasting core features: that is, a revolutionary, reflective, contextual, collective-transformative, and systemic form of practice. These five features represent different political, cultural, and developmental psychological stances toward children, education, and democracy when compared to the standard idea of education for deliberative democracy. In the paragraphs that follow, I will briefly summarize their differences and the key findings of this book.

First, while education for deliberative democracy is evolutional, deliberative democratic learning is *revolutionary*. Educational theory influenced by what I call "Piagetian Geist"[8] informs a practice that follows an evolutional path. On this account, human development is biologically conditioned by age-appropriate nonskippable stages, and education aims to help children move through these stages in the appropriate order with sufficient support from adults. It assumes the presence of a "standardized" model of children in the "normal" human social environment that "construct[s] the same basic rational competencies in the same sequence at about the same time" (Moshman 2020, 11–12). Inspired by this assumption, education for deliberative democracy tends to define children as politically immature beings who are assumed to follow a "right path" through which they become competent citizens in the future. The main problem with the evolutional approach to development and education is that it presupposes adults' superiority over children and expects children to be integrated into an adult-centric model of development. Education of this kind recognizes the significance of empowering children, but it does so by focusing intensively on "what children and young people are deemed to be lacking and what adults are deemed to be possessing" (Hartung 2017b, 55). After all, an evolutional view of education starts from "what children cannot do," which is the book's object of criticism.

Guided by deliberative theory and sociocultural developmental psychology theory, this book illustrates how and why democratic education ought to be a revolutionary practice. The term "revolutionary" here does not refer to an ideologically guided rebellious activity but is instead as a bottom-up activity of re-creation and co-construction of one's habit and environment that guide his or her further learning (Newman and Holzman 1993). The revolutionary nature of Vygotsky's theorization of children's development can be summarized as "creat[ing] new meanings for everything" (Newman and Holzman 1993, 83) or "learning what is not yet there" (Engeström 2015). Grounded in this theory, deliberative democratic learning, to be formulated in this book, aims neither to facilitate children's deliberation in a way that helps them fit into predetermined developmental stages nor to let them act as small adults. Rather, it aims to encourage children to use and develop various cultural mediating tools (e.g., language) to question, examine, reconstruct, and re-create "what democracy ought to look like," thereby enabling them to form and shape their own democratic practice in their own terms. Simply put, deliberative democratic learning is a practice that promotes the return of ownership of (re)defining and implementing deliberative democracy back to children themselves. From chapter 2 onward, I will offer a more specific explanation and justification of why deliberative democratic learning should emphasize revolutionarity rather than evolutionarity by drawing on arguments by Vygotsky's left-wing theorists,[9] namely, Yrjö Engeström's expansive theory of learning.

Second, education for deliberative democracy is reproductive, while deliberative democratic learning is *reflective*. According to Gutmann, socialization in the context of democratic education is often geared toward what she calls "unconscious social reproduction" (Gutmann 1999, 15), whose core aim is to adapt to existing social order and norms for societies to perpetuate themselves. Democratic education along this line is designed to create socially and politically "desirable" citizens who complete a set of pedagogical trainings to be recognized as full-fledged members of democratic society only when they successfully gain desirable competencies as an achievement of democratic education (Crittenden 2002).

Meanwhile, deliberative democratic learning, which takes a revolutionary view of development, disagrees with such a reproductive goal of democratic education. If democratic education is equivalent to the mere acquisition of and adaptation to something that already exists, it deprives children of their basic human rights of envisioning and defining what democratic society and citizens should look like in their own terms. Democratic education for reproduction is, from children's perspective, questionable, because it vests solely in adults the task of defining what democratic citizens and necessary competencies are, which underestimates the fact that democracy is codesigned by both adults and children. As Holzman, a Vygotskian practitioner, indicated, such socialization-oriented educational practice treats "young people more as passive recipients of what adults create than as creators" (Holzman 2017, 86).

In relation to this point, democratic education for reproduction risks neglecting the value of repertoires and strategies for child-led participation that children themselves create. As will be discussed in chapter 3, for example, democratic education scholars have emphasized the value of the rational form of argumentation but have rarely focused on the role of other forms of communication such as silence, boycotting, dancing, joking, and online communication. Although these communication strategies serve as an important means for children to participate in the process of deliberation, democratic education for reproduction normally rejects the deliberative potential of such communication as nondeliberative or even anti-deliberative. By contrast, the idea of deliberative democratic learning puts greater value on how children act as creators of a new vocabulary and strategy for democratic deliberation. In this practice, children deliberate not only controversial topics in question as presupposed by many existing studies but also how deliberation and democracy should work in practice. They sometimes question, challenge, problematize, and, if needed, modify the legitimacy of existing adult-defined norms and expectations of human development, the image of ideal citizens, and meaning of desirable democratic competencies and then repeatedly apply these modified ideas. A self-reflective process of deliberation and learning, called meta-deliberation, is the key to go beyond the reproductive goal of democratic education.

Third, education for deliberative democracy orients itself toward generalizability and universality, while *contextuality* is a focus of deliberative democratic learning. Nancy Thomas (2010, 4) suggested some *general* competencies for effective democratic deliberation, including skills for effective communication, effective dialogue skills, public reasoning, collaborative decision-making, and critical analysis of knowledge and information. Supporters of education for deliberative democracy frequently share this desire for a kind of all-rounder who can effectively deliberate at any time and in any context (e.g., Crittenden 2002; Noddings 2013). Chapter 2 of this book reveals that such desire is derived from the Piagetian Geist's universalist take on human development.

Deliberative democratic learning is skeptical about the decontextualized take on human development and instead argues that both development and deliberation are socioculturally constructed practices embedded in different contextual factors, norms, communities, language codes, and so forth. Deliberation and development are universally observable, but the manner in which they appear in practice largely depends on various contextual elements. Rather than investing all efforts to create decontextualized all-rounders, learners must be encouraged to analyze the various contextual elements that enable or inhibit their deliberation (e.g., gender norms, gender composition of the deliberative group, cultural taboos, and power imbalances between students). Learners practice social democracy by testing the degree to which the deliberative strategies they learn in one context apply to another context and continually updating their own understanding of what deliberation is. In other words, deliberative democratic learning enables learners to develop their habit of recognizing their embeddedness in broader sociocultural historical contexts and critically engaging with such contexts.

Fourth, education for deliberative democracy is an individual-transformative practice, while deliberative democratic learning is a *collective-transformative* one. Both focus on group deliberation, and in this sense, both are collective actions. However, the individualistic nature of education for deliberative democracy is due to its unit of analysis. Education for deliberative democracy, which aims to create a deliberative all-rounder, is mainly concerned with the question of how each individual can acquire deliberative competencies as a result of deliberative practice. If many individuals acquire such required competencies at the end of their deliberation, then the practice is a "success"; if not, then it is assumed that there is room for improvement. As Engeström (2016) constantly noted, such perspective is grounded on the Cartesian idea that skills and competencies belong to each individual's mind, and what is overlooked here is the ecological perspective where skills and competencies are collectively and intersubjectively produced, shared, and sometimes modified within the complexity of human and environmental systems.

Vygotsky was aware of this point. In his research on children with disabilities, he identified a process in which children with severe and mild cognitive disabilities collaborate to develop a kind of reciprocity and mutually develop their social skills (Vygotsky 2006). In his view, any attempts to remove each disabled child from such groups to see whether they are capable of doing something will only tell us an extremely superficial picture of their development. Vygotsky believed that successful learning is possible and observable only when learners collectively participate in a shared learning context and negotiate with one another's capabilities, which ultimately leads to a collective mastery and transformation of the context. This means that learning and its dynamics may not be understood properly while our unit of analysis is an isolated individual. Rather, it should focus more on a complexity of shared meaning-making and transformative action in each context.

Finally, education for deliberative democracy is a spatially discrete practice, while deliberative democratic learning is a *systemic* project. To date, classrooms have been viewed as the central space for education for deliberative democracy, and research has shown how classrooms function as important forums for deliberative learning (Hess 2009; Journell 2017; Molnar-Main 2017). Yet we must acknowledge that the classroom is not a magic box that addresses all of democracy's pathologies at once. Even if children learn how to act as good citizens in the classroom, this does not guarantee that they can do the same outside the classroom. If we want to solve the pathologies of democracy through education, we must look *both* in and beyond the classroom. Moreover, many factors may inhibit education for deliberative democracy in the classroom precisely because classrooms are often conditioned by various undemocratic characters (e.g., discrimination, bullying, teacher-student power imbalances). In short, there might be many classrooms in the world that cannot afford to introduce education for deliberative democracy.

Deliberative democratic learning seeks to avoid relying solely on classrooms and adopting such an elitist perspective on democratic education. In so doing, it broadens the scope of democratic education. This strategy is largely informed by the latest theory of deliberative democracy, called the deliberative system theory, which emphasizes the functional division of labor as well as vertical and horizontal networking relations among various deliberative practices (Dryzek 2010; Mansbridge et al. 2012). As will be discussed in detail in chapter 1, adopting the systemic theory of deliberative democracy provides two distinct benefits for retheorizing democratic education. First, it provides an overarching framework for understanding where and how children act as deliberative agents, allowing us to approach their various experiences (e.g., private space, public space, empowered space) and their interactions. Second, it helps us recognize where and how children learn deliberative democracy. The deliberative system, for example, enables us to observe the different democratic functions of classrooms and schools within the broader system: while the former serves as a deliberative forum where children engage in creating their own deliberative norms, the latter functions as a mediating space that bridges their everyday and public experiences. In addition, the deliberative system considers the activist group as an important democratic organization inside and outside the system and allows for an analysis of deliberation occurring within the organization and the deliberative consequences of organizational practice relative to the system. In such deliberative activities, we can find a more naturalized practice of deliberative learning, which can contribute to the theorization of a novel view of democratic education that is not limited to the confines of the classroom. In short, deliberative democratic learning does not take place in a single discrete space. Different spaces have various deliberative and learning potentials, which eventually allow us to examine democratic education from multiple angles.

The book will shed light on three optimal spaces where deliberative democratic learning occurs: classrooms, schools, and activist groups. These spaces have different social and political functions, yet they have all recently served as hosting spaces for various forms of democratic innovation and learning. As we shall see in the main body of the book, children in these spaces initiate their deliberative practice with relevant support from adults, learn about and engage with democracy, empower themselves, and become recognized members of a democratic community and society.[10]

Importantly, the idea of deliberative democratic learning outlined here is not a preconstructed theory arbitrarily assumed at the beginning of my project. Rather, its theorization is informed and developed through a process of reflective iteration, wherein the findings of my theoretical study and my field research are continuously brought together, reflected upon, and developed in tandem. Theory provides a guiding framework for deepening our understanding of how children, democracy, and education work in tandem, while empirical research offers insights into how we understand such a theory in real contexts. This is what Diana Mutz (2008) calls a nonideal falsifiable middle-range theory—a theory consisting of a critical iteration of normative theorizing and empirical insights. With multiple iterations of both theory and practice, the book attempts to give a more concrete shape to the idea of deliberative democratic learning. The main cases used in this book are taken from Japanese and Australian educational practice, but its theoretical as well as practical implications are wider than these two contexts.

Chapter Roadmap

Children, Democracy, and Education consists of three independent yet interrelated parts that include seven total chapters. Each chapter (except chapter 5) begins with a critical examination and consolidation of key concepts, theories, and philosophies that form the chapter's main topic, followed by an empirical elaboration of these (titled "Lessons from the Field").

Part 1, "Theory," provides a theoretical ground for rethinking the complex relationship between children, democracy, and education from a deliberative perspective. Starting with the question "Can children deliberate?" chapter 1 introduces the theory of deliberative democracy with a view to establish what it requires of agents in deliberative democracy. Although both the Rawlsian and Habermasian accounts of deliberation as a rational and consensual practice in the public sphere does not fully capture children's democratic role and agency, deliberative systems theory can offer an inclusive and effective framework to theorize what children can do in deliberative democracy. This chapter explains how deliberative systems offer a broader, albeit not stretched, concept of deliberative agents, deliberative space, and the deliberative consequence of one's deliberative act. With this theory in mind, the chapter then suggests the *deliberator model* to define the role of children in deliberative systems. After justifying the model's normative and methodological benefits, the rest of the chapter provides an example of the global-scale climate strike movement to demonstrate how deliberative systems theory and the deliberator model help address children's deliberative experiences and contributions in both micro and macro terms.

With the deliberator model, chapter 2 critically examines the concept of development in democratic education. This chapter consists of two elements: diagnosis and treatment. The diagnosis part reveals how the traditional theory and practice of education for deliberative democracy reinforce the idea of "children as future citizens" as a result of their unconscious and uncritical acceptance of the Piagetian Geist. Through the critical examination of two core concepts anchoring the Piagetian Geist (evolutionism and universalism) from the lens of deliberative systems theory and the sociocultural theory of psychology, the chapter discusses how key premises of education for deliberative democracy are in conflict with the deliberator model. Then, the treatment part of the chapter follows Vygotskyan developmental psychology, namely, Yrjö Engeström's expansive learning theory, therefore retheorizing what "growing into deliberators" means in democratic education. This developmental psychology tellingly explains why democratic education should be grounded in a revolutionary approach to development and competency-building. On the basis of these arguments, the chapter theorizes the idea of deliberative democratic learning.

Part 2 and part 3 discuss how the theory of deliberative democratic learning can be brought into practice and how empirical insights inform and give a more concrete shape to the theory.

Part 2, "Classroom," is a theoretical as well as empirical inquiry into the implications of the theoretical trajectory presented in part 1 for classroom deliberation. Based on the author's action research on classroom deliberation conducted in two different settings (Japan and Australia), part 2 investigates how deliberative democratic learning is brought into context. Chapter 3 aims to provide empirical and practical insights into how reason-giving, as a core component of deliberation, is designed and practiced. Starting with a conceptual analysis of the key differences between two trends of reason-giving (*reason*-giving and reason-*giving*), the chapter shows that the plurality of reason-giving blurs the boundaries of how we define deliberative, nondeliberative, and anti-deliberative reason-giving. The question then would be how deliberative democratic learning can keep reason-giving as an epistemic anchor while accommodating the plurality of reason-giving. The paternalistic instruction of "this is what deliberative reason-giving should be" is a common approach in education for deliberative democracy, but deliberative democratic learning adopts a more reflective approach—*meta-deliberation*. It encourages students to innovate and practice various forms of reason-giving and then lets them assess whether their practice counts as deliberative, nondeliberative, or anti-deliberative. In meta-deliberative practice, students can elaborate their self-reflective capacities for assessing the quality of deliberation and, more importantly, enable themselves to act as creators of deliberative norms who formulate, practice, negotiate, and retheorize new repertoires of reason-giving in their own terms. To explain how and what kind of meta-deliberation works in practice, the second half of the chapter draws on my action research in Japanese classrooms.

Chapter 4 explores another key component of deliberation—listening. Quite often reason-giving alone does not work well, as children intentionally avoid listening to one another for various reasons. Facilitating listening in classroom deliberation is, however, not straightforward compared to facilitating reason-giving, precisely because of the difficulty of assessment. The chapter first reviews the philosophical and theoretical ground on the deliberative role of listening to explore how we assess the quality of listening in a deliberative process. The chapter welcomes some key implications gained from Mary Scudder's (2021) novel idea of the Listening Quality Index (LQI). However, because the LQI is designed for assessing the quality of listening in public deliberation, I will also point out the LQI's practical and intrinsic limitations when it is applied to classroom deliberation. By combining the LQI's core idea with meta-deliberation, I then suggest a more revolutionary and participatory way for democratizing the LQI (which I call the uncapitalized *lqi*). In the second half of the chapter, I draw on my action research experience to illustrate how creation of the lqi is possible in the real classroom.

Chapter 5 discusses the role of the facilitator in classroom deliberation. Deliberative democratic learning without a facilitator is, at least in the classroom context, unrealistic, although various powers that facilitators can exert run the risk of inhibiting children's democratic deliberation. This is the dilemma addressed in the chapter. Unlike other chapters, the chapter begins by sharing empirical findings, as the topic of facilitation of classroom deliberation is still an underdeveloped area. Drawing on action research in Australian schools, the chapter identifies three key challenges (facilitator's power, testimonial injustice, and disagreement) that I, as a facilitator, experienced during classroom deliberation. To investigate how we facilitate in the face of these three challenges, I will examine three theoretical arguments about facilitative teachers: the banking facilitation (informed by Paulo Freire), the ignorant facilitation (informed by Jacques Rancière), and the community of inquiry (informed by John Dewey).

Despite the general significance and advantage of each model, the first two models focus mostly on individualized facilitative techniques that make it difficult for a facilitator to address the socioculturally constructed structural challenges I experienced. By contrast, the Deweyan model of the community of inquiry theorizes facilitator's involvement not only as an intervention in children's communicative interactions but also as an environmental design that provides further discursive scaffolding and structure. Some examples of such facilitative design I practiced with children shall show how they mitigate three challenges to a greater extent.

Part 3, "Beyond the Classroom," seeks to dispel myths that limit the scope of democratic education within the classroom. This part focuses on schools and activist groups, demonstrating how deliberative democratic learning occurs in a different way from classrooms. The central topic of chapter 6 is democratic schools. While mainstream studies on democratic education tend to mix schools and classrooms uncritically, this chapter makes a case for distinguishing students' deliberative engagement in schools from those in classrooms and then explores schools' deliberative capacity. The chapter first analyses three key functions of democratic schools and then suggests the integrative concept of schools as a *mediating space* that contributes to the growth of deliberative systems by connecting children's everyday experiences and the wider public spaces. To identify conditions under which schools provide opportunities for deliberative democratic learning while functioning as a mediating space, this chapter discusses some empirical findings from two case studies of Japanese schools. These case studies call for further attention to the democratic role of schools' horizontal and vertical networks, which enable a naturalized deliberative learning moment.

Chapter 7 shifts our attention away from the traditional learning settings (classrooms and schools) toward a wider public space, which shapes the idea of deliberative democratic learning from a different angle. In this chapter, I report on my two and a half years of ethnographic research with a group of teenage climate activists in Kyoto City, Japan, with a specific focus on Fridays for Future Kyoto's deliberative form of self-transformative experience. The chapter is written on the basis of teenage activists' publicly invisible deliberative experiences (e.g., weekly group meeting, dialogue workshop) and its interplay with their protesting activities in the public sphere (e.g., standing protests, protest march). Teenage activists have inevitably put themselves in conversation with changing and unforeseeable situations such as the global-scale climate crisis and the COVID-19 pandemic, and thus they have to deliberate on a regular basis in order to (re)examine the raison d'être of the movement and their identity as climate activists. By doing so, they transformed power structure within the group and the meaning of the climate activism they have engaged, thereby redefining and redesigning their movement itself. Through this series of deliberative experience, teenage activists grow into *deliberative* activists.

Part I

Theory

Part 1 deals with two theoretical tasks. The first task is to locate children in deliberative democracy. Like many other theories of democracy, however, deliberative democracy has so far failed to recognize children's political agency due to its implicit assumption that children are less mature than adults, and therefore less able to deliberate. In order to combat this assumption, it is worth returning to a fundamental question: What does it mean to "be able to deliberate?"

Drawing on deliberative systems theory, chapter 1 establishes what is required of agents in a deliberative democracy. Moving away from the traditional ideal of deliberation as a one-off instance of authentic and inclusive argumentation in the public sphere, deliberative systems focus on the functional division of labor among different deliberative practices that happen across different spaces. In a deliberative system, not all political institutions, organizations, and individuals need to be deliberative in a normatively rigorous fashion; what is more important is the way in which different deliberative agents interact and connect with each other, so that authentic and inclusive norms of deliberative democracy can be realized in the system as a whole. Viewed in this light, the exclusion of children from deliberative systems on the basis of their age and immaturity would be unjustifiable because, even though their political engagement itself is less deliberative from a normative point of view, their voice, when connected with other deliberative opportunities, can make the deliberative system more multivocal and reflective. Chapter 1, then, advocates the adoption of a deliberator model in conceptualizing the agency of children in democracy, as opposed to the traditional "future citizens" model. While the traditional model theorizes the role of children in comparison with adult citizens, the suggested model understands children with respect to their agency, their various deliberative spaces, and their various deliberative contributions. To see a concrete instance of how the deliberator model works, chapter 1 analyses the systemic contributions of the transnational Fridays for Future movement.

The next task is to consider how the previous chapter's argument speaks to the aims and scopes of democratic education. Chapter 2 first reviews literature in the field of education regarding deliberative democracy to identify what deliberative thinkers expect for democratic education. Many people believe that democratic education should help children become citizens of future democracy. Chapter 2 shows how this view is underpinned by evolutionism and universalism, both of which are inspired by Jean Piaget's developmental psychology paradigm. On the one hand, evolutionism postulates that adult citizens are the goal of development, thereby ensuring that children are seen as immature individuals who are incapable of creating a political community. On the other hand, universalism presupposes that children who are at present incapable should be educated to be "deliberative all-rounders," or individuals who have acquired universally applicable deliberative competencies. Overall, both ideas inevitably define children as future citizens, which contradicts the deliberator model theorized in chapter 1. Drawing on deliberative systems theory and Lev Vygotsky's sociocultural psychological theory of development, I argue against the implicit evolutionist and universalist assumptions. I do so by outlining the difficulties faced when trying to identify a universal must-learn competency prior to actual contextualized deliberation. In lieu of these difficulties, the value of a sociogenesis understanding of competency and human development is emphasized. In particular, Vygotsky and Vygotskyan theorists define development as a contextualized reflective meaning-making process by which children negotiate and interpret their learning environment (e.g., learning space, friends) and then co-construct and redefine the value and norm of their activity. Viewed in this light, rather than focusing on the mere acquisition of a predetermined set of deliberative competencies, democratic education should allow children to have a primary ownership of determining for themselves what kind of competency are required for deliberation and then updating their vision of what deliberation ought to be through a continuous deliberation. On the ground of these arguments, I finally theorize this vision of democratic education as deliberative democratic learning that is characterized by the five core features: revolutionary, reflective, contextual, collective-transformative, and systemic practice.

Chapter 1

Children in Deliberative Democracy

James Bohman's landmark article entitled *The Coming of Age of Deliberative Democracy* (Bohman 1998) was a rather visionary work in the sense that deliberative democracy is currently one of the most vibrant research fields in political theory and political science (see Curato et al. 2017; Bächtiger et al. 2018; O'Flynn 2021). Today, deliberative theory cuts across various disciplines, ranging from communication studies to psychology, international relations, philosophy, public administration, environmental politics, and education, among others. Unfortunately, though, rather little is known about how deliberative theory relates to childhood studies. While several democratic theories such as liberal democracy (Callan 1997) and citizenship theory (Invernizzi and Williams 2008) consider the role of children, many deliberative democrats remain silent. Their silence is probably based on the assumption that *children cannot deliberate* (and thus are not key agents of deliberative democracy).

This chapter challenges this widely shared view from a theoretical angle, arguing that children can deliberate, and deliberative democracy is indeed the effective framework to capture how children can act democratically. This chapter, in particular, has three goals geared toward responding to the question "Can children deliberate?" The first goal is to set out the theory of deliberative democracy with a view to establishing what it requires of agents of deliberation. Deliberative theory now experiences a *systemic* turn, and this chapter illustrates how deliberative systems theory offers a better framework to understand how children help constitute democracy than its classic theory.

To the extent that children can make various contributions to deliberative systems, we need to shift our attention away from a traditional model of children as future citizens to an alternative one. The second goal of this chapter is to theorize a new model of children with respect to deliberative democracy. The suggested model examined in this chapter can overturn the conventional understanding of (a) agency (Who can deliberate?), (b) space (Where does deliberation occur?), and (c) consequence (What is a consequence of deliberation?), thereby revealing children's various roles in and contributions to deliberative systems. As we shall see, this model takes priority over the future citizen model in normative and methodological terms.

The third goal is to show how the suggested model can be effective in interpreting the meaning of children's democratic engagement from multiple angles. To this end, the recent case of student-led climate activism, known as the Fridays for Future movement, is examined. It demonstrates children's deliberative agency exerted across empowered space, public space, private space, and transmission of discourses.

The Deliberative Turn in Democratic Theory

Around the 1990s, an increasing number of people began to take notice of and point out some of the limitations of the traditional understanding of election-centric democracy. Citizens of democracies around the world contended that their political institutions were undemocratic because their voices were not being heard and their collective will was not adequately represented by political elites. This in turn accelerated citizens' distrust in government. Political elites, however, found it difficult to appropriately take up and represent the public will and make legitimate decisions given the variety of citizens' needs and preferences, as well as the contradictions and competitions that come with that variety. Moreover, they felt that there is no guarantee that citizens' voices are always reliable, because some voices are provided on the basis of a significant lack of information or of a shortsighted and highly opinionated justification. In the face of such political gridlock, or the so-called "crisis of democracy" (Ercan and Gagnon 2014), deliberative theory has gradually begun to receive attention from citizens and decision-makers alike. For citizens, deliberation allows room for citizens to be heard publicly and to learn from the voices of others. For decision-makers, deliberation creates a novel pathway through which they can more effectively listen to well-considered collective inputs from citizens. Such an important theoretical shift toward a citizen-centric communicative theory of democracy has been called a *deliberative turn* in democratic theory.[1] Although the crisis of democracy remains salient in contemporary politics (especially in the age of post-COVID, climate crisis, and global conflicts), many democratic theorists continue to propose "more deliberative democracy" as a key solution, which has recently been called a "deliberative wave" (OECD 2020).

But what exactly is deliberative democracy? Minimally defined, deliberative democracy is a communication-centered normative project of democracy. Yet this does not mean that norms of deliberative democracy accept all forms of communication. Normatively, deliberative democracy is an idea for making informed consensus through *authentic* and *inclusive* communication by all those subject to the decision.

Authentic communication refers to a process in which one has "to be truthful in what one says, to respect the arguments of others, to give good reasons for one's own arguments, and to be open to changing one's position by the force of the better argument" (Steiner 2012, 3). Authentic communication is differentiated from mere conversation or debate precisely because it focuses more on a collaboration between differently situated people in sharing their own view in a noncoercive manner (Dryzek 2000). For this, authentic communication, in principle, places rational, reciprocal, and reflective reason-giving in the foreground.

Early deliberative democrats believed that a legitimate outcome is achieved when people justify their positions, negotiate with opponents, and exchange mutually agreeable reasons by rejecting manipulation, indoctrination, propaganda, and coerciveness (Cohen 1989). However, when people do not listen to others and understand the interests, concerns, and beliefs underlying their opinions, deliberation becomes less rational and more disruptive and conflictual. Hence, rational argumentation must be supported by the idea of reciprocity that "requires a favorable attitude toward, and constructive interaction with the persons with whom one disagrees" (Gutmann and Thompson 1996, 79). Guided by rational and reciprocal ideals, citizens should deliberate in a reflective manner. Citizens test their assumptions and beliefs "which were found in public debate to be wrong or short-sighted or otherwise indefensible" (Kymlicka 2002, 291). Rather than sticking to their given opinions and beliefs, citizens are encouraged to deliberate in ways that learn from different, or even opposing, opinions, and transform their preferences, judgements, and views, thereby forming better and well-examined collective opinions.[2]

The idea of inclusiveness is normatively demanded as another key principle. Although inclusiveness is, as André Bächtiger and John Parkinson (2019, 9) point out, a general democratic principle, it plays a particularly essential role in deliberation. To understand this, Iris Young's (2000) well-known two classifications of inclusiveness in deliberative democracy, or what she calls "communicative democracy," are worth mentioning. First, deliberation should be open externally. Opportunities should be created for all voices to be heard and considered. External inclusion requires conditions under which all those subject to the decision can physically participate in a deliberative process. Second, deliberation should also be internally inclusive. No structural, social, and cultural barrier should prevent people from being recognized and heard within the process of deliberation. Adopting this approach means that deliberative theory should recognize multiple forms of reason-giving, including nonverbal and emotional ones, that can enrich the inclusive quality of deliberation.[3]

To realize such authentic and inclusive deliberation in the real world, in the past 20 years, various kinds of deliberative innovations have been implemented in the global, national, and local public spheres in the form of citizens' assembly, consensus conference, citizens' jury, or planning cell, all of which are usually called deliberative minipublics (see Gastil and Levine 2005; OECD 2020; Reuchamps, Vrydagh, and Welp 2023). Perhaps one of the most famous deliberative minipublics is James Fishkin's pathbreaking Deliberative Polling (DP). DP is a combination of an opinion poll and public deliberation. In the DP, randomly selected citizens provided with balanced documents deliberate together. Before and after their deliberation, they are asked to respond to the same questions so that the researcher can identify what sorts of effects (e.g., preference shifts, increased knowledge about the issue in question, further political participation) result from deliberation. Participants' opinions are presented publicly as a more sophisticated and elaborated opinion of citizens than the conventional form of opinion polling. Consequently, deliberation is used as a means to rebuild collaborative capacities of democratic politics by including interests and voices of ordinary citizens. As Nicole Curato et al. note, deliberative democracy is not utopian, because "it is already implemented within, outside, and across governmental institutions worldwide" (Curato et al. 2017, 29).

The Systemic Turn in Deliberative Theory

Now we return to the main question: Can children deliberate? Unfortunately, though, it is difficult to answer this question at this stage because what I have illustrated above is the view of deliberative thinkers in the *previous generations* (Elstub, Ercan, and Mendonça 2016). Even if deliberation is implemented in the global, national, and local public spheres, deliberative democracy as conceived by previous generations may not be able to provide an effective ground theory of the role of children in democracy. The first reason is linked to the authentic principle that is still likely to set a high epistemic threshold about what meaningful deliberation ought to be, and some deliberative democrats think that children cannot deliberate in such a meaningful manner. For example, a key deliberative theorist Christiano argues:

> Children are not capable of elaborating or reflecting on moral principles; they adopt moral ideas from their parents not out of a sense of conviction but out of a desire to please and a sense of trust in their parents. For the same reasons, children do not have a developed sense of their own interests. As a consequence of these points, children are not likely to have elaborated or reflected on ideas of justice and whatever ideas they do express are not likely to reflect their interests. (Christiano 2001, 207)

The second point relates to inclusiveness. As Carole Pateman (2012) points out, early deliberative thinkers tended to link deliberative democracy intensively with deliberative minipublics while paying little attention to other deliberative-participatory opportunities in the public sphere.[4] Although some early deliberative democrats paid attention to the deliberative capacities of out-of-forum citizen activities (Mansbridge 1999; Dryzek 2000), evidence for Pateman's claim can be found in various examples of deliberative minipublics showcased in *The Deliberative Democracy Handbook* (Gastil and Levine 2005) that have a quite limited case of informal or nonformal deliberative engagement of citizens, such as social movements. If deliberative democracy is understood mostly through the lens of deliberative minipublics, it may justify exclusion of children for two reasons. In terms of external inclusion, children are normally not allowed to participate in deliberative minipublics. Quite often, those aged 18 or below are not the subject of random sampling for participating in deliberation, even if they are affected by the issue at stake (Nishiyama 2023). Furthermore, even if children are recruited to participate in deliberative minipublics, they face a risk of internal exclusion because adult participants sometimes underestimate children's experience and capacity. This tendency is illustrated by a statement made by a state government representative in Queensland, Australia, who talked with children about community planning in a deliberative forum. He said, "I am a bit skeptical of young people being involved in this [forum]. . . . What life experiences did they bring?" (Grant-Smith and Edwards 2011, 8).

Hence, using a narrow understanding of deliberative democracy is not enough to understand the place of children in democracy. I argue instead that we need to take the "new generation," or frontiers of current deliberative theory, into account. While deliberative democracy in prior generations tend to focus exclusively on the extent to which deliberative democracy's norm is realized within the confines of a single, isolated, and one-off forum, deliberative theory as formulated by the new generation is more concerned with how different forms of citizens' democratic activities interact and connect to establish a wider network of deliberative democracy. This theoretical position of deliberative democracy, known as *deliberative systems*, has recently received widespread attention from deliberative democracy researchers (Dryzek 2010; O'Flynn 2021).[5] As Jane Mansbridge et al. (2012) note, a "system" means "a set of distinguishable, differentiated, but to some degree interdependent parts, often with distributed functions and a division of labour, connected in such a way as to form a complex whole" (3).

Like previous manifestations of deliberative theory, the concept of deliberative systems takes authentic and inclusive communication to be one of its core elements. Unlike previous generations, however, in deliberative systems, these communications do not need to "be sought for the same people in the same place at the same time" (Ercan, Hendriks, and Dryzek 2019, 10). In other words, each deliberative space does not need to serve as "the best possible single deliberative forum" (Mansbridge et al. 2012, 1) where all normative aspects of deliberation (e.g., rational argumentation, reciprocity, reflection, and internal and external inclusion) are realized at once. Instead of seeking for normatively "perfect" deliberations that rarely occur in reality, the idea of a deliberative system values *division of labor* among different communication locations. As Mansbridge et al. note, "a single part, which in itself has a low or even negative deliberative quality with respect to one of several deliberative ideals, may nevertheless make an important contribution to an overall deliberative system" (13).[6]

For example, deliberative minipublics usually play a salient role in forming citizens' collective will through informed and facilitated deliberation. However, as already pointed out above, the disadvantage of such minipublics lies in their limited capacity to include children. In contrast, some child-friendly and well-designed deliberative practices (e.g., children's parliaments) can provide children with a valuable opportunity to engage in quality deliberation about controversial political issues in contemporary society (e.g., climate change), but their limitation generally lies in their lack of connection with official decision-making processes. No matter how high the quality of children's deliberation in such spaces, their voice and decision are rarely reflected in official spaces. Consequently, neither deliberative practice consistently meets a normative standard with respect to inclusiveness. Nonetheless, the idea of a deliberative system is more concerned with enabling interaction between these two practices, so that a limitation of each practice is compensated by another and each advantage is strengthened.

In Scotland's Climate Assembly, held 2020–2022, such interaction became a reality. Before the Climate Assembly, members of the Children's Parliament, an organization consisting of over 100 children aged 7 to 14 from across Scotland, undertook surveys and interviews to collect data about children's opinions and demands with respect to climate change. Members deliberated together to write their collective report, which was entitled *It's Up to You, Me and All of Us.* This report was used as one of key sources of information for adult participants during the Climate Assembly's process of deliberation. Their report was also included in the Climate Assembly's final report and submitted to decision-makers (Nishiyama 2023). Even if the deliberations that took place in the Climate Assembly and the Children's Parliament were not in themselves always fully inclusive, their division of labor contributed to forming an inclusive deliberative system of climate governance in Scotland.

Hence, given that deliberative theory goes beyond a single forum, it necessitates reconsideration of our conceptual understanding of *agency* (how we define agents of deliberation), *spaces* (where deliberation takes place), and *consequence* (what deliberation can bring about). Reconsidering these concepts is important, because an expanded understanding of deliberative agency, spaces, and consequences allows room for accommodating children as *deliberators*, not mere future citizens. The next section elucidates how the idea of deliberative system expands these three concepts with a specific focus on implications for children in democracy.

Children in Deliberative Systems

AGENCY

A deliberative system distinguishes democratic deliberation from deliberative democracy. While the former refers to a set of deliberative *practices,* the latter focuses on multiple *functions* of deliberation (see Bächtiger and Parkinson 2019, 25). Democratic deliberation envisages a classic core of public deliberation characterized by reasoned and reflective communicative interaction coupled with listening and reciprocity (Cohen 1989). The idea of deliberative systems, on the other hand, defines democratic deliberation as one key source of democratic legitimacy but, at the same time, acknowledges the role of other forms of communications (e.g., storytelling, emotion, rhetoric, silence) contributing to different ways of achieving goals of deliberative democracy. In Edwina Barvosa's systemic analysis of US public engagement on LGBT equality, for example, she focuses on the role of Ellen DeGeneres, a top comedic entertainer in the United States, who came out publicly as a lesbian. With a detailed description of DeGeneres's story, Barvosa (2018, 86–95) makes a case for how DeGeneres has enhanced and allowed for deliberation across the public sphere and changed US public opinion on LGBT equality over the last 10 years. Even though DeGeneres herself does not engage in democratic deliberation, Barvosa argues that DeGeneres uses various communicative strategies (e.g., humor) and acts as a deliberative entrepreneur who provides people with rich opportunities to reflect on and reconsider what LGBT equality and social acceptance ought to be. Similarly, as we will see later, Greta Thunberg and Emma González,[7] whose political expressions are not always rigorously deliberative, can play such an entrepreneur role.

John Dryzek and Jonathan Pickering's idea of formative agents (Dryzek and Pickering 2018, 105–6) provides another example of how people can contribute to enhancing the overall quality of deliberative systems without engaging in democratic deliberation. Formative agents do not involve themselves directly in an official decision-making process through democratic deliberation. Their primary work is instead to formulate the meaning of a contested concept used in a process of public deliberation (e.g., justice, equality, stability) and consider how the concept should be redefined and applied in practice. Before a specific concept is implemented in practice by politicians or decision-makers, formative agents question its meaning and legitimacy, create a counterdiscourse or a supportive discourse, and then appeal to the broader public. In the past several years, we have witnessed various cases in which children and young people act as the formative agents. They employ various communicative strategies that do not always fit neatly into normative standards of democratic deliberation, as they often use various nondeliberative expressions (e.g., protests, coercion, rhetoric, visual representation). With these nondeliberative strategies, they challenge and reformulate controversial concepts used in the public sphere, such as "safety" (the March for Our Lives protests initiated by survivors of mass shootings), "sustainability" (the global climate protest initiated by Greta Thunberg), and "women's rights" (the women's rights movement launched by Malala Yousafzai).

Sometimes, children's presence can exert a quite powerful influence over the process of public deliberation. Presence itself is not a deliberative practice, because there is no speech action. According to Dewey, children's presence has a power "to enlist the cooperative attention of others" ([1916] 2004, 42). Children are physically so vulnerable and immature that they cannot survive alone. This enables them to receive sympathetic care and responses from adults—Dewey calls it social capacity. Because of social capacity, children's voices and activities can have an effective impact on society in ways that call for attention and recognition from people who previously were not concerned about the issue at stake. Drawing on the case of the children's peacemaking movement in Colombia, for example, Sara Cameron notes "the voices of children against violence can be inspiration for adults . . . their power seems to lie not just in the eloquence of their words, but in the fact that they are said by children" (Cameron 2000, 44)

In sum, the idea of deliberative systems can provide an effective framework that allows us to approach and take into account children's democratic contributions with respect to the functions of their activities in a broader system. It should be made clear that I am not claiming that children cannot deliberate democratically. While democratic deliberation is still a salient component in deliberative systems, we should also pay attention to various deliberative functions of their diversity of communicative acts.

SPACE

The idea of deliberative systems "expands the scale of analysis beyond the individual site and allows us to think about deliberations that develop among and between the sites over time" (Mansbridge et al. 2012, 2). In addition to the well-established deliberative forums that are usually not accessible for children, deliberative systems theory allows us to focus on the deliberative potential of other spaces, ranging from legislatures to both virtual and physical public spaces (e.g., NGOs, cafés, universities, online forums) or even private spaces (e.g., family) (Dryzek 2010; Tamura 2014).

Accordingly, the expanded perspective on deliberative spaces provides multiple interpretations about where children's deliberative activities can take place. *Empowered space*, land for producing public authority through collective decision-making, is one example of this (Dryzek 2010). The systemic framework of deliberative democracy has been able to recognize many democratic efforts and projects for children's involvement in official decision-making. Since the UNCRC (1989), more and more children have participated in deliberative decision-making processes in child congresses, community planning, consultative forums, and so forth (Percy-Smith and Thomas 2010).

Having said that, the traditional approach to children's participation is, despite its important impact, problematic, because it can recognize children as agents of democracy only when they engage actively and voluntary with the selected and substantive issue at empowered space. This limited understanding of children's participation overlooks the fact that not all children can have an equal opportunity to access deliberation in such an empowered space. Meanwhile, the salient advantage of deliberative systems is that it allows us to approach children's formal, informal, and nonformal experiences in *public space*. Compared to empowered space, public space is a relatively freer and more accessible communicative space with few legal and authoritative restrictions (Dryzek 2010). With a deliberative systems framework, we can see how children appear and act politically in public spaces in ways that connect with particular adult-initiated civil society initiatives and initiate child-led participatory projects.

Even *private space* can be the core entity for children to engage in deliberative acts. Mansbridge argues that "when many individuals engage in everyday talk, update their earlier ideas, and coordinate on a new, temporarily settled conviction, the society itself may be said to have 'decided' and a new 'authoritative allocation of values' is born" (Mansbridge 2007, 267). While most children do not usually enjoy the opportunity to participate in both empowered and public space, they carry out deliberative activities in their everyday settings. For example, Constance Flanagan (2013) shows how family discussion on current political events can provide children and young people with a chance to question and contest dominant narratives, thereby cultivating their political awareness and building a foundation for social change.

Not only do children deliberate in a particular physical space, but they also contribute to deliberative systems by connecting different deliberative spaces. This is what Dryzek (2010) calls *transmission*. It refers to the activities that make a linkage and transmit a discourse between one component of a deliberative system and another. Social media can be one of the most important means for children to engage in transmission of different discourses. Benjamin Lyons (2017) shows that a specific type of Internet memes shared via hashtag and hyperlink on Twitter and Facebook make transmission possible, thereby provoking emotional and reflective reactions among viewers and triggering their political conversation across online as well as offline spaces. Although Internet memes per se are not deliberative, they represent a communitive action that can vitalize public deliberation in ways that allow for new spaces of linkage across different parts of the system.

CONSEQUENCE

Given that children can and should be understood as agents of deliberation in deliberative systems, what is the consequence of their deliberative practices? That achieving rationally motivated consensus is a primary consequence is one of the common views of deliberative democrats (Cohen 1989). However, this view has been challenged by agonistic democrats and difference democrats alike on the grounds that disagreement is another key attribute of politics and comprehensive consensus-making may ignore a plurality of irreconcilable interests and values in a deeply divided society (Mouffe 2000).

Consensus is certainly one of the key goals that deliberative democracy pursues, but it should also be acknowledged that not every single deliberative space needs to reach this goal, because, as already discussed, the focus of deliberative systems is the degree to which each contributing part can function so as to achieve the authentic and inclusive ideal of deliberative democracy as a systemic whole. The merit of deliberative systems theory is that it enables us to approach both clear-cut consequences and more nuanced, albeit significant, ones.

Consequence as defined by advocates for deliberative systems may include not only formal (e.g., informing public policy) but also informal one (e.g., building reciprocal relationships among previously hostile groups). Kuyper (2017) also classifies instrumental value in deliberative systems into three: micro, meso, and macro consequences. Micro-scale consequence is about an individual's learning opportunity, including learning different perspectives and preference transformation. Meso-scale consequence relates to collective and group experiences, such as collective will-formation and creation of counter-discourse. Context is also an important factor in considering deliberative consequence because the meaning of the most desirable consequence can be altered in different spaces. Consider Bora Kanra's (2012) research on deliberation in Turkey, for example. By analyzing agonistic interactions between Islamic and secular discourses in Turkey, he empirically unpacks that a social learning moment is more important and even desirable than the classic Rawlsian and Habermasian consensual ideal of deliberative consequence, because social learning deepens participants' understanding about how to live together more productively in a divided society. Take another example where context matters. Lucy Parry (2017) also draws on the case of animal activism with the specific focus on activists' performative acts in deliberative systems. Although, she argues, some grotesque images of animal suffering used by animal activists may potentially represent an animal's unheard "voice" and trigger further deliberation in one context, she notes they also may prove counterproductive (e.g., facilitating further polarization between activists and lay citizens by invoking the latter's negative psychological reaction) that may not always contribute to authentic and inclusive ideals of deliberative democracy in another context.

Recognizing various democratic consequences in deliberative systems opens a new avenue through which children are interpreted as deliberators, insofar as their deliberative engagements function well in a way that carries micro, meso, or macro consequences contributing to the overall authentic and inclusive quality of deliberative systems. Deliberative systems theory does not require children to act as perfect deliberators in all places at all times. Nor does its theorists always expect children to behave like adult deliberators in an exact fashion. In a healthy deliberative system, deliberators should be defined not by age, individual's discrete capacity, or the degree of official policy influence but by the expanded understanding of agency, spaces, and consequences of deliberative actions.

As I have discussed, the systemic understanding of deliberative democracy allows us to see children as deliberators, and not mere future citizens. Insofar as children wish to express their views, preferences, and feelings on matters affecting them, exclusion of children from deliberative systems on the basis of their age and supposed immaturity is unjustifiable. This is so because the main task of the deliberative system is not to force children to wait until they become adults but to find or create a pathway for connecting children's voices with other elements of the system. The traditional image of children in deliberative democracy has been dominated by the *future citizen model*, where children are defined as lacking essential abilities when compared to "mature" and "competent" adult citizens. In contrast, the idea of a deliberative system assumes what I label the *deliberator model*, which defines deliberators with respect to one's *deliberative agency* (how children deliberate), *deliberative space* (where children do something deliberative), and *consequences* (how children's deliberative practice works). The deliberator model understands deliberative democracy not only as the communicative engagement of citizens in a deliberative forum, but also as the whole variety of democratic experiments that citizens engage in, which help make the deliberative system more authentic and inclusive. Even though each contributing individual may be less competent than what the future citizens model expects, a deliberative system opens the door for various agents to broaden the range of debates, maximize the opportunity to make the system itself more democratic, and facilitate citizens' further collaboration.

Normative and Methodological Implications

The deliberator model has also the normative and methodological advantage when we consider the role of children in deliberative democracy.

The deliberator model requires us to pay sufficient attention to what children can do for democracy, which is a neglected perspective in traditional normative theory of deliberative democracy. Adult citizens, including guardians, teachers, and politicians, often justify exclusion of children from a democratic process on the ground of children's lower age and their limited suffrage. However, the idea of deliberative systems provides a normative rationale for understanding how and where children express themselves and why it is unjust to ignore their voices on the ground of their age and immaturity if the consequence of deliberation can affect children's everyday, social, cultural, and political lives. A *democratic* deliberative system is anchored by a process that "must not exclude any citizens from the process without strong justification that could be reasonably accepted by all citizens, *including the excluded*" (Mansbridge et al. 2012, 12; emphasis added).

The deliberator model also provides a normative basis that requires us to reconsider what democratic society ought to be and who constitutes democracy. In particular, the systemic lens enables people to be self-reflective about how existing democratic order naturalizes biased, namely, adult-centric, norms. Despite the increasing interest in children's participatory projects in the past several decades (particularly since the 1990s), mainstream discourse strongly rests on the assumption that it is "too early" for children to engage in democracy. As Mattheis (2020) argues, a widely shared view that reinforces this assumption emphasizes the apolitical nature of childhood, indicating children's low level of political responsibility, their limited suffrage, and lack of required competencies. On the basis of this view, it is believed that democracy is in principle run by fully competent and responsible adult citizens, while children are expected to wait until they hold official political rights. This attitude is exemplified by the former Australian prime minister Scott Morrison's criticism of youth climate activists: "What we want is more learning in schools and less activism in schools."[8] However, as we shall discuss in the next chapter in more detail, setting competent adult citizenry as a standard for healthy democracy is undesirable because it unjustifiably excludes children from deliberative systems.

The deliberator model's methodological implications are twofold. First, it provides a comprehensive framework to approach children's different experiences, roles, and contributions to deliberative democracy. Rather than investigating a yes-or-no question (e.g., whether children can deliberate or not), the model asks about the degree to which deliberative ideals can be applied to a specific context where children act politically. The deliberative system does not reject deliberative ideals, but its primary focus is the way in which such ideals can be distributed and achieved across different spaces and different times. This is particularly helpful in understanding children's seemingly "intangible" activity. As Hartung (2017b, 45) cautions, overemphasis on "tangible" and "immediate" impacts may limit our understanding of what children's participation means by downplaying their varying "intangible" but democratically important activities. The advantage of deliberative systems theory is that it provides a novel framework for recognizing the deliberative potential of activities that are normally understood as "meaningless" but that could be interpreted as "reasonable" strategies for children to act as deliberators in a deliberative system.[9]

Second, the deliberator model allows us to focus on both macro and micro experience of children and to analyze inhibiting factors that induce dysfunction along their deliberative engagements. As is often reported, for example, children can engage in high-quality deliberation in a well-designed forum, such as youth parliament (Bulling et al. 2013). However, deliberative systemic diagnosis can identify that this sort of deliberation alone is, despite its high deliberative quality, not sufficient if such a forum does not have channels though which children's collective opinion is adequately transmitted to an officially empowered decision-making body. Alternatively, when the deliberative system itself is characterized by an oppressive structure, the system may not become democratic, no matter how much children engage in consequential deliberation. For instance, in societies where adults do not recognize children as legitimate epistemic agents and grant them low credibility for their knowledge and experience, only adults take primary ownership of defining what to talk about, how children communicate, and how to inform decision-makers, while children may have quite limited control over these issues and need to engage in "better" and "consequential" deliberation in accordance with adult's expectations. By approaching children's lived experience both from micro (e.g., whether children are fully included in a process of authentic deliberation) and macro (e.g., how the deliberative engagements function in a wider system in an authentic and inclusive way) angles, the deliberator model helps us come up with mechanisms that supplement the weaknesses of the existing practice and system itself.

Importantly, deliberative systems is not a theory of accommodating everything. Nor does it romanticize all children's activities uncritically, even though it allows us to assess their various communicative engagements, including nondeliberative ones, from a deliberative point of view. Deliberative systems is a theory of sharping deliberative possibilities in the real world.

Forming a Deliberative System

Thus far, I have discussed how the deliberator model underpinned by deliberative systems theory provides a useful framework to analyze and understand the deliberative role of children and suggests prescriptions, if any, for improving the weakness of their deliberative engagements. In what follows, I use the model to show how it frames children's various deliberative engagements as a contributing constituent of democracy. To this end, I pay attention to a global and student-led climate activism, known as Fridays for Future (henceforth FFF). It should be made clear that this section does not aim at providing a comprehensive account of FFF's contribution to democratizing global climate governance. Its primary goal is to sketch a broader view of how FFF can formulate and sophisticate the deliberative system on global climate governance. A more specific context-based analysis of FFF shall be discussed in chapter 7, with a specific focus on the interplay between their publicly visible protests and publicly invisible deliberative engagements.

FFF is an international student-led climate activist movement that problematizes world elites' irresponsibility and inaction toward climate change through nonviolent and nonpartisan means. The Swedish female activist Greta Thunberg is the symbolic icon of this movement. She started the protest in front of the Swedish national parliament when she was 15 in 2018. People call her protest activity Fridays for Future because the movement was started by Thunberg sitting alone on every Friday. Her action resonated with a massive number of students, adults, politicians, parents, and climate activists through old and new media.[10] Inspired by Thunberg and her fellows, on March 15, 2019, more than one million people in more than 120 countries joined the cross-national climate protests. Some countries have their own school strike groups run by students themselves (e.g., School Strike 4 Climate in Australia, Fridays for Future Tokyo in Japan).[11] At the time of writing this chapter (May 2024), FFF is an ongoing and longitudinal, project, and some scholarly findings are already available that shed light on multiple inclusive aspects of the movement.[12]

One clarification might be needed before we examine the deliberative contributions of FFF, because some might be quite skeptical about my case selection. For skeptics, protests and deliberative democracy are by nature strange bedfellows because, while deliberative democracy puts much value on an authentic form of communication, protests highlight strategic and nondeliberative use of language such as rhetoric, visual language, or performative language (Medearis 2005). Others also think that children's active involvement in protests can be undesirable for both society and children simply because there is a risk of manipulation and illegality (Hart 1997).[13] Because of these objections, children's protest engagement is seen as neither deliberative nor democratic. However, this is the very reason why FFF shall be analyzed through the lens of deliberative systems. The lens can portray the way in which previously unrecognized action (protests) initiated by previously ignored agents (children) make children deliberators in the context of global climate governance.

The following discussion examines the role of children in constituting a deliberative system on global climate governance. Its primary concern is various systemic contributions children make within the deliberative system that has been formed (mainly by adults) prior to the FFF movement, while the way in which teenage climate activists exert their deliberative agency both within and outside the system is to be discussed in chapter 7.

PUBLIC SPACE

On May 9, 1992, the United Nations Framework Convention on Climate Change (UNFCCC) was adopted. Since then, citizens, civil societies, and nongovernmental organizations have jointly engaged in activism related to climate change. Dryzek's (2005) analysis reveals that various actors and organizations have created and shaped different climate discourses over the past several decades. Some protests went beyond domestic borders and created the transnational public sphere by involving individual citizens, companies, policymakers, journalists, young people, and so forth, worldwide (Stevenson and Dryzek 2014). Some movements problematized the specific issue of climate change, while some other groups foregrounded broader political questions that emerged from climate change (e.g., global inequality between the North and South). Irrespective of global or domestic scale, the public space is the most essential space for climate activists to express their interest, represent various voices, and forge solidarity.

FFF can be situated within such a historic sequence of climate activism, yet the movement is described as "a historic turn in climate activism" (Wahlström et al. 2019, 6). This is so not because FFF is distinctive in terms of its deliberative authenticity. Like other existing climate movements, participants in FFF bring cheerfulness and joy to the forefront of the movement through rhetoric, cosplays, marching, rallies, dances, singing, and so forth (see Bowman 2019; Catanzaro and Collin 2021), that do not fit neatly into the authentic ideal of deliberative democracy. Nonetheless, we can say that one of the salient features of FFF is its inclusiveness. It has offered various pathways through which children and young people can express their concerns, interests, and emotions and shape climate discourse in local, national and global public spaces.

Historically, there have been many instances of involvement by children and young people in activism, yet the recruitment process was often strategic (e.g., adult citizens, organizations, and civil society organisations invited children to gain sympathetic response from the public) or occurred by default (e.g., children had no choice but to participate in a movement because their parents actively joined it) (Rodgers 2005). In contrast, the large-scale research on FFF conducted on March 15, 2019, by Mattias Wahlström and colleagues in European cities reveals how the movement made active, voluntary, and free participation by children possible (Wahlström et al. 2019). The researchers' short interviews (N = 1561) and surveys (N = 1925) show that the majority of youth participants joined or were recruited through their peer networks (e.g., friends, schoolmates). Using such peer networks enabled many children who had never previously demonstrated to take action in a public space for the first time (11). Accordingly, the movement offered a more inclusive platform where more and more children (including first-timers) could engage in claim-making in the public space with few institutional, organizational, or parental restrictions. The inclusive atmosphere of the movement may also affect gender composition as compared to climate activism in general. Wahlström and colleagues revealed that 66.4 percent of the protestors across the sample were women (9).

Moreover, FFF can be an inclusive project, as it has attempted to ensure an opportunity for participants to enjoy their activities by encouraging them to engage in protest through their everyday activities. By translating teenager-friendly means of action (e.g., music, school uniform, dance, marching) into their contentious action in the public space, children created and developed their own vocabulary to make their own claim, to appeal to wider publics, and to enjoy their activities (Bowman 2019; Catanzaro and Collin 2021). Such practice can also be found in online public space, including social media, online discussion platforms, and viral engagements[14]. Importantly, irrespective of the online or offline public space, participants join protest actions without relying on unfamiliar or unsafe pactices that are far from their everyday activities (e.g., property destruction), which in turn lowered the threshold of participation and sharpened participants' creativity in making their claim in the public space.

In this manner, children have continuously appeared in public spaces not through conventional channels (e.g., civil society, nongovernmental organizations) but through their personal networks and the practical applications of their everyday deeds. Consequently, FFF has facilitated inclusion of children in the process of (counter)discourse-making, redefinition of taken-for-granted concepts used in climate governance (e.g., "future," "sustainability"), and further mobilization of people affected by the climate crisis.

PRIVATE SPACE

Although few studies have examined the role of private space in deliberative systems,[15] FFF would offer insights into how children's everyday talk enhances the inclusive capacity of public deliberation about climate change. The key point here is that the more children engage in everyday political talk, the more opportunities people can gain to participate in demonstrations, thereby, ultimately, increasing the possibility of diversifying voices in the public space. For example, research shows that 482 students participating in FFF have engaged in everyday talk with their friends (including schoolmates), family members, teachers, and acquaintances to ask them to join the movement (Wahlstöm et al. 2019, 13). Michelle Catanzaro and Philippa Collin (2021) also analyze various homemade placards held at the Sydney School Strike for Climate protest, which imply how their protests in the public sphere are supported by their political paintings in their home. In addition, Greta's initial motivation for starting her school strike arose, according to her parents, out of her daily talk with them (Ernman et al. 2019). Again, their everyday talk in the private space is normally far from the authentic ideal of deliberative democracy. Nonetheless, the private space could create a precondition for further deliberation in the public space.

EMPOWERED SPACE

The increasing presence of young protestors in the public space, partially fostered by their everyday talk in the private space, produces various claims that problematize politicians' and decision-makers' inaction toward the contemporary climate crisis. That being said, children and young people usually have quite limited institutional setup and channels through which they directly persuade the authorities in the empowered space. Scholars have pointed out that this is one of the crucial limitations of child-led participation (e.g., Nishiyama 2017). However, even though all young protestors are unable to directly influence official decision-making, their collective voice can be represented by a few powerful leaders or icons of the movement who have opportunities to represent others, make a claim, persuade others, and exert pressure on decision-makers. Just as Malala Yousafzai has been invited to a number of empowered spaces as a symbol of women's rights and peace, Greta Thunberg has also appeared in various empowered spaces (including the United Nations, COP 24, the World Economic Forum, the European Parliament, London Assembly, the Austrian World Summit, and so forth).[16]

Some political maneuvers might have facilitated the invitation of Thunberg (e.g., symbolic use of the presence of Thunberg in the context of climate change), yet Thunberg and her collaborators have given public speeches intended to galvanize further deliberation across the deliberative system. From a deliberative democratic perspective, however, her speeches in the empowered spaces can be considered as effective expressions to the extent that they can provide an authentic or inclusive ground for deliberative systems. Indeed, a close reading of her speeches from 2018 to 2020 shows how they create opportunities for children's reason-giving in the empowered space.[17]

Her reasoning takes various forms. *Justification of opinion through reason-giving* is one of the key components of authentic reasoning, as early deliberative thinkers (e.g., Cohen 1989) point out. For example, Thunberg often draws on the Intergovernmental Panel on Climate Change (IPCC) report to underscore the significance of achieving a 50 percent reduction of CO_2 emissions within the next decade.[18] She also draws on multiple forms of resources to justify her claim. For example, in her speech at the London Assembly on April 23, 2019, she referred to the official report of the Global Carbon Project, a 2001 EU Directive on Air Quality, and the research report of the Tyndall Manchester Centre for Climate Change.

She also attempted to make her speech effective through *persuasion and demand*. In some speeches, she suggested redefining several key concepts such as "emergency" instead of "climate crisis" to change how people speak about the problem (the R20 Austrian World Summit, May 28, 2019). Quite often she suggested that climate activists would stop engaging in school strikes when the authorities pay continued attention to what the scientists say. For example, in the European Economic and Social Committee (February 21, 2019), she argued as follows: "We know that most politicians don't want to talk to us. Good, we don't want to talk to them either. We want them to talk to the scientists instead. Listen to them. . . . We don't have any other manifests or demands, you unite behind the science, that is our demand." Importantly, while her speeches were made with a critical tone, her reasoning is not limited to speech that takes a purely authentic form. Her reasoning is sometimes *emotional*, intended to express her disappointment and anger at political elites. She defines adults and politicians as "liars" to criticise their optimistic view of the future world[19] or to charge adults with irresponsibility for children's future in an emotional manner.[20]

Rhetoric is the other important and influential element of her speeches. Over the past two years, she has made a number of speeches in empowered spaces and produced widely recognized phrases. This includes, for example, "Our house is on fire" (World Economic Forum, January 25, 2019), "Unite behind the science" (Assemblée Nationale, July 23, 2019), or "How dare you!" (United Nations, September 23, 2019), among others.

On some occasions, Greta explains her thoughts through *storytelling*. On December 3, 2018, she was invited to COP 24 to give a speech. In her speech, she shared her early experience of school strikes with a specific focus on some adults' critical response:

> So when school started in August this year I sat myself down on the ground outside the Swedish parliament. I school striked for the climate. Some people say that I should be in school instead. Some people say that I should study to become a climate scientist so that I can "solve the climate crisis." . . . Why should I be studying for a future that soon may be no more, when no one is doing anything to save the future?

In this manner, Thunberg has given reasons in the empowered space. At this moment, no evidence exists on how her series of speeches influence climate policies and agendas and transform politicians' minds and decisions. Since FFF and Thunberg's strike are an ongoing project, further research is needed to understand the movement's short-term and long-term policy impacts. From a deliberative perspective, however, her series of public speeches in the empowered space can be assessed positively to the extent that children, albeit selected ones, can have a voice in the empowered space and that messages and claims made in the empowered space can inform the public space through a well-functioning transmission mechanism that shall be discussed below.

TRANSMISSION

Some expressive and performative activities observed in FFF are transmissive practices delivering a message produced in one space to another space or creating a new link between different parts of a deliberative system. Dryzek (2010) defines transmission as a process in which public space can influence empowered space, but FFF demonstrates that transmission is not limited to such a one-way process.[21]

Transmission can occur in such a way that empowered space influences public space when the movement's symbolic icon gives a powerful speech in an empowered space. For instance, as Malala Yousafzai said in her well-known UN speech, "one child, one teacher, one book, one pen can change the world," which was a signal to so many audiences worldwide. Likewise, Thunberg's aforementioned rhetoric has traveled to the public space worldwide and facilitated solidarity among many other climate activists who cannot express themselves in the empowered space, which is what Dryzek (2010, 76) calls the "bonding feature of rhetoric." Social media plays a crucial role in linking a message produced in a particular forum with informal activities of citizens such as social movements. Once Thunberg makes her speech in the empowered space, the speech is shared via newspapers, climate activists' official websites, YouTube, Facebook, and Twitter (X), coupled with hashtags and hyperlinks, thereby sending a signal to a wide range of global audiences (Wahlström et al. 2019). Thunberg initially used the term School Strike for Climate, but children and adults who were inspired by Thunberg's climate strike created a number of hashtag variations (e.g., #FridaysForFuture, #SchoolStrike4Climate) for jointly expressing students' concern to global audiences. According to Boulianne, Lalancette, and Ilkiw's (2020) research, FFF participants' use of a variety of hashtags allows young activists who live far apart from one another to share their collective opinions and key information about climate crisis and climate strike, and collectively blame government and other institutions for their inaction.

SOME INHIBITING FACTORS

When seen through the lens of the deliberator model, we can also find some missing mechanisms that prevent children from acting as effective deliberators.

The lack of adequate *accountability* and *protective mechanisms* are examples of the weakness of deliberative systems in the context of global climate governance. Some deliberative systems theorists (e.g., Dryzek 2010) contend that democratic legitimacy requires the empowered space to be accountable to claims made in public spaces. However, for children who are not given the suffrage, elections are not the best means for rendering politicians accountable. Demanding accountability from those in power, such as politicians, in the public sphere is also risky for many young people. When young participants in the March for Our Lives movement called for accountability from progun politicians, youth activists were abused and criticized publicly by right-wing politicians and the national rifle association. Likewise, children and teenagers participating in FFF faced public criticism, intimidation, insulation, and opposition,[22] which would have a withering effect on children's protests. As to be described in chapter 7, the fear of possible criticism from adults has affected Japanese climate activists' activities in many ways (i.e., postponement of all protest activities in the public space during the state of emergency under the COVID-19 pandemic situation). Given the limited nature of mechanisms that protect children and young people from public abuse as well as accountability mechanisms, voices expressed in the public space and empowered space would not reach opponents effectively.

There is also lack of publicly shared consensus about the difference between nondeliberative expressions and anti-deliberative ones, which prevents people from assessing the democratic contribution of FFF appropriately. This is due to the lack of reflective opportunities within the deliberative system regarding what constitutes deliberative, nondeliberative, and anti-deliberative criteria. As will be examined in depth in chapter 3, deliberative systems theory highlights the significance of nondeliberative acts as a potential component of the system, but it is highly critical about anti-deliberative acts that undercut both authentic and inclusive principles of deliberation. Even though both forms of expression somehow have a particular influence on the wider systems (e.g., promoting further deliberation in public spaces), this does not mean that they can be valued equally. As for FFF, we can find varieties of nondeliberative activities of protestors, but we can also find some anti-deliberative engagements (e.g., the overinsulation of political elites) that may result in making a society more deeply divided. Of course, as Mattheis (2020) rightly indicates, some "unruly" acts should be justified, as these are quite effective means for children whose activities are restricted under existing rules. Nevertheless, to enhance authentic and inclusive capacity as a systemic whole, it would also be important for deliberators to be self-reflective about whether their expressive acts are deliberative, nondeliberative, and anti-deliberative. We will revisit this issue in chapter 3 in more detail.

Conclusion

This chapter has described deliberative democracy, especially the systemic account of it, as a key theoretical framework for locating children in democracy. Deliberative systems theory has both normative and a methodological benefits in that it shifts our attention from a static understanding of agency, spaces, and consequences of deliberation toward an expanded one. This is because it allows us to approach children's various forms of communicative activities, including previously ignored ones, across different spaces.

On the basis of this argument, the chapter has theorized and offered a justification for adopting the deliberator model, which overturns some of the assumptions associated with the idea of children as future citizens. The core idea of the model is to define deliberators with respect to the expanded view of deliberative agents, spaces, and consequences. According to this model, there is no single transcendental threshold to distinguish deliberators from nondeliberators. Competencies, age, or social status could be important criteria, but these are not necessarily so. Deliberators do not need to be able to engage in authentic and inclusive communication anytime and anywhere: instead, what is essential is their *function*, or the way in which their communicative engagement plays a meaningful role in a specific context, as well as contributes to the overall authentic or inclusive quality of the wider deliberative system. In this sense, deliberative systems theory defines deliberators as not only individuals who engage directly in public deliberation but also individuals, such as deliberative entrepreneurs or formative agents, who can form and elaborate a deliberative system on a specific topic and create a foundation for further democratic deliberation across the system. We thus need to have a broader perspective of the kinds of spaces where people engage in deliberative acts.

As the case of FFF illustrates, children act as deliberators not only in physical spaces (e.g., private, public, and empowered space) but also in the invisible or connective sphere (e.g., transmission). Consequences produced by deliberators in deliberative systems can sometimes be immediate and tangible but are often not. Despite the intangibility of the consequences of their acts, the deliberator model must be viewed in both macro and micro terms, because an intangible consequence in a macro sense can serve as a key impetus for further deliberation in a micro sense. Again, the purpose of drawing on the case of FFF is to show how systemic theory creates room for incorporating children's previously downplayed communicative acts as a legitimate form of deliberative participation. In chapter 7, we will revisit the more micro and everyday story of FFF in the context of Japan and its implications for democratic education.

With the framework of the deliberator model, I contend that children should be recognized as deliberators rather than mere future citizens. But if children are not future citizens, what should democratic education be? This is a difficult question, because education's essence is generally understood as a *preparation for future*. The next chapter shall tackle this puzzle.

Chapter 2

Theorizing Deliberative Democratic Learning

Education is a recurring theme in democracy studies. A widely held view says that a healthy democratic society delivers a good-quality democratic education to develop children's minds, attitudes, and participatory skills in terms of democracy (see Callan 1997; Gutmann 1999; Nussbaum 2012; Noddings 2013). Likewise, staunch democrats have also envisaged education as a key driving force for making society more deliberative and democratic. Over the past 20 years, deliberative theory has appeared in the classroom in many countries in both formal and informal manners. This application of deliberative theory in classrooms is generally called *education for deliberative democracy* (Samuelsson 2016).

In the previous chapter, I discussed problems associated with the conceptualization of children as future citizens and suggested the deliberator model as an alternative. Given that children are deliberators, not future citizens, what is the role of democratic education? Despite a rich number of theoretical, empirical, and practical findings reported over several decades, both the theorization of democratic education and its practical application contradict the deliberator model for several reasons: namely, a trusting acceptance of the assumption of children's incompetency, the narrow understanding of the meaning of development, and an overreliance on a rigid understanding of deliberation and competency building.

I agree that such trends of education for deliberative democracy can, whether implicitly or explicitly, be located within Jean Piaget's developmental psychology paradigm. Although education for deliberative democracy scholars rarely refer to Piaget's work itself, the way in which they frame human development is significantly informed by the typically (mis)interpreted version of Piaget's work that I call the *Piagetian Geist*. As we will see, what characterizes the Piagetian Geist shared in education for deliberative democracy is evolutionism and universalism, and the chapter will problematize their underlying assumptions from the two distinct perspectives: deliberative system theory and sociocultural human development theory. Both criticisms reveal that the logic of evolutionism and universalism limit the potential of children's deliberative acts, justify the exclusion of children from deliberative processes, and ultimately reinforce the idea of "children as future citizens."

These two criticisms necessitate a transition away from the Piagetian Geist theory of the aim of democratic education, the meaning of development of competency, and the space of education for deliberative democracy. Instead, they require us to focus on theories of scholars inspired by Lev Vygotsky (or, so to speak, the Vygotskian Geist), in particular, Yrjö Engeström's expansive learning theory. Engeström's reformation of Vygotsky's concept of socioculturally mediated activity offers key insights into the revised idea of education for deliberative democracy, renamed *deliberative democratic learning*.

This deliberative democratic learning is underpinned by five distinct characteristics: *revolutionarity* (the aim of deliberative democratic learning is to enable children's agency of meaning-making), *reflection* and *contextuality* (deliberation and its competence should be understood as a socioculturally embedded tool that is open for reflective reinterpretation), *collective transformation* (the unit of analysis of democratic education is a transformation of a process of collective engagement in meaning-making), and *systemic practice* (democratic education occurs across the system of deliberative democracy). Deliberative democratic learning defines learning and development as a meaning-making process in which children deconstruct, reconstruct, and co-construct the theory and norms of deliberation. Deliberative democratic learning is also not a universalist project because it places more value on the contextuality, reflection, and creativity of children's deliberative activities than the mere acquisition of one-size-fits-all deliberative competencies. Deliberative democratic learning does not ask, "How do children practice deliberation as predetermined deliberative norms expect?" Instead, its attention is on the circular process where children themselves take primary ownership of problematizing, analyzing, modelling, (re)theorizing, and implementing their own deliberative norm and activity.

The way in which education for deliberative democracy has become a key trend in democratic education is illustrated in the first two sections. The subsequent sections then challenge its core assumptions informed by the Piagetian Geist and go on to theorize about deliberative democratic learning.

Deliberative Democracy and Citizens' Competencies

Deliberative theorists often expect citizens to have a specific set of competencies prior to their participation. The competencies required for democratic deliberators are quite varied. From a normative point of view, deliberators must, first and foremost, be equipped with effective communication skills, including logical inference, reasoning, rational judgement, listening and talking, and they must be able to use these skills with people who have different, or even opposite, opinions. Deliberators are also expected to put their self-interest aside in consideration of the public's best interest by using skills like collaboration, conflict management, and openness. Furthermore, deliberators should be able to collect relevant information and evidence and analyze these factors appropriately to generate better solutions to complex social and political problems. Table 2.1 outlines some typical examples of competencies expected of citizens in normative theory.

Table 2.1a–b. Examples of normatively required deliberative competencies.

Table 2.1a. Norm: Authenticity.

Competencies	Normative requirements	Reference
Reasoning	Individuals express their views through evidence, which should be as logical, persuasive, and noncoercive as possible.	Habermas (1996) Dryzek (2000)
Rational judgement	Individuals should be able to make a judgement based on their reason-exchange rather than their immediate feelings or biased information.	Goodin (2003) Cohen (1989) Habermas (1996) Bohman (1996)
Public-spiritedness	Individuals should put their narrow self-interests aside and instead take the common good into account.	Gutmann and Thompson (1996) Benhabib (1996) Bohman (1996)
Information collection and analysis	Individuals should be informed through a full examination of the provided data and evidence.	Fishkin (2009)
Reflective thinking	Individuals should be able to examine their own preferences in a reflective manner and, if necessary, change them.	Fishkin (2009) Goodin (2003)

Source: Created by the author.

Table 2.1b. Norm: Inclusiveness.

Competencies	Normative requirements	Reference
Respect and care	Individuals should acknowledge the integrity of others and respect different perspectives, especially if expressed by disadvantaged people.	Young (1997) Gutmann and Thompson (2004)
Openness	Individuals should be open to various perspectives, interests, and concerns, even if these are opposite to one's own opinion.	Gutmann and Thompson (1996) Young (1997)
Empathetic imagination	Individuals should deliberate in a way that considers benefits of interlocutors and people outside a deliberative forum.	Goodin (2003) Morrell (2010)

Source: Created by the author.

However, some deliberative democrats believed that this sort of normative theorization of deliberative citizens and their competencies was too demanding. Daniel Bell, for example, argued "not all citizens have the same capacity to reflect upon and apply principles of deliberation to complex cases" (Bell 1997, 74). More recently, Ian O'Flynn summarized the concern that "ordinary people may lack the motivation and the capacity for meaningful deliberation" (O'Flynn 2021, 7).

In the past two decades, two findings have addressed this worry in two different ways. Some theorists and psychologists support Bell's argument, demonstrating how citizens have poor deliberation skills. For example, Shawn Rosenberg (2014) concluded that the vast majority of adult citizens are not equipped with the necessary analytical, logical, communicative, and rational judgement skills. Cass Sunstein (2000) also questioned citizens' deliberative competencies (particularly critical and reflective thinking skills) by illustrating real world cases where citizens are vulnerable to groupthink, especially in the context of deliberation in a like-minded group. These findings lead to the pessimistic conclusion that citizens' deliberative competencies do not meet the normative standards of classic deliberative theory.

While the above findings were mainly observed in a laboratory setting, deliberation in the real world provides opposite, more optimistic insights. For example, Marlène Gerber et al. (2016) challenged the conventional negative view on citizens' deliberative competencies by drawing on the case of EuroPolis, a transnational deliberative poll. Their study measured the quality of citizens' deliberation, which shows that the normative require-ment of deliberative democracy is not so demanding because participants scored high on deliberative standards (including justification, rationality, common good orientation, respect, empathy, and inquisitiveness). Thus, Gerber et al. concluded that it is unfair to treat citizens as incompetent beings because, to use their term, "the ideal deliberator scoring high on all deliberative dimensions as envisaged by classic deliberative theory exists" (1113).

Some may not be fully persuaded by this conclusion, because, as Gerber et al. acknowledge, they have analyzed only a small number of deliberative groups. Often, people are not willing to participate in such deliberative public matters because they prioritize their private affairs over public matters, they are not interested in the issue in question, or they may prefer not to talk with strangers (Jacquet 2017). Consequently, even if people *inside* the deliberative forum are highly deliberative, this conclusion does not lead to another conclusion that citizens, including those *outside* the forum, can also be deliberative.

Perhaps, in my view, we should be neither too pessimistic nor optimistic about citizens' deliberative competencies. Although Gerber et al.'s research reveals that highly competent citizens exist, it does not show whether citizens at large (including nonparticipants of deliberative forums) can also engage in a high-quality deliberation. Thus, for many people, it may be natural to conclude that citizens can deliberate *to some degree* even if they are not equipped with all competencies required for democratic deliberation. However, it is also believed that deliberation becomes more meaningful if more and more citizens have a clearer understanding of how to deliberate together prior to participation. This view then leads to growing attention on the significant role of education for deliberative democracy.

Education for Deliberative Democracy

Many deliberative researchers have envisaged education in general as a key driving force for realizing deliberative democracy in the real world. After analyzing citizens' deliberative qualities in different countries, Jürg Steiner (2012, ch. 11) argued how education contributes to the realization of better deliberative democracy by cultivating students' cognitive skills and creating deliberative cultures in schools and society. Michael Morrell (2010, 187), a deliberative theorist researching the place and role of empathy in deliberation, also argues that empathy training is a key responsibility of the public education system. Likewise, Sharon Krause (2008, 135), a scholar of deliberation and emotion, recommends the education of moral sentiment and the development of sympathy. Gutmann and Thompson (1996, 359), leading deliberative democrats, also define educational systems as the single most important institution outside government that can make democracy more deliberative. Even though their main argument does not center on education, their concluding argument often discusses how education can be an important supplementary element in the theorization of deliberative democracy.

After the deliberative turns occurred in democratic theory, studies on democratic education also experienced the same turn. To date, a series of joint works between practitioners and theorists has facilitated a number of theoretical, practical, and empirical studies of deliberation in educational settings, and their diversity is attributed to the different ways in which scholars and practitioners interpret what deliberation is and ought to be. For example, some practices are driven by a collaborative and consensual approach (Molnar-Main 2017), while other practices bring the agonistic and conflictual aspect of deliberation to the fore (Stitzlein 2014). Despite the difference, it is usually agreed that the purpose of education for deliberative democracy is to cultivate in students' the competencies required for their future engagement in public deliberation (see table 2.1).

In spite of a variety of different theoretical takes on the concept of deliberation, when it comes to practical implementation many people employ the learning-by-doing approach. Walter Parker (2010) argues that the key to democratic education lies in a shift from learning about deliberation toward involvement in deliberative democracy. Parker divides such participatory democratic education into two kinds: seminar and deliberation. The former is a text-based discussion where learners read and interpret a text together "to see the world more deeply and clearly thanks to the selection of the text, the opening question and the multiple interpretations and experiences that are brought to bear by discussants" (2826). The latter focuses on a controversial public issue, and strives to create an environment wherein learners "are finding, studying and weighing alternatives in order to decide a course of action" (2826). Regardless of whether we take the seminar or deliberative discussion approach, the general features of such learning-by-doing practice can be summarized as follows:

- *Controversial topic*: Students talk about controversial social, economic, cultural, moral/ethical, and political questions (e.g., climate change, immigration policy, ethics of genome editing) (Lipman 2003; Hess 2009).

- *Preparation and instruction*: Students are asked to prepare prior to deliberation, including collecting necessary information about the topic for deliberation, or teachers offer such information prior to deliberation. Usually, teachers give some instruction about good deliberation (Luskin et al. 2007; McAvoy and Hess 2013).

- *Deliberation*: Students discuss the topic to deepen their understanding of the issue in question, frame and analyze the issue, solve a specific problem, or, if possible, reach a consensus, thereby developing the abilities, knowledge and attitudes they are expected to learn (Samuelsson 2016; Mehltretter Drury, Kuehl, and Anderson 2017; Molnar-Main 2017).

- *Facilitation*: While students deliberate, a teacher serves as a facilitator to assist students' effective deliberation and competency building (Hess and McAvoy 2015; Nishiyama et al. 2023; see also chapter 5 of this book).

With these features, education for deliberative democracy is practiced in many educational institutions, ranging from higher education (Thomas 2010; Schaffer et al. 2017) to primary as well as secondary schools across the globe (Hess 2009; Molnar-Main 2017; Steiner and Jaramillo 2019; Nishiyama et al. 2023). Advocates argue that experiencing deliberation in the classroom allows students to become fully competent deliberators in the future, which in turn contributes to addressing various political gridlocks in contemporary societies and improving the democratic quality of the public sphere. For advocates, various competencies developed through education for deliberative democracy are "essential to civic engagement in the twenty first century" (Mehltretter Drury, Kuehl, and Anderson 2017, 192).

Piagetian Geist in Education for
Deliberative Democracy

The availability of a good-quality democratic education is one of the key indicators of the democratic quality of society, and this is the reason many political theorists and education scholars have jointly pursued designing and implementing deliberation in educational settings over the past 20 years. In these attempts, the term "development" frequently appears.[1] Even if people do not use this term explicitly, there could be no scholars working on education for deliberative democracy without considering what development means. Surprisingly, however, little is known about what sort of "development" people share and assume when they talk about education for deliberative democracy. Their use of the term development might be directly or indirectly informed by developmental psychology, but we have rarely examined what sort of developmental psychology paradigm carves out the conventional understanding of development in the context of education for deliberative democracy.[2]

As will be illustrated below, French psychologist Jean Piaget's developmental psychology paradigm anchors the concept of development within the discussion of education for deliberative democracy. Piaget is one of the "main geniuses in the field of developmental psychology" (Lourenço 2012, 281) who "dominated thinking around children and young people in the latter half of the twentieth century, particularly Western legislative and educational initiatives regarding children and young people's competence" (Hartung 2017b, 15).

Equally important to note here is that Piagetian developmental theory, especially in comparison with Lev Vygotsky's, has been read in a particular fashion. The most popular reading is to understand Piaget as an individualist. In this reading, Piaget focused intensively on individual process of development, while Vygotsky acknowledged the significance of the social interaction in one's development. As "genuine" Piagetian and Vygotskian theories both commonly argue, however, such "stereotypic" reading oversimplifies Piaget.[3] However, such a stereotypically individualistic reading of Piaget's theory resonated with the dominant Cartesian tradition of Western science that dichotomizes the individual and the social, thereby becoming "canonical" (Cole and Wertsch 1996, 250) in our understanding of development. Martyn Griffin (2011) indicates that education for deliberative democracy is also not an exception, as its underlying concept of development relies largely on the *Piagetian* interpretation and reading of what Piaget argues. Thus, I henceforth call the widely shared *post-Piaget* scholars' interpretation and reading *Piagetian Geist*.

Piagetian Geist gives us two distinct characteristics of human development: *evolutionism* and *universalism*. Although Piaget himself did not use these terms, they are nonetheless widely discussed by many psychologists. In what follows, I shall summarize how Piagetian Geist's evolutionism and universalism is still alive in the concept of development in education for deliberative democracy.

EVOLUTIONISM

Piaget's psychological theory is interpreted as *evolutionism* or an evolutional theory of human development (Reimer, Paolitto, and Hersh 1990; Griffin 2011). On this interpretation, childhood is defined as a transitional process embedded in humans' biological and natural mechanism, where children as tabula rasa become competent humans (or adults). Piaget explained how humans' internal biological mechanism enables children in a different developing age group to adapt to the environment in a different manner and thereby develop their cognitive and mental abilities (Piaget and Inhelder 1969). To explain this, Piaget suggested the framework of *stages* based on his observation of a number of infants. This concept illustrates that human beings have a fixed internal structure and mechanism (or what Piagetian scholars call scheme). In light of this view, there are some distinct evolutional stages where the structure and mechanism define what people can and cannot think and perceive. In particular, Piaget divides children's cognitive development into four sequential stages (Piaget 1952, 1962; Piaget and Inhelder 1969): (1) the sensorimotor stage (the first phase of development), where infants use the basic sense and motor abilities they were born with to understand the environment; (2) the preoperational stage (the second stage occurring between the ages of 2 and 7), where children apply their basic language and reasoning abilities to the environment yet are normally unable to see things from a different viewpoint (this is what Piaget calls egocentrism); (3) the concrete operational stage (the third phase occurring between the ages of 7 and 12) in which children gain abilities in terms of logical thinking, hypothetical and abstract inference, and understanding what others think, and (4) the formal operational stage (the final stage that lasts into adulthood) where children are able to think in a more sophisticated manner than the previous stages.

The idea of the stage of development led to several derivative interpretations. First, children in a lower stage are essentially helpless in isolation and therefore expected to grow up gradually with the help of education and then become adults. Here, adults are regarded as a standard or stage of completion. Second, adult educators are expected to get a clearer understanding of the final goal of children's development and make various assistive efforts to help children reach such goals effectively. It is important that children adapt to educational processes prepared by adults, and, in this sense, children are expected to intentionally reproduce what the society (adults) expects. Some researchers point out that such understanding distorts Piaget's own intentions; for example, Piaget did rank the top and bottom stages or try to explain everything about child development from a biological point of view, as his psychology's core question was "What is intelligence and how is it developed?" rather than "Who is intelligent?" or "When does one become intelligent?" (Piaget 1952, 1962). As I have already noted, however, the significance for this chapter is not what Piaget himself actually thought and said but rather the question, "In what way is the Piagetian Geist imported into democratic education, and how does it give shape to education for deliberative democracy?"

Often, the Piagetian Geist makes an important influence on the idea of political socialization. The core idea behind political socialization is that children must prepare to conform to the future democratic society through a well-designed educational program. Abendschön's definition of political socialization shows that this is "the process of how individuals find their place within a political community by acquiring knowledge, skills, and attitudes with respect to the political system" (Abendschön 2014, 1). Whether implicitly or explicitly, political socialization postulates that adult citizens, who can create a political community, are the goal of development, whereas children are thought of as agents fitting into the (adults') political community and assumed to be individuals who do not have sufficient skills, virtues, and attitudes required for democracy. David Moshman (2020), for example, defines rationality and various social and civic competencies as "the *outcome* of developmental process" and calls for democratic education that fosters children's development (90; emphasis added). For this reason, advocates for political socialization of this kind tend to emphasize the significance of preparation, and children are understood as those preparing for the goal of development.

Insights gained from political socialization studies then appear in education for deliberative democracy studies and establish the view that children are less mature than adult deliberators. As one of the most popular theorists of deliberative democracy and democratic education, Amy Gutmann insists that "deliberative democracy underscores the importance of publicly supported education that develops the capacity to deliberate among all children as *future* free and equal citizens" (Gutmann 1999, xii; emphasis added). As a practitioner, Stacie Molnar-Main indicates that the primary mission of education for deliberative democracy is to ensure "*the next generation of citizens* has the skills needed to act on the pressing issues facing our nation and communities" (Molnar-Main 2017, 28; emphasis added). Jack Crittenden also argues that "the assurance that we as citizens want is that our *future* fellow democrats have knowledge and judgement sufficient to make informed decisions and the thoughtfulness or critical-thinking skills to deliberate politically" (Crittenden 2002, 112; emphasis added). For him, children can be more autonomous, deliberative and thoughtful "once they *become* citizens" (112; emphasis added). The underlying logic behind these arguments is that children are at present neither citizens nor deliberators precisely because they are not adults and are regarded as immature and incompetent beings.

Moreover, the emphasis on the future of children may also lead to conceptualizing schools and classrooms not as a space for children's current democratic practice but as a place to prepare for the future. For instance, Gutmann and Thompson argue that "without a civil society that provides *rehearsal* space for political deliberation, citizens are less likely to be politically effective" (Gutmann and Thompson 2004, 35; emphasis added).

Consequently, scholars in the education for deliberative democracy camp tend to situate children in the middle of the evolutional stage. They assume that, if children as positioned at an immature stage are appropriately educated, "the likelihood that they will be capable of doing so will increase" and thus "the possibility of successfully implementing more deliberative practices in society would also increase" (Samuelsson 2016, 3). Thus, the Piagetian Geist's evolutionism requires primarily adults to be responsible for identifying the ideal goal of deliberators (mostly adults with specific competencies) and then implementing a deliberative practice in a way that allows children to successfully reach the goal (e.g., Luskin et al. 2007). Conversely, if children do not deliberate like adults or fail to deliberate in accordance with the predetermined milestones set by adult educators, they are regarded as neither developed nor competent deliberators. Crocco et al. (2018, 7) studied education for deliberative democracy with children and concluded that children failed to practice "true deliberation" because the majority of children did not talk democratically in an expected manner. Their judgement of "failure" comes only from adult researchers' points of view, which may be underpinned by the assumption that adults prepare everything (e.g., final goal, ideal outcome, process) and children should be adaptive to what is prepared.

UNIVERSALISM

Piaget identified the importance of the natural and spontaneous psychogenesis characteristics of the individual as key to understanding the development of this biological intelligence (Piaget 1952; see also Lourenço 2012, 285). For him, an individual is an autonomous being and the process by which she internally constructs and dialectically refines a cognitive element in relation to the environment and others. Eduard Martí (2013) thus describes Piaget's theory as an inside-out theory of development, and, for Piaget, such a theory is a universal aspect of human development, which in turn leads some scholars to depict Piaget as a *universalist*. Matusov and Hayes (2000) indicate that Piaget "believed that rationality, logic, and principles of scientific thinking have universal applicability for all developing individuals in all societies" (224). Coupled with the evolutionism interpretation, Piaget's universalism is also interpreted as a process where children, regardless of the context, can become intelligent adult humans if they progress with a biologically predetermined "normal" course of development. Inspired by Piaget, Moshman indicates that, while he acknowledges that development does not always happen at the exact same age, he also arguess that "biologically *normal* children in *normal* human social environments construct the same basic rational competencies in the same sequence at about the same age" (Moshman 2020, 112; emphasis added).[4]

Griffin (2011) indicates that the universalist view of development is shared by education for deliberative democracy researchers because they often presuppose that each individual child has to acquire universally applicable deliberative competencies. Such presupposition leads to "an overarching agreement that students and future citizens learn the skills and values necessary for deliberative democratic participation by partaking in deliberative discussions" (Samuelsson 2016, 1). Much ink has been used for identifying what such universally meaningful deliberative competencies children should acquire. Molnar-Main (2017, 19–20), for example, shows how education for deliberative democracy enables students to "learn content and make personal connections to issues," "learn about others' concerns and experiences," "argue for and evaluate different approaches to a problem," "practice expressing agreement and disagreement," "learn how to find common ground with those who have different views and experiences," and "maintain their own views about the issue, which may differ from those of others in the class." Thomas also summarizes three general competencies students should learn through classroom deliberation: "effective communication skills in a variety of contexts and among diverse groups of people," "effective dialogue, deliberation, public reasoning and collaborative decision-making skills," and "competent understanding and critical analysis of knowledge and information" (Thomas 2010, 4). Griffin summarizes the current argument, saying, "If Piaget's theory provides an account of how children become internally competent deliberative citizens in one society, it provides an account of how they can become internally competent deliberative citizens in any society" (Griffin 2011, 10). Importantly, the presupposition that and these deliberative competencies are applicable in any context leads to a strong aspiration toward what Bächtiger and Parkinson (2019) call *deliberative all-rounders*, who "simultaneously give reasons [that] are common good oriented, and listen respectfully" (52; see also Gerber et al. 2016). As table 2.1 shows, there are various competencies that ideal adult citizens need to have prior to deliberation, and the core mission of education for deliberative democracy is considered to mold incompetent beings into all-rounders.[5]

In addition, the primary unit of analysis in Piagetian Geist's universalism is an individual, and practice of education for deliberative democracy tends to follow the same line. Luskin et al.'s (2007) experiment on deliberative polls in the classroom compares pre- and post-deliberation surveys in order to understand each student's development and transformation of opinion and desirable civic attitudes through deliberation. Alternatively, Steiner's long-term projects on deliberation in Brazilian schools attempt to measure how each student in a treatment group acquires good deliberative competencies and civic virtues such as reasoning skills or empathy (Steiner and Jaramillo 2019). What these practices share in common is that both focus on an *individual's* internal transformation. Both aim to measure how each individual child acquires the desirable deliberative competencies, knowledge, civic attitudes, and civic virtues through deliberation. They presuppose that the more assessment boxes are ticked, the more a competent deliberator each child becomes.

People inspired by the Piagetian Geist, namely, its evolutionism and universalism, tend to imagine education for deliberative democracy as a

direct step-by-step lineal process: (1) deontologically predetermine competencies (e.g., reasoning, communication skills, sympathy) that children
must learn; (2) design a deliberative process in a way that fits into children's current developmental stage; (3) practice deliberation with children;
and then (4) measure how each child acquires required competencies
and the degree to which she or he is molded into an ideal deliberator
(or deliberative all-rounder). The ultimate purpose of such educational
process is, according to Crittenden, "to prepare *all* future citizens for
active democratic participation," and thus the publicly supported democratic education should "ensure that *every citizen* meets the requirements
of such participation regardless of what any individual state, family, or
leader wants" (Crittenden 2002, 200; emphasis added). In other words,
as Crittenden's argument shows, it is *normatively* expected that everyone
becomes deliberative all-rounders.

Two Potential Critiques

As a researcher of democratic education, I agree with the *significance* of
education for deliberative democracy but object to the existing *rationale*
provided for supporting and justifying its significance. My criticism derives
from two different yet interlinked theories: deliberative systems theory
and the sociocultural psychology theory. The first, which I introduce
as *systemic critique*, argues that aspiring to be a deliberative all-rounder
allows little room for incorporating children in a deliberative system;
therefore, it undercuts the deliberator model suggested in chapter 1. As
already explained, a well-functioning deliberative system does not rely
on the discrete competencies of individual citizens. Even though each
contributing individual may not be capable of deliberating in ways that
meet a normative threshold, deliberative democracy puts a lot of focus on
the collaboration and division of labor between those individuals. Overall,
while the Piagetian Geist underpinned by evolutionism and universalism
defines children as future deliberators on the grounds of their lack of
competency, empirical findings counteract this assumption by showing
how difficult it is to identify a universal "must learn" competency prior
to actual deliberation.

Another criticism, which I introduce as *sociocultural critique*, is
informed by the developmental psychology theory formulated by Lev
Vygotsky. When seen through the Vygotskian sociocultural lens, the

existing theory of education for deliberative democracy underpinned by evolutionism and universalism weakens the contextual, or more specifically sociogenetic aspect of competency and human development. From the sociocultural critique's perspective, we need to shift our understanding of development of one's competency, away from something that is able to be predetermined, toward a more contextual and comprehensive process.

SYSTEMIC CRITIQUE

As we explored in chapter 1, one of the core features of deliberative systems is the strong emphasis on a functional division of labor where each differentiated contributing part makes effective use of the strength of the others. As Bohman rightly notes, we "do not need to idealize deliberation in each dimension . . . but rather test the deliberative system as a whole and how it functions overall according to a basic list of democratic functions" (Bohman 2012, 85). Given that deliberative systems function in this way, we should reconsider the following two questions: (1) Should education for deliberative democracy aim to create deliberative all-rounders who have universally applicable deliberative competencies? (2) Is it possible and desirable to rigorously identify the "useful" and "necessary" competencies before actual deliberation takes place?

Regarding the first question, the answer is "no." Although research shows that deliberative all-rounders exist in the real world (Gerber et al. 2016), this sort of finding does not immediately lead to the normative claim that everyone should be deliberative all-rounders. One reason can be found in Gerber et al.'s own research on EuroPolis, which suggests that, while deliberative all-rounders scored high on all deliberative dimensions, "less privileged people in the European "polis"—lower-class participants, particularly from the European periphery—were also the least skilled deliberators" (1113). This implies that there is no crucial difference in deliberative quality between differently skilled participants if they face a highly controversial question. Put simply, deliberative all-rounders are a favorable condition for a successful deliberation, but they are not a necessary condition for realizing it. In addition, the ambition for deliberative all-rounders tends to neglect the role of nondeliberative acts and actors in deliberative systems. As we saw in chapter 1, a political expression, with a limited deliberative quality with respect to the normative standard can contribute to galvanizing further public deliberation or mobilizing more and more people into public debate about the issue in question, thereby supporting the authentic and inclusive quality of deliberative systems (Mansbridge et al. 2012; Nishiyama 2017). A healthy and well-functioning deliberative system relies significantly on the functional division of labor between varieties of acts and actors rather than on the single powerful and high-skilled individual. Even though we can be a deliberative all-rounder, it does not justify the claim that education for deliberative democracy should aim to create a deliberative all-rounder.

Furthermore, if we accept the claim that we use developmental (im) maturity as a threshold for inclusion and exclusion of children, logically speaking the same must be applied to adult citizens. In reality, there are children who are more psychologically as well as physically mature than adults in general or there are adults who are less mature than children in general. If so, should we include mature children and exclude less mature adults instead? If this seems a curious question, it is necessary to acknowledge the curiosity of excluding children on the grounds of their developmental immaturity as well. Some may explain the difference between adults and children in terms of levels of linguistic ability, but this explanation offers a weak foundation for understanding children in democracy. Donaldson and Kymlicka (2016) worry that, if linguistic ability serves as the only entrance ticket to participate in public deliberation, it excludes not only children but also people with cognitive disabilities, thereby producing an exclusive democracy founded upon ableism and elitism. Given that the original goal of deliberative democracy is to promote marginalized voices rather than legitimizing voices of the powerful (Bohman 1996), the exclusion of children from deliberation based on their limited linguistic ability cannot be justified in any way.[6]

My response to the second question is, likewise, "no," due to the impossibility of identifying "useful" and "meaningful" deliberative competency prior to actual deliberation. A deliberative system is comprised of multiple ways of deliberating; therefore, the same person may take different roles in distinct deliberative settings. This means that one person's same quality of deliberative engagement does not necessarily have the same consequence in different contexts. Imagine the situation where a person has strong logical reasoning skill. Many deliberative theorists think of logical reasoning as one of the essential skills for enabling rational deliberation in the public sphere (e.g., Habermas 1996; Rawls 2001; Moshman 2020). However, the heavy use of this skill, or a sort of hyperrationalism, may have a risk of depriving the marginalized of opportunities to have a voice in some situations (Young 2000). Similarly, while openness is one of the key deliberative attitudes in democratic education studies (Molnar-Main 2017), Robert Goodin (2018) argues that in a deliberative system "it may be deliberatively undesirable for all stages in the process to be fully open to public scrutiny" (891), because some decisions must inevitably be made behind closed doors. Even if openness is seen as a desirable attitude, open deliberation does not need to be available anytime and anywhere.

Moreover, defining a "competent" deliberator is hard work in itself, because the degree to which one can exert one's own deliberative competency depends significantly on the context. Christopher Karpowitz and Tali Mendelberg's (2014, ch. 5) empirical study shows that female participants in a deliberative forum, despite their high deliberative potential, tend to be in a disadvantaged position in most mixed-gender deliberative groups, because male participants are more likely to decide whose voice predominates. However, once such disadvantaged female participants have a chance to deliberate in a well-designed structure in a group setting, they can deliberate at high quality levels. An important lesson from Karpowitz and Mendelberg's study is that whether one can be a "competent" deliberator is determined not by how she or he develops and internalizes the required competencies but by the context under which the opportunity to participate in deliberation is afforded.

Empirical findings also proved that some assumptions regarding the competencies anchored by evolutionism and universalism are irrelevant. Evolutionism in the Piagetian Geist leads to a sort of ageism that understands children as future citizens on the ground of their lack of competencies *in comparison with adult citizens* (Crittenden 2002). Moshman notes that "adults at their best are rational in ways beyond the competence of children" (Moshman 2020, 88). In light of this view, "true" deliberators, or a final destination of development, are supposed to be adult citizens who have completed the process of cumulative training of deliberation. It is taken for granted that older is better; however, this is a problematic assumption from the perspective of the deliberator model. As theorized in chapter 1, many children, as best exemplified by participants in the FFF movement, show their deliberative competencies within multiple components of the deliberative system differently. Furthermore, it has gradually been proved that many adult citizens are, in reality, less deliberative than the normative theory presupposes. As already noted, some deliberative thinkers question adult citizens' deliberative competency, and Rosenberg's psychological study proposes a more critical conclusion that "individuals' thinking appears to lack the objectivity, complication, integration and abstraction to enable them to appreciate the complexity of social problems and to imagine effective, novel ways of addressing them" (Rosenberg 2014, 112).

The systemic critique proposes that everyone, regardless of age and developmental stage, has the potential to act as deliberators across different contexts of a deliberative system. This proposal offers an important implication for democratic education. A widely shared view says that the goal of education for deliberative democracy is to *create* the educated deliberative citizens (Englund 2022), but what is missing here is that children can already be active deliberators in a specific context of a deliberative system. While education for deliberative democracy tends to assume that well-functioning deliberation relies on the presence of competent citizens and that well-educated children can act as good deliberators when they become adults (Moshman 2020), evidence shows that this is not always so. Even though each child lacks set of deliberative competencies, she or he can collaborate with others to act as a powerful deliberator, collectively formulating and refining the democratic quality of deliberative systems through multiple pathways and means. Therefore, the question that democratic education should be asking is not "What competencies do children not possess?" but "What competencies of deliberation do children potentially have, under what conditions can children deliberate, and how can we refine potential competencies that children possess?"

SOCIOCULTURAL CRITIQUE

Piagetian theory of human development focuses on Piaget's organic and biological approach that asks how individuals develop their cognitive ability in a way that adapts their organic mechanism to the new environment around them. On this account, the organic mechanism is a sort of guide creating an effective channel for enabling what Piaget calls assimilation (a process where individuals encounter a new environment and fit themselves into it) and accommodation (a process of complete alternation of their preexisting framework to see the world around them) (Piaget 1952). As we can clearly see here, the Piagetian take on psychological development is a lineal process moving from individual to social. Grounded on this view, as Lourenço (2012) notes, Piagetian psychologists and their supporters interpret the term "development" as a purely *individual-centric* psychogenesis phenomenon. If a child fails to assimilate or accommodate the given environment, she or he is seen as a less matured person. Competency is thus a production of an *individual's achievement* of a predetermined developmental milestone, and "the responsibility for development lies with the individual themselves" (Griffin 2011, 17).

Vygotsky casts skeptical eyes toward such an understanding of humans in isolation. For Vygotsky, children's development should focus on the dialectical relationship of one's biological factors and one's participation in shared sociocultural activities. In *Thought and Language*, Vygotsky (2012) attempted to explain this point by contrasting himself with Piaget in terms of children's egocentric speech. For Piaget, children at an early developmental stage are psychologically egocentric and therefore their speech acts are oriented toward themselves. Piaget took young children's frequent use of inner speech (e.g., a speech act directed to and for oneself, like a soliloquy) as an example of children's egocentricity and analyzed such inner speech as an undeveloped form of speech act that is unique to early childhood and is unrelated to the development of children's thinking. Such inner speech may disappear or be replaced by social communication (outer speech) as they become psychologically mature. This transition process from inner to outer speech is, for Piaget, a key for measuring children's cognitive development. As indicated, his theory is therefore summarized as inside-out theory of development (Martí 2013).

Vygotsky's study of children's inner speech is contrastive. He summarizes his claim as follows: "The primary function of speech, in both children and adults, is communication, social contact. The earliest speech of the child is therefore essentially social. . . . At a certain age the social speech of the child is quite sharply divided into egocentric speech and communicative speech. Egocentric speech emerges when the child transfers social, collaborative forms of behavior to the sphere of inner-personal psychic functions" (Vygotsky 2012, 36–37). In another work, *Mind in Society*, Vygotsky suggested a similar claim: "Every function in the child's cultural development appears twice: first on the social level, and, later on, the individual level; first *between* people (*inter*psychological) and then *inside* the child (*intra*psychological)" (Vygotsky 1978, 57; original emphasis).

Vygotsky emphasized the social origin of cognitive development of children; language is a socially and culturally[7] constructed and embedded tool, and speech and thinking are impossible without language. Vygotsky conducted an experiment where children were asked to draw pictures. In this experiment, he intentionally added a series of "difficulties" (e.g., unprepared papers or pencils) to frustrate the children. The result showed that children expressed a significant number of inner speeches when they address the problems, such as "Where's the pencil? I need a blue pencil. Never mind, I'll draw with the red one and wet it with water; it will become dark and look like blue" (Vygotsky 2012, 31). Vygotsky argued that this result suggests that inner speech is a way for children to interact with and define the world around him, and that such social process can help children's development of thinking (32). For Vygotsky, inner speech is not a psychological action that disappears with the biological development of children's outer speech but a social activity that attempts to understand oneself and the outside world using a socioculturally constructed tool (language). In this sense, inner speech is essentially a social and cultural activity. For this reason, in contrast to Piaget, Vygotsky's theory is referred to as "outside-in" (Martí 2013). In other words, while Piagetian Geist assumes human development is a psychogenetic phenomenon, Vygotsky stressed that it is a sociogenetic one (see Lourenço 2012).[8]

Urie Bronfenbrenner updates the theory of the social origin of development of human competency in his landmark study of *bioecological* development. As a Vygotsky-inspired scholar, Bronfenbrenner attempts to understand how exactly and in what sense human development is embedded in social and cultural elements. He defines his bioecological model of human development as follows: "The ecology of human development involves the scientific study of the progressive, mutual accommodation between an active, growing human being and the changing properties of the immediate settings in which the developing person lives, as this process is affected by relations between these settings, and by the larger contexts within which the settings are embedded" (Bronfenbrenner 1979, 21). For Bronfenbrenner, development cannot be understood without an emphasis on the reciprocal and dialectical interaction between human organisms and environments. More specifically, he proposed five nested systems of developmental influence (microsystem, mesosystem, exosystem, macrosystem, and chronosystem). The microsystem is the environment that affects children's daily lives (e.g., family, schools), and the mesosystem refers to the interconnections between multiple microsystems (e.g., the relationship between family, friends, and schools). The exosystem is the environment that has an indirect but significant influence on children's development (e.g., the quality of parents' workplace, the quality of teacher training), and the macrosystem is the overarching environment that is invisible but has a greater influence on children's lives (e.g., culture, tradition, language). Finally, chronosystem, introduced in Bronfenbrenner's later work, is "change or continuity across time and influencing each of the other system" (Hayes, O'Toole, and Halpenny 2017, 17), referring, for example, to changes in cultural norms.[9]

Viewed in the light of Vygotskian sociocultural theory of human development, there are at least two requirements for education for deliberative democracy. The first is that education for deliberative democracy should acknowledge the *sociocultural nature of competency*. There is no guarantee that children with good deliberative competencies (e.g., a skill for logical inference) in one context can act in the same fashion in another context, because, as Hayes, O'Toole, and Halpenny (2017) put it, "no one factor will automatically predict the behavior and development of a child" (75). Different contexts (e.g., classroom, out-of-school public space) and different interlocutors (e.g., classmates, teachers, parents) define "competent deliberators" differently. In this sense, there is no universally applicable competency as regards deliberation. Educators adapting the sociocultural approach therefore should place value on the way in which children reflectively examine whether their deliberative acts can adequately accommodate or respond to different contextual requirements (e.g., topics, human relationship, classroom atmosphere) rather than how they achieve given decontextualized milestones of learning. They are also expected to learn not only adaptation and accommodation of the contextual requirement but also flexible and reflective transformation of their communicative acts in response to different contextual requirements. In other words, we should provide children with rich opportunities to engage in collective inquiry, self-reflection, and retheorization regarding their deliberation in each context.

Second and in relation to the first point, education for deliberative democracy should take into account the fact that *competency is a comprehensive concept*. Here, comprehensiveness has two meanings. On the one hand, competency is comprehensive in a sense that it is not something like an unchanged and fixed object that is internalized as a result of one's development. Rather, it is a creative, or what Vygotsky himself calls *revolutionary* activity embedded within a sociocultural context that is characterized by "periodicity, unevenness in the development of different functions, metamorphosis or qualitative transformation of one form into another, intertwining of external and internal factors, and adaptative processes which overcome impediments that the child encounters" (Vygotsky 1978, 73). As Vygotsky's example of inner speech illustrates, a child who could not find a specific-colored pen to draw a picture attempted to change his or her environment by defining the situation through the use of inner speech or through the process of using another color as an alternative. Competency, therefore, is not something that comes from accomplishing a given task. Rather, it is a process of interacting with one's environment to define the task or change the meaning of the task.

On the other hand, competency is comprehensive because children's development of competency is observed elsewhere insofar as they engage in an activity using a sociocultural tool (e.g., language). As Bronfenbrenner's bioecological model of human development illustrates, this society and culture, and even the world per se, is important learning material that gives different learning contexts to children. Education for deliberative democracy scholars normally focus on the role of classrooms as a primary site for democratic education (Molnar-Main 2017). Although a classroom is one of the key spaces for learning deliberation (see chapters 3–5 of this book), this is not the only space for learning deliberation. Children can learn different deliberative competencies beyond the wall of the classroom, and some competencies (e.g., using political rhetoric, designing social movement) may rarely be learned in the classroom (see chapters 6 and 7 of this book).

The above two critiques call for some radical modifications of education for deliberative democracy informed by evolutionism and universalism, which can be summarized as follows:

- *Aim*: Education for deliberative democracy does not need to aim to create deliberative all-rounders by molding children into the predetermined and idealized evolutional path because a well-functioning deliberative system relies not on a discrete capacity of a single deliberator but on the functional division of labor of different individuals.

- *Competency*: We do not need to stick to the idea of universally applicable deliberative competencies. A one-sided solid, fixed, and decontextualized definition of deliberative competencies may treat children as one-way recipients and reproducers of adult knowledge and practice, ignoring the fact that they have creative agency to form and refine their own competencies from within their sociocultural context. The key for the way forward is to acknowledge the comprehensiveness and context-responsiveness of competency.

- *Space*: The classroom is one of the key spaces for education for deliberative democracy, but it is not the only space for this, because children can nurture their deliberative agency differently in a different space in the deliberative system. The deliberator model, deliberative systems theory, and sociocultural development theory all require us to have a broader perspective on where a deliberative form of learning occurs.

However, if the primary purpose of education for deliberative democracy is not to develop children's competencies normatively required to be deliberative all-rounders, what is its raison d'être? Additionally, given that the development of children's competencies is socioculturally constructed, how can and should the educational process be designed and implemented?

Vygotsky, whether directly or indirectly, influences many leading psychologists and educationalists (Wertsch, Cole, Bronfenbrenner, and many more), and what Newman and Holzman (2014, 67) call scholars of "Vygotsky's left-wing" share the similar abovementioned questions. For these theorists, including Newman and Holzman themselves, the mere acquisition of children's socioculturally constructed competencies is not different from subordinating them to a script prepared by adults. For them, learning and development is not just a *tool* for accommodating a given socioculturally constructed environment but also a *result* of constantly updating the meaning of such an environment. This is what Newman and Holzman call "a tool and result methodology," in which learning and development need to be understood as a unity of tool (adaptation to culture) and result (reexamination of culture). Viewed in this light, learning democracy and developing as a democratic agent is neither about the acquisition of predetermined "desirable" skills for deliberation nor about becoming an all-rounder, but about a deliberative process of meaning-making itself where children deconstruct, reconstruct, co-construct the normative and practical meaning of democratic citizenry. Such a dynamic relationship between tool and result does not treat context and norm as a mutually exclusive but mutually evolving element that is not reduced to a mere evolutionist or universalist take on human development. Yjrö Engeström, one of the Vygotsky's left-wing scholars, theoretically pushes this tool-result idea forward and describes a comprehensive picture of how we translate the idea into practice. As we shall see below, his "Vygotskian Geist" gives us a great clue to retheorize education for deliberative democracy.

Expansive Learning

As the leading critic of the Piagetian developmental psychological paradigm, Engeström objects to the view that defines the nature of human development only from a biological point of view, arguing that "there is no single biologically determined universal appropriate or good way to learn among humans" (Engeström 2016, 14). In addition, like Bronfenbrenner and other Vygotskian psychologists, Engestörm criticizes the traditional psychology paradigm located in the line of Kant, Descartes, and Piaget on the ground that its unit of analysis is mostly an individual action in isolation and that "these theories seem to have difficulties in accounting for the socially distributed or collective aspects as well as the artifact-mediated or cultural aspects of purposeful human behavior" (Engeström 1999, 22). He attempts to overturn such traditional paradigms by shifting our attention away from an individual-focused action and toward networked and contextually embedded collective actions where individuals collaborate with each other and negotiate, analyze, and transform themselves and the environment where they are embedded. Put simply, like Bronfenbrenner, Engeström attempts to understand the nature of human development from the perspective of dialectic interactions between human and environment.[10] However, their biggest difference is that, while Bronfenbrenner unpacks the diversity and multilayeredness of the learning environment where learners are embedded, Engeström's distinct attention is on the complexity of learning process in such a multilayered environment and on how learners transform themselves and their learning environment itself.

For Engeström, the universalistic theory of development leads to a fallacy, because "you will tend to impose it upon your data and examples so that you will indeed find evidence confirming that your theory works in practice" (Engeström 2016, 14). He thus suggests an alternative learning theory that emphasizes the significance of "the possibility that learning gets out of the hands of the instructors and takes a direction of its own" (9). To this end, he takes a clue from Vygotsky's theory of learning and updates it.

In particular, Engeström focused on the idea of *mediation* in Vygotsky's theory. The Piagetian paradigm of psychology, according to Engeström, focused only on the consequences arising from the relationship between the subject and the object. For instance, in the act of reading a book, we understand whether or not a child (subject) has the competency to read (outcome) from the relationship between the child and a book (object). For

Vygotsky, however, such a linear understanding of learning and development was problematic in that it treats the subject and object as separate entities. Vygotsky instead pointed out that there is a culturally constructed and shared mediating artifact (e.g., language, symbol, sign) that bridges the subject and the object. According to this idea, the act of reading a book cannot be understood without broadening the unit of analysis as a process in which the child uses language (mediating artifact) to read the object. Being able to read is, therefore, measured not only by the subject's interaction with the object but also the subject's mastery of the mediating artifact. Vygotsky illustrated this socioculturally mediated act as shown in figure 2.1.

Importantly, while traditional psychology considers the relationship between subject and object to be one that proceeds along a one-way arrow (subject→object), in Vygotsky's socioculturally mediated action, the object sometimes interacts with the subject through the mediating artifacts. Vygotsky, for example, often attempts to illustrate this with the example of play. When children engage in playing house, they create an imaginary house setting as the object. The cultural artifact (language) bridges the children and the house setting and then constrains children's behavior (for instance, when I was a kid, I was always asked to play the role of a dog and be forbidden to speak human language). In this way, the subject not only works on and interacts with the object, but the object may also work on the subject, transforming the subject's actions and behaviors. As Vygotsky (1978, 100) indicates, "play gives a child new form of desire," so the relationship between the subject and the object cannot be explained by a one-way arrow but is a reciprocal and dialectical relationship.[11]

Figure 2.1. Vygotsky's socioculturally mediated act model. *Source*: Vygotsky (1978, 40).

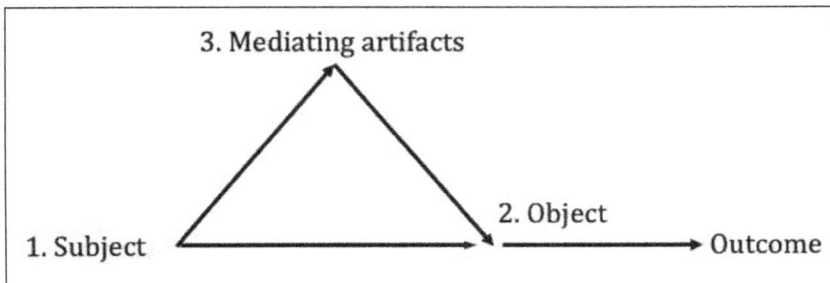

Engeström notes that a key theoretical contribution of Vygotsky is that "the objects ceased to be just raw material for the formation of the subject as they were for Piaget" (Engeström 2015, xiv). Still, he problematizes part of Vygotsky's theory because, while Vygotsky explains how an individual's engagement in a process of meaning-making within a sociocultural system works, "what is left unexplained is how the socioculturally mediated forms of behavior, or the activity settings, or even societies, are generated or created in the first place" (252).

Thus, Engeström ameliorates Vygotsky's triangle to capture the dynamic and dialectical mechanism of human learning and development more effectively. Inspired by post-Vygotsky Soviet and Russian researchers,[12] Engeström distils three additional aspects of human development: the division of labor, the rules for regulating or sophisticating the division of labor, and the community where the division of labor occurs. Engeström argues:

> A collective activity can only be carried out by dividing the labor among the members of a community, that is, by assigning different actions to different participants. . . . The cultural meaning and personal sense of an individual action can only be deciphered by seeing it in the context of the activity it realizes. (2016, 107)

> Human activity always takes place within a community governed by a certain division of labor and by certain rules. A group of people are responsible for a shared object of a community. Community is thus seen as the carrier or bearer of activity. (122–23)

In the case of play, as indicated here, *community* refers to the context or environment within which a collective and shared activity is practiced. Children's play happens in different spaces, including school, park, street, or home. Different spaces allow children to engage in different forms of play. For instance, they are more likely to engage in playing house at home or in a sandpit, while they tend to engage in a more physical play with a claiming frame or on the streets. *Rules* include laws, cultural norms, and social expectations, which define how people should act and behave. When it comes to the example of play, children create their own rules that regulates their activity to some degree. For instance, when I acted as a dog in playing house, I could not speak a human language and my female friend internalized the gender role construed in our society and acted as a mother who washed dishes and cooked. On the street, when children play football, they usually do not play without limits, but rather tentatively determine the area for football and play within it. *Division of labor* means the separation of work to achieve a specific object, or, in other words, the combination of what one can do by oneself and what one can do with the help of others. In a nutshell, Engeström (2015) contends that learning is, by its essence, a social and shared meaning-making activity that is intertwined with specific sociocultural structures, rules, and human relations. Figure 2.2 is a visual summary of how Engeström himself modifies and expands Vygotsky's learning theory.

Some may think that his learning theory equates to environmental determinism, the core idea of which is that the environment or context can determine every human behavior, but Engeström rejects such criticism. For Engeström, learning and development are not merely an uncritical adaptation to the environment but rather a dialectical and innovative interaction between humans and the environment that requires "reflective analysis of the existing activity structure—one must learn and understand what one wants to transcend" and "reflective appropriation of existing culturally advanced models and tools that offer ways out of the internal

Figure 2.2. Engeström's expansive model of Vygotsky's triangle. *Source*: Engeström (2015, 63).

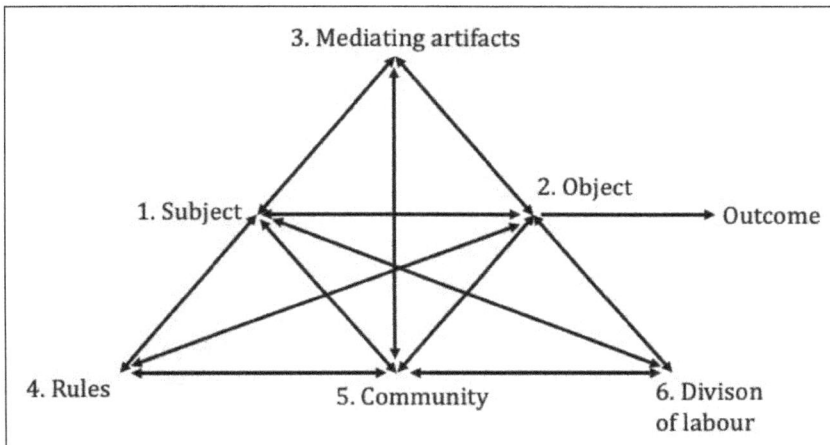

contradictions" (Engeström 1999, 33). He thus summarizes his expansive learning as "learning what is not yet there" (2016, 37). This implies that learning is not simply an adaptation to the environment but also a reflective creation of a new one. He also notes that successful learning and development leads to "a qualitative transformation of all components of the activity system" (Engeström and Sannino 2017, 113). Learning and development are not just a change of subject but a transformation of subjects and conditions of their shared task.

Engeström identifies six key components within the expansive learning framework (Engeström 2016, 47–8). The first component is *questioning*, in which children challenge the value of the activity itself and/or some taken for granted rules regulating the activity. The keyword here is *contradiction*. For Engeström, contradiction means that an individual must pause his/her current activities, take the problem s/he is facing seriously and try to cooperate with others to address the problem. Grounded on Gregory Bateson's theory of double bind (a dilemma in communication) as a typical form of contradiction, Engeström (2015) argues that "a double bind may now be reformulated as a social, societally essential dilemma that cannot be resolved through separate individual actions alone—but in which joint cooperative actions can push a historically new form of activity into emergence" (131). Put simply, contradiction (or dilemma) serves as an important driving force for motivating people to engagement in a shared action. To understand this, let's return to the example of playing house. When a child tries to play house, she or he may find various contradictions, such as:

- *Subject*: There is the gap between who she or he is as an actual child and his or her imaginary role (i.e., she wants to play as a mother, but she knows she is not a real mother).

- *Object*: The degree to which is she or he trying to make the imaginary house space as realistic as possible (i.e., she knows that she is trying to make her imaginary kitchen as realistic as possible, but she knows that she does not have a real vegetable).

- *Mediating artifacts*: Which code of language does she or he use during playing house (i.e., a boy playing as a dog wants to speak to his friend, but he is prohibited from speaking human language)?

- *Rules*: How much do all participants share in the rules that regulate their acts (i.e., is it acceptable to pretend to eat mud dumplings, or must they eat it for the sake of realistic playing house, and who is allowed to administer the rule)?

- *Community*: Who can define, and how, the best place for playing house (i.e., she wants to do playing house with her friends at her real house, but her father does not wish it)?

- *Division of Labor*: Several participants want to play the same role (i.e., three boys say they want to play as a dad).

These contradictions are consciously recognized and scrutinized in the second component, *analysis*, so that children find a way to understand and resolve problems. For example, if one child wants to play house while another child wants to play basketball (contradiction in the object), they have to find common ground, which leads to the third component, *modelling*. Based on the analysis, children create a new set of rules, practices, and ways of working with others to solve the problematic situation. In the above situation, the children can agree to play house as the imaginary family of the basketball player. The fourth component is *examining the model* to check whether the suggested model addresses the original problem. The fifth component is *implementing the model*, which is the practical application of the suggested model to identify problems or to check whether further experimentation is needed to amend its practice. Finally, the sixth component is *reflection* on the overall process and its *theorization*. Taken together, children examine various contextual factors (e.g., rules, community, division of labor) that regulate or enhance their activity. Through these practices, children can generate and define a new meaning of their action and the environment where they act.

For Engeström, learning and development mean the reflective analysis of contradictions and the effort to transcend them, not merely a process of internalizing given knowledge or predetermined skills. In other words, the essence of learning and development is a process in which a learner (a) is immersed within an activity system, (b) reflectively examines various contradictions emerging from their activity, (c) transforms both environments and the learner so as to make one's action more sophisticated, and (d) applies a new model of action in another context to update their act. As Engeström (2015) himself summarizes: "The essence of learning activity is production of objectively, societally new activity structures (including

new objects, instruments, etc.) out of actions manifesting the inner contradictions of the preceding form of the activity in question. Learning
activity is *mastery of expansion from actions to a new activity*" (98–99).
As long as we accept this definition of learning, competency is defined
quite minimally. It does not specify a particular set of practices defined
by others in a top-down manner but rather refers to a meaning-making
process itself in which people reflectively analyze and examine contradictions in their activity and, if necessary, transform their actions or the
environment constraining their actions.

From Education for Deliberative Democracy to Deliberative Democratic Learning

Engeström's theory resonates with both systemic and sociocultural critiques
of education for deliberative democracy. It sets the goal of learning not as
a creation of a "perfect," autonomous, and independent individual but as
a facilitation of one's revolutionary agency developed through a collective
engagement in contradiction resolution and meaning-making about their
behavior and actions embedded in a socioculturally constructed environment. Both Vygotsky and Engeström clearly show that our action (namely,
a communicative action) is always mediated by a sociocultural tool, but
Engeström unpacks that the potential of human beings lies in the fact
that we are not subordinate to such a tool. Rather, when learning occurs
in Engeström's sense, we humans have the power to master such a tool
and remake its meaning. In simple words, we do not learn to get what is
already there but to transcend it.

Thus far, we have taken a long detour into a discussion of developmental theory. Now we return to the discussion of democratic education.
Note that my intention here is not to test democratic education with
Engeström's framework. His expansive learning theory is not a deontological framework about what learning ought to be, but rather an explanatory framework for understanding how and when learning occurs. The
important task here is to distil core implications for understanding the
relationship between children's deliberation, learning, and development
from Engeström's theory, thereby emancipating democratic education
from the Piagetian Geist.

First, the development of children's *revolutionary* agency should
be situated at the heart of the aim of democratic education. Children
learn not only those deliberative norms that have already been defined

by adults but also act as agents who give new meanings to such norms through deliberation. It is important to note that revolutionarity here does not mean rebellion. Revolutionarity in the Vygotskian Geist is, as Newman and Holzman (2014) discuss, *the iterative process of deconstruction, reconstruction, and co-construction of one's own activities and environment* in a way that guides his or her further learning. Rather than aiming at becoming an ideal deliberator in an evolutionary way, democratic education must allow room for children to take primary ownership of generating, defining, and implementing their own deliberative acts.

To this end, the process of democratic education should be as *reflective* as possible. As we have seen in the first half of this chapter, the systemic critique problematizes education for deliberative democracy on the grounds that it sustains the ideal of the deliberative all-rounder. By contrast, if democratic education is to be a revolutionary practice, it ought to encourage children to deliberate about their own deliberation in a way that consciously examines what their deliberation is and how it ought to be implemented in the context where they are embedded. In this practice, (a) children as the subject deliberate various (b) topics as the object by using multiple forms of (c) communicative actions defined as a mediating artifact. During this process, they shall also deliberate about various socioculturally constructed environmental factors that enable or constrain their deliberation, such as (d) shared presuppositions about deliberation, (e) situations of deliberation, and (f) the degree to which children collaborate with each other. In particular, it is important for children to deliberate various contradictions that they (potentially) face; these six elements might also provide children with different sorts of contradictions and children are encouraged to address them collaboratively. For example:

- *Future citizens vs. deliberators*: Many children know that they are often treated as future citizens, while deliberation enables them to realize their democratic agency.

- *Consensus vs. dissensus*: Many children would initially deliberate over the prospect of resolving the problem or making a consensus. Yet they may realize that there is quite limited room for a full consensus, especially when they deliberate highly controversial topics.

- *Verbal vs. nonverbal expressions*: During deliberation, some children, namely, those from disadvantaged communities, would realize that the most effective form of expression is not just rational and logical argumentation but also some nonverbal or even nondeliberative expressions, such as gestures, silences, or drawing a picture.

- *Authenticity vs. inclusiveness*: The more deliberators value rational forms of communication, the more risk there is of deliberation becoming exclusive, as cautioned by difference democrats. Thus, the balance between authentic and inclusive deliberation should be considered through a negotiation with and reflective analysis of each other's deliberative acts.

- *Homogeneity vs. heterogeneity*: Some children may want to hear various opinions including opposite ones, but others do not.

- *Individual Insight vs. collective insight*: Whether a few clever and intelligent children should lead deliberation or whether the opinions of a diverse range of ordinary children should be more respected.

Through the critical and reflective analysis of such contradictions, children are encouraged to suggest a new deliberative norm and practice that can potentially resolve the problems they face. Then children can refine and apply the norm and practice into their next practice. Thus they gain a clearer understanding of what deliberation ought to be in a given context. However, this is not the final goal of their meaning-making. As figure 2.3 shows, what children learn as an outcome of their deliberation is used as their new repertoires of deliberative expression, and children practice this new form of expression to examine whether it plays a meaningful role in different contexts. Continual practice, reflection, and sophistication enable children to update their understanding of what good deliberation is and thereby habituate such reflective engagement.

The above argument leads to the third and fourth point: learning deliberative democracy (or meaning-making of deliberation) is a *contextual* and *collective-transformative* practice. Contextuality is not equivalent to a hands-off approach that accepts all children's contextualized activities as deliberative. Goodin's (2018) article title clearly summarizes its problem: "If Everything Is Deliberation, Maybe It's Nothing." As the existing theory and practice of education for deliberative democracy stresses, I do not object to a practice of teaching children core normative principles

Figure 2.3. A revolutionary process of deliberative meaning-making. *Source:* Created by the author.

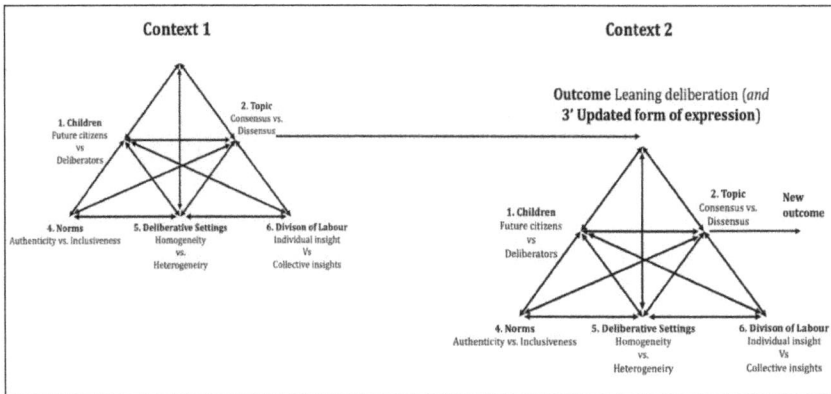

(authenticity and inclusiveness) and key forms of deliberation (e.g., reasoning, listening). However, even if teaching deliberative norms is important, thinking and defining how to translate the norms into practice in their deliberative situation must be both participatory and context-responsive (Burgh and Thornton 2022). By taking the integration of their deliberative acts, contexts, and norms into account, children examine and transform their acts, their environments, and even their deliberative norms by themselves, not only to deepen their understanding of good deliberation but also to make their deliberative agency more sophisticated. Children need to experience many contradictions in the course of their practice of "something deliberative," to take such contradictions seriously and to overcome them collaboratively. The unity of such process and deliberation defined and practiced by the children themselves should be recognized as a competency. It is not something that can be reduced to an individual's mind but something that is created interactively and collectively.

Finally, democratic education should be more *systemic.* More specifically, democratic education should not be limited to the confines of the classroom. Although I agree that the classroom is one of the key sites for learning deliberation, I disagree with the view that it is the only site. As Bronfenbrenner's sociocultural developmental theory illustrates, children's learning can happen within broader and networked systems (micro-, meso-, macro-, exo-, and chronosystems), and different systems provide different learning opportunities. The same can be applied to the existing model of education for deliberative democracy. As we have seen in chapter 1, we must acknowledge the fact that children already deliberate in various sites within a broader deliberative system, and they can enjoy various learning opportunities through different forms of deliberative participation. In this book (particularly chapters 6 and 7), I will pay particular attention to two distinct spaces beyond the classroom (i.e., school and activist groups) and their deliberative learning potential.

Hereby I finally suggest *deliberative democratic learning* as an alternative of education for deliberative democracy. Deliberative democratic learning is characterized by the above revolutionary, reflective, contextual, collective-transformative, and systemic practice of deliberation.

Conclusion

Educational practice is often designed to guide children's development. However, since education for deliberative democracy research and practice are influenced by the mainstream Piagetian Geist's evolutionism and universalism, they guide children's development in a way that justifies exclusion of children from deliberative democracy, which contradicts the deliberators' model discussed in chapter 1. This chapter also shows how this mainstream view on development is vulnerable to two key criticisms—systemic and sociocultural critiques—due to its narrow understanding of deliberators, deliberative competency, and the purpose of education for deliberative democracy.

This chapter thus shifts our attention from the traditional narrow scope of education for deliberative democracy toward a more revolutionary, reflective, contextual, collective-transformative, and systemic practice, which I define as deliberative democratic learning. It is possible that some deliberative democrats may criticize deliberative democratic learning, arguing that it may risk accepting everything as deliberation. For critics, deliberative democratic learning leads to an uncritical stretching of the concept, neglects the core democratic value of deliberation in democracy, and devalues some key components of deliberation, as illustrated in table 2.1. This sort of criticism can be answered in at least two ways.

First, my suggestion is not about education for deliberative democracy but about deliberative democratic learning. They sound similar but look quite different. If we consider the former, the practice should be designed according to a normative conceptualization of deliberation. However, in the latter, it is children who practice, analyze, retheorize, and reimplement deliberative norms in a revolutionary way. As we will see in subsequent chapters, different norms of deliberation are respected, implemented, and transformed as necessary in different contexts. The conditions under which they are possible in a specific context will be examined in more detail in subsequent chapters. These chapters offer different perspectives on the kinds of norms of deliberation that can be theorized when children's agency is placed at the center of children's deliberative activities.

Second, because deliberation is not mere discussion or conversation, but a specific form of communication, reason-giving and listening are treated as core elements of its practice. In this sense, deliberative democratic learning is not a theory open to infinite concept stretching—both reason-giving and listening are important anchors in the practice. However, as we shall see through my fieldwork described in chapters 3 and 4, in particular, deliberative democratic learning practiced in the classroom does not always require children to reason and listen together based on predetermined norms, but encourages children to make their own deliberative norms and reflectively scrutinize them through deliberation. By doing so, children can learn various repertoires and potential ways of reason-giving and listening.

As noted in the introduction, the idea of deliberative democratic learning as a middle-range theory opens it up to critical iterations alternating between theoretical elaboration and empirical insights. In the chapters that follow, our attention will shift toward how theory travels into the realm of practice so as to give a more concrete shape to the theory.

Part II

Classroom

Part 2 is a theoretical as well as empirical inquiry into the implication of the theoretical trajectory presented in part 1 for classroom deliberation. To this end, this part 2 focuses on three key elements that constitute deliberative democratic learning in the classroom—reason-giving, listening, and facilitation.

Chapter 3 examines the meaning of "teaching reason-giving." Deliberative democrats have argued that reason-giving is an essential element of authentic deliberation. But the degree to which we give weight to the "reason" and the "giving" parts of this term varies. Some focus on the term "reason" by emphasizing a process of rational argumentation, while others value the process of "giving" by highlighting various ways in which people give reasons (e.g., rhetoric, storytelling, nonverbal expressions). Consequently, the term "reason-giving" is open to a diverse array of interpretations and practical applications. This, however, makes differentiating deliberative, nondeliberative, and anti-deliberative reason-giving all the more essential. For example, the excessive use of logical argumentation may run the risk of draining the elements of empathy and emotion from a deliberative process, thereby actually making reason-giving antideliberative. Alternatively, silence is normally seen as a nondeliberative practice, yet it sometimes serves as a means of expressing reasons of politically disadvantaged people. Subsequently, the question becomes how deliberative democratic learning can be designed and practiced in a way that maintains reason-giving as an epistemic anchor while accommodating the existence of a variety of reason-giving practices. Chapter 3 shows that the key to addressing this question lies in the creation of an optimal environment where students not only internalize the predetermined norms of reason-giving but also engage in and ameliorate the norm itself through deliberation. This sort of deliberation about deliberation is called *meta-deliberation*. In meta-deliberation, students can elaborate their self-reflective capacities for assessing the quality of deliberation and enable themselves to act as creators of deliberative norms who formulate, practice, negotiate, and retheorize new repertoires of reason-giving in their own terms. To explain how meta-deliberation works in practice, the second half of the chapter draws on my action research in an Australian primary school. The study shows three different types of meta-deliberation (meta-deliberative session, meta-deliberative moment, and anteroom meta-deliberation) that all expand the ways in which students are able to give reasons and otherwise engage in deliberative democratic learning.

Having said that, reason-giving alone is ineffective if your inter-locutor intentionally avoids listening. Chapter 4 thus explores the democratic value of listening and its implication for deliberative democratic learning. It begins by elucidating what listening means, as well as why and how listening is important for deliberative democracy. When these kinds of theoretical arguments travel to the classroom, however, things become complicated: listening is a difficult thing to observe and assess. Chapter 4 acknowledges some key insights gained from Scudder's novel methodological toolkit, known as the Listening Quality Index (LQI); but it also identifies some practical as well as theoretical limitations of the LQI when applied to classroom deliberation. On the one hand, the LQI is designed for researchers who assess the quality of public deliberation, and therefore teachers find it difficult and burdensome to use for assessing classroom deliberation. On the other hand, the LQI implicitly promotes a top-down paradigm, insofar as only adults and researchers are permitted to define what good listening ought to be—a privilege that comes at the expense of students' contextualized lifeworld. Thus, chapter 4 suggests a less burdensome and more context-responsive form of quasi-LQI, or the uncapitalized *lqi* whose normative core is reconstructed based on the lifeworld of students as it is exhibited in their meta-deliberation. With the help of a facilitator, students create a list of their own listening norms by collectively analyzing and reconstructing their listening experiences and habits, and then deliberate on the basis of that list. By sharing ownership of definition and practicing democratic listening with students in this way, students exercise their agency of deliberative norm-making and, at the same time, become sensitive to their own listening habits, which ultimately motivates them to be self-reflective and self-corrective about their own more democratic listening habits. The second half of the chapter draws on my action research in Japanese classrooms to show how the lqi works in a real context.

Chapter 5 shifts our attention to the role of adults. More specifically, the role of the adults/facilitators in classroom deliberation is the main focus of the chapter. At least in context of the classroom, deliberative democratic learning without a facilitator is unrealistic. However, a facilitator is not a miracle-performer who can always achieve a state of perfect deliberation anywhere and anytime. Through the self-reflective analysis of what I experienced as a facilitator in classroom deliberation, chapter 5 first identifies three key challenges that can prevent both a facilitator and students from engaging in deliberation in a meaningful fashion. The challenges include the facilitator's power, students' disagreement-averse attitude, and testimonial injustice. The sections that follow shall consider how a facilitator should cope with these challenges by examining three theoretical models of facilitation: involved facilitation (informed by Paulo Freire), passive facilitation (informed by Jacques Rancière), and the task-sharer (informed by John Dewey). The first two models primarily focus on an individualized understanding of the facilitator's techniques, identity, and ethical responsibility that are, however, less effective in addressing the above socioculturally constructed challenges. By contrast, the Deweyan model of a facilitator as a task-sharer theorizes the facilitator's involvement as a process of environmental design that provides further democratic scaffolding and structure. Drawing on another praxis story from my Australian classroom experience, chapter 5 makes a case for the importance of shifting from the paradigm of facilitation by *technique* to that of facilitation by *design* in order to mitigate the risk of unethical facilitation and deliberation in the classroom.

Chapter 3

Reason-Giving in the Classroom

Talk is a key element of deliberation. However, this does not mean that all of its forms are valued equally. Some specific types of talk may lack persuasiveness and legitimacy because of the absence of justifiable reasons. When one's opponent states an opinion underpinned by a good reason, one may feel a degree of sympathy for the speaker despite their opinion's lack of acceptability. A single argument that is supported by multiple reasons can possess a sophisticated quality. As empirically demonstrated by Fishkin's set of Deliberative Poll projects, deliberative participants can drastically modify their original opinion when listening to the reasoning of different positions. Hence, Cohen (1989) argues that deliberation must weigh and test the quality not only of an opinion itself but also of its underlying reasons. Now, *reason-giving* is deemed an essential element of updating mere talk to authentic deliberation that produces better decisions, better agreements, and better democratic legitimacy (see Habermas 1996; Rawls 2001; Landemore 2013; Bächtiger and Parkinson 2019).

The term "reason-giving" consists of two words, "reason" and "giving," which vary in the degree to which they are given weight. The earliest deliberative democracy theorists were more inclined to discuss *reason*-giving, an application of Rawlsian and Habermasian theory of rational discourse that purges a strategic, coercive, dominative, and illogical use of language. Other scholars also explored the plural meanings of reason by examining, for instance, the role and place of emotion in the traditional rationalistic view of reason-giving (Krause 2008; Maia and Huber 2020). However, scholarly attention has recently shifted toward reason-*giving*, explaining various ways and forms of giving reasons, including rhetoric, joking, storytelling, dancing, marching, and even silence, all with diverse democratic goals contributing to deliberative ideals (e.g., Young 2000; Rollo 2017; Ercan, Hendriks, and Dryzek 2019).

A challenge that this chapter will address is the ability of reason-giving plurality to blur boundaries of *deliberative, nondeliberative,* and *anti-deliberative* forms of reason-giving. If we define reason-giving using the rigorous normative standard, the differences among these three practices might be clear. Yet, if reason-giving forms and meanings become more diverse, things become more complicated. A provided reason that plays a deliberative democratic role in one situation may not always guarantee that the same practice is equally valued in another. This is because our reason-giving strategy is influenced by various contextual factors (e.g., Who participates? What is discussed? Is the deliberation institutionalized?), and thus, in a specific context, a seemingly "banal" and "nondeliberative" reason-giving can serve as a deliberative function that shapes our understanding of the issue in question. To identify whether the expressed reason takes a deliberative, nondeliberative, or anti-deliberative form, a more context-sensitive discussion is essential.

What does this argument imply for democratic education? Educating how to reason together has long been a popular topic among education philosophers and practitioners (e.g., Englund 2000; Lipman 2003; Moshman 2020). Conventionally, much thought has been given to a deontological and normative definition of reason-giving, which is then applied to students' activity. Yet the plurality of reason-giving challenges this trend. Precisely because what counts as *reason* and *giving* is constructed contextually, we should not assume that there is a single form of reason-giving that can apply to any context and any time. A theoretical puzzle emerges: How can democratic education keep reason-giving as a normative anchor and, in parallel, accommodate the fact of reason-giving plurality in practice?

Building upon the idea of deliberative democratic learning formulated in chapter 2, this chapter addresses the above question. In light of deliberative democratic learning, the key to resolve the question is the creation of an optimal environment where students not only internalize the predetermined norm of reason-giving but also engage in and, if needed, ameliorate the norm itself. Specifically, the process necessitates a critical and reflective circle in which students, on the one hand, acquire a clearer understanding of the normative value of reason-giving and, on the other, rethink their conventional reason-giving habit and transform the meaning of the reason-giving norm. As discussed in the theoretical part of this chapter, deliberation about deliberation, which deliberative theorists call *meta-deliberation*, is key to practice such a reflective and critical circle. Public deliberation, such as deliberative minipublics, tends to locate meta-deliberation at its sideline, while the chapter makes a case for the central role of meta-deliberation in deliberative democratic learning.

As Markus Holdo (2020) rightly indicates, however, there is no guarantee that meta-deliberation is more democratic than normal deliberation. On his account, the uncritical use of meta-deliberation indeed poses the risk of facilitating the majority's justification of their oppressive and anti-deliberative use of reason-giving rather than improving their deliberative quality. Against this backdrop, the empirical part of the chapter highlights the significance of allowing room for various forms of meta-deliberation so that the quality of students' different forms of reason-giving can be checked and improved from multiple perspectives. A case of deliberation with year 5 students in Australia will emphasize three distinct forms of meta-deliberation (meta-deliberative session, meta-deliberative moment, and anteroom deliberation) and their different contributions to reason-giving in the deliberation process.

Before highlighting meta-deliberation in theory and practice, we begin this chapter by explaining why reason-giving should be considered a core element of deliberative democracy with respect to its democratic and epistemic value.

Reason-Giving and Reason-*Giving*

Dennis Thompson's landmark article titled "Deliberative Democratic Theory and Empirical Political Science" (2008) offers an influential summary of the trend of deliberative democracy studies in the 2000s. Thompson argued that democratic deliberation anchored by mutual justification, or "presenting and responding to reasons intended to justify a political decision" (504), is and must be the primary source of democratic legitimacy. Around 5–10 years before and after 2008, a large and growing body of literature discussed what reason-giving exactly means and how we can bring theory into practice. Henceforth, the former ("what"-oriented argument) was labeled *reason*-giving, while the latter ("how"-oriented argument) was called reason-*giving*—and their difference is attributed to the extent to which they assign weight to "what" (reason) and "how" (giving), respectively. Chronologically, scholars mainly debated *reason*-giving based on the

Kantian concept of public reason; then, as part of the critical response to this trend, deliberative theorists and feminism scholars jointly introduced reason-*giving*; afterwards, the emphasis on reason in public deliberation reemerged and was retheorized by epistemic democracy theorists.

The earliest study on *reason*-giving was tinged with an Enlightened overtone alongside Kantian autonomous and transcendental reason (or what he calls practical reason). Specifically, the idea of public reason theorized by the neo-Kantian philosopher John Rawls and those influenced by him drew a starting line for thinking about what reason means in deliberative democracy. Although Rawls was mostly oriented toward the deontological and transcendental deliberative situation known as the original position, his idea of public reason reveals what philosophically grounded legitimate communication among citizens ought to be. Rawls asserted that public reason normatively demands citizens "to present to one another publicly acceptable reasons for their political views in cases raising fundamental political questions" (Rawls 2001, 91). Jürgen Habermas, another contemporary neo-Kantian philosopher, also foregrounded people's use of reason in the public sphere by postulating rational moral discourse in which people collaboratively engage in finding norms and making moral claims that every participant could accept without being coerced except for the unforced force of the better argument (Habermas 1996).[1]

Echoing Rawls and Habermas, Joshua Cohen situated the normative concept of reason-giving in deliberative democracy. His frequently cited argument defines deliberation as

> *reasoned* in that the parties to it are required to state their reasons for advancing proposals, supporting them or criticizing them. They give reasons with the expectation that those reasons (and not, for example, their power) will settle the fate of their proposal. In ideal deliberation, as Habermas puts it, no force except that of the better argument is exercised. Reasons are offered with the aim of bringing others to accept the proposal, given their disparate ends and their commitment to settling the conditions of their association through free deliberation among equals. Proposals may be rejected because they are not defended with acceptable reasons, even if they could be so defended. (Cohen 1989, 74)

As clearly illustrated, these philosophers share the view that the legitimate form of reason-giving in the public sphere must be a rational practice in the sense that opinions expressed in public disputes should be publicly acceptable, well-reasoned, and noncoercive; otherwise, democratic legitimacy would be difficult to realize.

The theory of public reason proposed by Rawls, Habermas, and Cohen—who, according to Elstub, Ercan, and Mendonça (2016), form the first generation of deliberative theorists—became an important starting point for deepening theorists' understanding of what reason-giving means. Bohman (1996), for example, situated reason-giving at the heart of deliberative theory, arguing that "the deliberative process forces citizens to justify their decisions and opinions by appealing to common interest or by arguing in terms of reasons that "all could accept" in public debate" (5). Gutmann and Thompson also theorized the reason-giving requirement where "leaders should therefore give reasons for their decisions and respond to the reasons that citizens give in return" (Gutmann and Thompson 2004, 3). For the early deliberative theorists, reason-giving is deemed as an indispensable normative anchor that provides a key standard for distinguishing democratic deliberation from a mere conversation, discussion, or debate.

The earliest deliberative theorist's account of reason-giving, however, faced a challenge that pertains to the concern that their public reason requirement unfairly undermines different "reasonable" claims made by marginalized groups of people. At the root of this concern, critics indicate that the underlying assumption in the Rawlsian and Habermasian understanding of a reason-giver is based on the image of the powerful majority, which disregards the value of various forms of reason-giving by politically vulnerable and marginalized individuals and implicitly regards their reason-giving as inferior to rational communication. For example, Young (2000, particularly chs. 1–2) problematized the hyper-rationalistic view of deliberation on the ground that it disregards and devalues the fact that seemingly "nonrational" methods of expression, such as greetings, narratives, and rhetoric, have been historically crucial in making democracy more inclusive and legitimate, especially if they are made by marginalized individuals, who are normally disadvantaged in rational argumentation.

Consider rhetoric in more detail as an example. According to Simone Chambers (2009), the Plato-inspired understanding of rhetoric abominates rhetoric itself, pointing out its monological, one way, nonresponsive, and nonreflective character. Interestingly, however, Chambers also argued that rhetoric is a way to avoid or minimize shallow reason in the public sphere if it "makes people think, makes people see things in new ways, conveys information and knowledge and makes people more reflective" (335).

Greta Thunberg is, in my view, one of the most successful deliberative rhetoricians in the contemporary world. As illustrated in chapter 1, she began her climate protest holding a handmade placard with the words *Skolstrejk för klimatet* (School Strike for Climate) in front of the Swedish parliament. She used different rhetorical phrases to assert her claims (e.g., "Our house is on fire"), which encouraged younger generations to be more seriously concerned about their future even at the expense of their present school lives. Consequently, for children whose voices are rarely considered in a conventional democratic institution, rhetoric can be part of their reason-giving strategy to deliver their voiceless voices, attract attention from wider audiences in the public sphere, encourage further reflection and deliberation about fundamental political issues, and influence public policies.[2]

Therefore, reason-giving occasionally takes a seemingly "irrational," "nonpolitical," "everyday," "nonverbal" form, which shifted scholars' attention and emphasis from *reason*-giving to reason-*giving*—or *the fact of the plurality of reason-giving*. Today, some deliberative theorists investigate the degree to which the normative scope of reason-giving can be relaxed by focusing on everyday talk (Mansbridge 1999; Beauvais 2020), exit (Rollo 2017), communication underpinned not by public spiritedness but rather by self-interest (Mansbridge et al. 2010), and others.

Meanwhile, skeptics argue that the fact of the plurality of reason-giving may hollow out the norm of deliberation. Gutmann and Thompson expressed doubt regarding the inclusion of any form of communicative activity into the recipe of deliberation because "it becomes indistinguishable from mere discussion and therefore its distinctive qualities and challenges get lost" (Gutmann and Thompson 2018, 904). Bächtiger and Parkinson (2019, 24) also acknowledged that storytelling has a deliberative function in wider deliberative systems but were quite skeptical about labeling it as a deliberative practice per se. Hélène Landemore (2017) also cautioned against the relativistic and nihilistic tendency in deliberative democracy studies, which greatly appreciate a contextualized take on deliberative reason-giving while tending to downplay and disregard the procedure-independent standard of truth, correctness, and betterment. Landemore (2013) would acknowledge the fact of the plurality of reason-giving but stress that such various repertoires of reason-giving ought to be accepted only when it meets the epistemic standard of deliberation, such as the production of better (or truer)[3] decision, agreement, and democratic legitimacy; otherwise, we might fail to distinguish democratic deliberation from mere discussion or conversation.

So far, I have illustrated the place and (contested) meaning of reason-giving in deliberative democracy studies. To date, deliberative democracy scholars may agree that (a) reason-giving should be situated at the heart of deliberation (*reason*-giving), (b) reason-giving is not limited to rational argumentation (reason-*giving*), but (c) this does not justify all stretched understandings of reason-giving—an uncritical expansion of its meaning would ignore the epistemic value of deliberation. Importantly, *reason*-giving and reason-*giving* are not an either-or choice; their balance ought to be checked, based on whether it has a valid orientation toward epistemically "better" and "truer" democracy.

(Non- and Anti-)Deliberative Reason-Giving

Meanwhile, can we make an a priori borderline about what epistemically "better" and "truer" reason-giving means? I ask this because deliberation has not only the "better" and "truer" aspect but also a "more real" aspect. In the real deliberative context, the fact of the plurality of reason-giving often poses a challenge because it blurs the boundary of *deliberative, nondeliberative*, and *anti-deliberative* forms of reason-giving. This is precisely because while a specific reason-giving form meets the epistemic standard of deliberation in one context, there is no guarantee that the same practice is equally valued in different ones. Many deliberative theorists today, especially those who employ a systemic framework, usually recuse anti-deliberative practice while promoting deliberative and nondeliberative measures (e.g., Bächtiger and Parkinson 2019). However, this section will show that what is often ignored here is that even seemingly deliberative reason-giving plays an anti- or nondeliberative role in a particular context, and, more extremely, anti-deliberative reason-giving in one context functions as nondeliberative practice. In such a situation, its boundary is set contextually and practically rather than procedure-independently, which finally raises one essential question with respect to classroom deliberation: What does "teaching reason-giving" mean?

A tentative definition is provided for each term. Deliberative reason-giving refers to a deliberative and democratic form of reason-giving—that is, a presentation of evidence-based, public-spirited, logical, and rational argumentation that aims to justify one's own arguments and examine those of others. Its epistemic standard requires people to express their reason as Socratically and democratically as possible; in this sense, reason-giving of this sort has an affinity for the aforementioned argument on *reason*-giving.

Nondeliberative reason-giving has an epistemic democratic orientation, yet it does not take a deliberative form. It is characterized as a strategic, less public, and performative use of political communication that can nonetheless become part of deliberative processes (Mansbridge et al. 2012; Beauvais 2020). Finally, anti-deliberative reason-giving is, as opposed to deliberative and nondeliberative reason-giving, takes neither a deliberative nor a democratic form but rather monological or coercive claim-making practiced through violent, exclusive, and less respectful means.

Because anti-deliberative reason-giving is equivalent to hate speech or different forms of harassment at a theoretical level, our normative mission should be to sanitize such anti-deliberative practice as much as possible and increase opportunities for deliberative reason-giving; otherwise, our deliberation would lack its normative edge. In reality, however, things are more complicated. Even though it is theoretically possible to clearly distinguish deliberative from nondeliberative and anti-deliberative reason-giving, their boundaries in the real practice of deliberation are highly contested precisely because of contextual factors.[4] To consider this point, we will focus on three boundary examples of reason-giving: *logical argumentation*, *silence*, and *disruptive expressions*. These practices are generally and theoretically categorized as deliberative, nondeliberative, and anti-deliberative reason-giving, respectively—but is this always so?

LOGICAL ARGUMENTATION

Logical argumentation pertains to a process in which one coherently explains the cause-and-effect relation of their own argument, states the problem with the opponent's claim, and justifies the validity of their opinion based on evidence. For epistemic democratic theorists, appealing to the logical validity of arguments is one of the most essential components of democratic deliberation. Conversely, offering a less evidenced or more biased statement or judging an opponent's argument based on impression rather than logic is often regarded as epistemically undesirable communicative practice because they normally fail to advance the argument. "Logical, scientific, principled and precedent-based reasoning" is, according to Moshman (2020, 132), an essential condition for people to act as rational agents in deliberative democracy.

While logical argumentation is considered as a key element of deliberative reason-giving, overly relying on it would sometimes work in an anti-deliberative fashion because it can make one's interlocutor more frustrated and silenced. Socrates—who may be the most classical example of this—laid bare his opponents' ignorance through logic and questioning, which then fueled the ire of many people, and he was consequently sentenced to death. His series of questioning is quite logical and rational, yet his story demonstrates that people are sometimes frightened and deflated by logical argumentation.[5] Moreover, people occasionally use logical argumentation to continue to force one's point.

In the Japanese context, this kind of logical argumentation is referred to as the buzzword "logical harassment" (see Allen 2020). Take the example of a pregnant wife who overeats because of the mental stress of pregnancy. One day, her husband says, "If you eat so much, you will have problems A, B, C, and D, which will lead to consequence E in the future. Overeating is therefore bad for our baby's health. So, you should not eat so much." Logically, this may be true, but what the wife wished may not be such a logical statement but rather sympathy for her mental condition. For her, such a statement would be perceived as a one-sided paternalistic attack that would be useless to her. Consequently, many situations do not require logical argumentation or even go off course because of it, depending on the time and occasion. A mere continuation of logical argumentation does not strengthen the democratic quality of deliberation. In the real context, finding a situation where people engage in reason exchange by only using logical argumentation is difficult. This is why we should not treat the link between logical argumentation and deliberative reason-giving as a given—real deliberation is more complicated.

SILENCE

Silence used to be considered as a sign of oppression (Karpowitz and Mendelberg 2014) or as a nondeliberative practice. Yet the recent systemic turn of deliberative theory opens a new avenue through which we assess silence as a nondeliberative but democracy-oriented reason offered by traditionally disadvantaged groups (Jungkuntz 2012; Rollo 2017; Curato 2019). Take a couple of recent examples. Emma González at the March for Our Lives rally in 2018 abruptly went silent for 6 minutes 20 seconds to "give reason" about why she felt anger, sadness, and misery and thereby to send a critical message to US society, which rarely values youth voices and lives. Meanwhile, during the Myanmar military coup in March 2021, activists called for a "silent strike" where many citizens, including the staff of the biggest supermarkets and delivery services, stopped working and stayed home to disrupt the economy through their silence, thus protesting oppressive military force. Each case of silence empowered politically disadvantaged people in the public sphere (e.g., young people, oppressed citizens) to publicly express their reason.

Nonetheless, we should not romanticize the power of silence, because it sometimes functions in an anti-deliberative manner. As we will see in chapter 4, some deliberative thinkers who theorize the role of listening in deliberation issued a warning that some types of silence may run the risk of broadening inequality and power imbalances between deliberators. This is demonstrated by the strategy that schoolteachers frequently use. If a teacher suddenly falls silent while students are talking, the silence pressure forces students to ask, "Did I say something wrong?" and mute themselves. Silence of this sort is not a practice for inducing further deliberation but rather a strategy for manifesting who holds power.

DISRUPTIVE EXPRESSIONS

Disruptive expressions used by both the radical right and left fall under anti-deliberative practice precisely because of their engagement in violence, tendency to bypass dialogue and argument, and advocacy for change via conflictual action rather than rational deliberation. In the normative study of deliberative democracy, considering a disruptive expression as a substitute for reason-giving is understood as a category mistake, and therefore it is believed that a deliberative democracy researcher's key mission is to find a way to avoid such anti-deliberative practice as much as possible. Christian Rostbøll problematized the controversial Muhammad comic about Muslim humor based on its significant lack of a "minimal degree of respect" even though this was one form of political expression practiced under freedom of expression (Rostbøll 2011, 13). Rostbøll also argued that such disruptive and racist expression is problematic in that it sees different others not as partners of deliberation but as targets of attack, which in turn induces fear and fight rather than learning and the pursuit of truth.

Rostbøll did not claim that we should eliminate all types of communicative expressions that potentially produce an anti-deliberative outcome. He acknowledged that testing the limits of deliberation is epistemically valuable only when (1) the expression is practiced around the limits, and (2) the test aims for a better understanding of the limits. If an expression clearly exceeds boundaries (e.g., racist hate speech), he suggested eliminating such expressions (Rostbøll 2011, 14). However, is it possible to set the limit a priori? This question is important because some disruptive expressions help otherwise oppressed voices to be heard and offer new reasons to the public debate under controversy. As Mansbridge et al. (2012 19) indicated, radical, anti-deliberative, and disruptive expressions can, despite their lack of rational argumentation, may significantly contribute to the inclusiveness of the deliberative system if such expressions give a voice to people whose sentiments and reasons have been traditionally ignored in the public sphere. William Smith (2016) also drew on the case of protests of anti-whaling groups and argued that their disruptive practice can be justified as a legitimate form of reason-giving if its purpose is to raise the issue in the public sphere and when people's shared priority is not deliberation but rather the enforcement of the international agreement on whaling prohibition.

Although Muhammad comics and cartoons are difficult to consider as a deliberative form of reason-giving because of their disruptive nature, this does not mean that all forms of humor should be excluded a priori from the public sphere. In November 2018, Australia's prime minister Scott Morrison criticized Australian youth climate activists (School Strike for Climate [SS4C]) by saying, "What we want is more learning in schools and less activism in schools." In December, students responded to Morrison's tirade not by deliberation (because they lacked access to the formal deliberative forum) but by humor in the public sphere in Sydney. Figure 3.1 shows a young man dressed in a Morrison costume holding a board stating that Morrison failed to understand the climate crisis and taking pictures with children who skipped school that day. Sometimes, the man would give kids a board with a poo emoji, which kids then rubbed and threw at the fake Morrison's face. From the perspective of a Morrison supporter, humor of this kind is totally unacceptable because it lacks a minimal degree of respect, nor does it treat Morrison as a partner in deliberation and dialogue. Nonetheless, for young school strikers who have long been unable to access formal democratic institutions, using such "disruptive" expression is a useful means for publicly criticizing authority and responding to powerful people.[6]

If such disruptive expression enhances the inclusive quality of the public sphere, enables people to use different methods of giving reason, makes the public sphere more multivocal, produces better collective knowledge and, as a result, achieves an epistemic value of deliberative

Figure 3.1. Fake Morrison in a climate protest in Sydney, December 8, 2018. *Source*: Photo by the author.

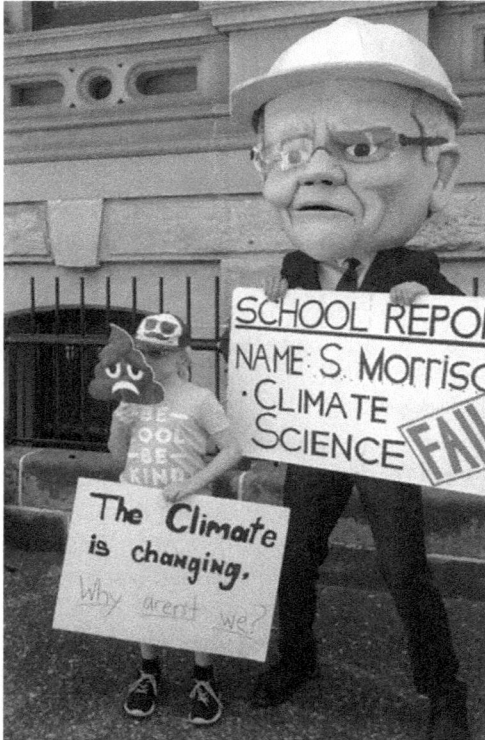

democracy, anti-deliberative disruptive practices can function in the same way as nondeliberative practices do. Again, Rostbøll's minimal degree of respect principle generally offers an important indicator to set a boundary between what is acceptable reason-giving and what is not. However, in practice, such a boundary is often blurred.

Thus far, I have described when and how reason-giving becomes deliberative, nondeliberative, and anti-deliberative and how their boundaries become vaguer than we assumed. As illustrated in the previous section, we must acknowledge both the fact of the plurality of reason-giving and the epistemic value of reason-giving; otherwise, we succumb to the "everything is deliberation" pitfall. Having said that, even though a reason is given for an epistemic purpose, its anti-deliberative crystallization fails to produce an epistemically valuable outcome, as summarized in table 3.1.

Table 3.1a–b. When reason-giving turns into a (non- or anti-)deliberative practice: Examples.

Table 3.1a

	Deliberative	Nondeliberative	Anti-deliberative
Normative definition	Deliberative and democratic practice characterized by rational, logical, evidenced, reciprocal, or public use of communication	Democratic but not deliberative practice characterized by strategic, less public, and performative use of communication	Neither deliberative nor democratic practice characterized by refusal of communication, violent, disruptive and exclusive use of communication
Typically practiced as	Facilitated deliberation Socratic dialogue	Nonviolent protests Some rhetoric	Hate speech Racist humor

Source: Created by the author.

Table 3.1b. Boundary examples.

	Deliberative	Nondeliberative	Anti-deliberative
Logical argumentation	(Normally) Yes	?	Excessively logical argumentation that lacks a sympathetic aspect
Silence	Silence expressed as a voice of voiceless people	(Normally) Yes	Selective silence and refusal to listen
Disruptive expressions	?	Disruptive act aimed at forcing the inclusion of marginalized voices	(Normally) Yes

Source: Created by the author.

With the above arguments in mind, in the subsequent sections, we shift our attention from reason-giving in the public sphere to in the classroom. We will see that the fact of blurred and contextualized boundaries of reason-giving requires a more critical as well as reflective—or what I call *meta-deliberative*—form of classroom deliberation that would be quite different from traditional ways of teaching and learning it.

Hands-On or Hands-Off?

Teaching and learning how to give reason is not a novel topic; it has long been discussed not only in democratic education (Molnar-Main 2017) but also in related fields such as critical thinking and philosophy education (Lipman 2003). In real deliberation, however, various types of reason-giving occur in different contexts and take various forms (e.g., deliberative, nondeliberative, and anti-deliberative). This begs the question: What does "learning reason-giving in classroom deliberation" mean, and how is it implemented? Perhaps a general response to the question would be twofold: hands-on or hands-off.

The hands-on approach focuses on an interventional process in which a teacher first defines what must constitute good reason-giving, and then students practice deliberation accordingly. The teacher then assesses the quality of students' deliberation based on their normative definition. If a student expresses a reason in an anti-deliberative fashion, the teacher must intervene in deliberation. Meanwhile, the hands-off approach emphasizes the significance of laissez-faire, where there are no restrictions and teacher's interventions about how students give reason together. Such a student-centric approach is a critical response to the hands-on approach, indicating its teacher-centric nature that prevents students themselves from developing their autonomy. The former is a traditional/mainstream approach to democratic education, whereas the latter is informed by a progressive education trend (see chapter 5 of this book).

Both approaches, however, do not fit adequately into what I have discussed in previous sections. Although a strict application of the normative view of reason-giving via the hands-on approach can maintain the value of reason-giving in deliberation and avoid concept-stretching, it runs the risk of ignoring the plurality of reason-giving. The instructional control over students' deliberation can also be criticized from the perspective of sociocultural developmental psychology, because the underlying assumption of the approach is roughly informed by the universalist account of reason-giving (i.e., there is a specific form of reason-giving that is always [un]useful). Again, as discussed in the previous section, we need not (or, I would say, should not) praise certain forms of reason-giving as a given. Meanwhile, the hands-off approach can consider the plurality of reason-giving to a greater degree by encouraging a student-centric practice of deliberation. However, this approach is also insufficient because students themselves lack the opportunity to check, assess, and examine whether their reason-giving meets an epistemic standard of deliberation. This approach does not respond to Landemore's aforementioned warning about the relativistic and nihilistic tendency in deliberative democracy. As Gert Biesta (2017) argued, the meaning of student-centric pedagogy is often distorted by many people who confuse it with nonintervention. Such practice seemingly values students' autonomy, yet in fact it is a form of teachers' abdication of teaching responsibility.

The Value of Meta-deliberation

One possible alternative way is a critical and reflective hybrid of the above two approaches. This begins with an instructor's explanation of *reason*-giving that provides sufficient room for multiple interpretations of reason-*giving*. Students then attempt to engage in various forms of reason-giving about the topic using their knowledge, experience, communicative habits, and capacities. At the next stage, with their teacher, students question and analyze their own deliberation aiming to sophisticate the quality of their reason-giving. Afterwards, students hypothesize ways to improve the quality of their *reason*-giving and, if needed, theorize a new reason-giving repertoire. For instance, if students' deliberation is analyzed as highly rhetorical, they consider whether and to what degree the rhetoric is useful in their current deliberative practice. If they agree that rhetorical expression is quite disruptive, a teacher asks them to consider better alternative expressions or improve their communicative habits and norms. Conversely, if they agree that the rhetorical deliberation is an important factor in strengthening the effectiveness of their deliberation, they are asked to update their communicative norms and habits.

This learning process is student-led and participatory in that it is the students who take the initiative of forming and giving structure to reason-giving and how it should be implemented in a given context in collaboration with a teacher/facilitator. As Engeström noted, "The acknowledgement of expansivity means that we accept the possibility that learning gets out of the hands of the instructors and takes a direction of its own" (Engeström 2016, 9). This process itself is also deliberative in that students exchange reasons to justify and explain why the reason-giving under discussion should be seen as deliberative, nondeliberative, or anti-deliberative. Such *deliberation about deliberation* (more specifically, deliberation about reason-giving) takes a divergent path in creating and examining various deliberative repertoires when compared to the conventional model of democratic education, where students deliberate only about the discussion topic. While the latter focuses on the process in which students deliberate about a specific social, ethical, or political *topic* (e.g., Hess 2009; Parker 2010; Journell 2017), the former encourages them to deliberate not only about the topic but also about their *communicative habits and norms* (including their epistemic bias and preferred communication style) *and deliberative contexts*, which then necessitates a self-reflective practice of deliberation, so-called *meta-deliberation*.

Scholars proposed the idea of meta-deliberation primarily to cope with various deliberative failures and deficits, such as a crucial gender inequality within a deliberative process. Bohman noted that "competent speakers may begin a phase of meta-communication, or communication about communication, to restore cooperation between speaker and hearer about mutual-understanding" (Bohman 1996, 205). Dryzek (2010) developed this idea by emphasizing the reflective capacity of meta-deliberation in a deliberative system. At a systemic level, Dryzek argued, we can find various meta-deliberative scenes where people discuss how to organize and formulate a deliberative system about the topic in question, about how to improve the democratic and inclusive quality of the deliberative system if there is significant injustice, and then about how the deliberative system is restructured.[7]

We will see in the empirical part of this chapter that meta-deliberation can take various forms in practice, yet its core should be a self-reflective and self-corrective reason-giving process. This practice encourages students to become conscious of their deliberative habits, question their relevance and adequacy in the context where deliberation takes place and, if needed, consider ways to improve their deliberative norms. Meta-deliberation also allows students to examine a seemingly "problematic" (non- or anti-deliberative) reason-giving to determine whether and in what sense it is really problematic. Building upon the self-reflective process, furthermore, meta-deliberators must be facilitated in a way that encourages them to collaboratively think about how to enhance their own deliberative habits.

Meta-deliberation ensures some key benefits to reason-giving in classroom deliberation. It eschews some pedagogical risks associated with hands-on practice (e.g., teachers' one-sided assessment of students' reason-giving, reinforcing power imbalances between teacher (as an evaluator) and student (as the evaluated)). Meta-deliberation also trusts and recognizes students' self-reflective and self-corrective capacities even though they initially engage in somewhat "problematic" reason-giving. Creativity is also an important benefit of meta-deliberation; while deliberation is practiced within the confines of a set of predetermined deliberative norms, meta-deliberation empowers students to innovate their deliberative repertoires (Nishiyama 2021).

Furthermore, meta-deliberation is an *appropriate* option in terms of students' deliberative agency and learning in the classroom. Deliberating in accordance with adults' (or, more specifically, teachers') definition of "better" deliberation will only reproduce the power relationship in which students act as mere consumers of what adults create. To be emancipated from the traditional adult-initiated top-down practice of pedagogy, students must be, first and foremost, free to exercise their deliberative agency while simultaneously reflecting on their deliberative habits and norms with the support of their teachers to sophisticate and redefine their current deliberative competency on their own terms (i.e., meta-deliberation). As already discussed in chapter 2, learning should not be limited to a traditional behaviorist account of a stimulus-response process but a synthesis that occurs in a revolutionary process of questioning, reflecting, and creating in a given context as defined by Vygotsky-inspired learning theory. Viewed in this light, meta-deliberation allows students to act as formative democratic agents who define and practice what deliberation ought to be and how it is applied in democracy.

Lessons from the Field

Now let us move to a practical question: How can we practice meta-deliberation in an actual classroom? If students discuss a specific topic (e.g., climate change, indigenous rights, the tax system), when is the best time for them to engage in such meta-deliberation? Moreover, as briefly mentioned in the introductory part of the chapter, how can we democratize the meta-deliberative process if, as Holdo (2020) noted, there is no guarantee that meta-deliberation is more democratic than normal deliberation? To consider these points in more practical terms, I draw on my action research on classroom deliberation in an Australian primary school.

From August to September 2018, my research collaborators (Drs. Wendy Russell and Pierrick Chalaye) and I conducted a funded deliberation project in the Deliberation in Australian Schools pilot. The primary purpose of this study was to reflect on our own lived experiences and understand the challenges and required competencies for deliberative facilitators in the classroom.[8] The first project was conducted at a primary school in Canberra with the year 5 cohort (aged 10–11 years). The school is one of the oldest schools in Canberra, with a socioeconomically and culturally diverse student body.[9]

The deliberative program proceeded as follows. The first day was an orientation, in which we introduced ourselves and explained the program's broader purpose, followed by icebreakers and a deliberation about good communication guidelines, which will be discussed later. On the second day, we introduced the main topic of deliberation, which was determined by a teacher and our research group: "How can we make school democratic?" We divided students into two groups—one observing and the other deliberating in rotation—and students attempted to define what a "democratic school" means. On days 3 and 4, based on their working definition of a democratic school, the students were divided into three small groups and deliberated about suggestions for democratizing their school. On day 5, the students prepared presentation materials based on their small-group deliberations and presented their ideas for creating a democratic school in front of the teachers and school principal. Each researcher served as a facilitator throughout the session.

Over the course of the five days, while we observed variety in students' reason-giving about the main topic (democratic school), we also had rich experiences of meta-deliberation conducted by various agents and practiced in different times and forms. Three forms of meta-deliberation played a particularly powerful role in shaping students' reason-giving practice: meta-deliberative session, meta-deliberative moment, and anteroom deliberation.

META-DELIBERATIVE SESSION

A *meta-deliberative session* is a purposefully organized meta-deliberation where participants are given sufficient time to share and examine their reason-giving experiences, knowledge, and habits from multiple angles to create a shareable, falsifiable, and temporary understanding of what their deliberation ought to be.

Honestly, before the first session, we had no idea about the degree to which year 5 students deliberate together, nor did we know the kind of deliberation knowledge and habits they had. We also did not even know how many of them knew the term "deliberation" in the first place. We then had two options. One was to adopt a hands-on approach by introducing to students what deliberation ought to be and then asking them to act accordingly. Precisely because we thought that this approach might risk the predominance of an adult's authority over an entire deliberative process, we took another approach—organizing regular meta-deliberative sessions.

On the first day, after we introduced ourselves to one another, the students engaged in what we called "a good communication guideline practice," where they created a working definition of what good communication is. We first decided to use the term "good communication" instead of "deliberation" because the latter was not a popular term for many children. In this work, the facilitator simply asked, "What is the key to good communication?" Then the facilitator gave the children a few minutes to think, after which they freely wrote their thoughts on Post-it notes and put them on the whiteboard. After sharing the content with the whole group, the facilitator asked them to group some ideas whose meanings overlapped. Interestingly, many children proposed a body-related idea of good communication. According to their explanations, relying excessively on verbal expressions may prevent listeners from obtaining a nuanced understanding of what a speaker intends to say. The children then asserted that "reading" what the other person is trying to say from their nonverbal signs (e.g., gestures, tone of voice) is an important element that makes communication effective. In addition, a male student suggested that we practice more creativity in making the guideline, that is, in a way that is more accessible and understandable to everyone. In response, we decided to summarize all Post-it notes into nine key items (Do not Interrupt, Engage, Listen, Body, Clear, Respect, Authentic, Think, and Everyone's Included) and then put them under the guideline DELIBERATE (figure 3.2), which was used throughout the project.

We used this guideline as material for the meta-deliberative meetings organized at the beginning and end of each session. At the beginning of the session, the facilitator asked, "Do you want to add more items or improve the contents of this guideline?" Meanwhile, at the end of each session, we also asked, "On the basis of today's deliberation, do you think the guideline needs more items?" and "Which items do you think made our deliberation better?" After asking these questions, we spent approximately

Figure 3.2. Students' own good communication guidelines: DELIBERATE. *Source*: Photo by the author.

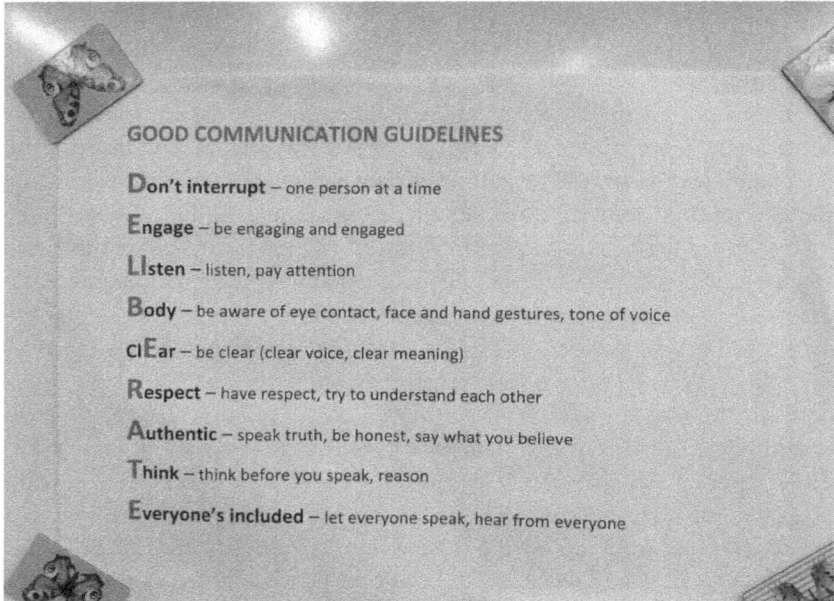

10 minutes deliberating about the guideline. As a result, for instance, a male student pointed out at the end of the session on the third day that body should include more diverse expressions such as drawing, and the other children agreed.

META-DELIBERATIVE MOMENT

Not only meta-deliberative sessions organized and initiated by a facilitator but also a contingently and spontaneously occurring meta-deliberation sometimes allowed students to check, examine, define, and theorize their good communication guideline. Meta-deliberation of this kind can be labeled as a *meta-deliberative moment*, which originates within a deliberative interaction between students, and ideally the facilitator must exert much effort in discovering and nurturing this moment. A meta-deliberative moment is less structured than a meta-deliberative session but is certainly meta-deliberation, as it is a reflective and critical examination of the legitimacy of the shared communicative norm practiced in various deliberation stages in a more naturalized way.

On the third day, for example, the students in my group deliberated about the suggestion of having pets as a means to make schools better and more democratic. The female student who suggested this proposal explained that she often felt that many children in her school were not responsible for their own actions and did selfish things, so she believed that they needed to develop a sense of responsibility to others—having a pet is an important step toward learning responsibility. In emphasizing this point, she referred to her own story of having a dog and talked about how owning a pet had helped her develop a sense of responsibility. One of the boys in my group suddenly responded as follows:

STUDENT A: That's a too personal story!

STUDENT B: What's wrong with my personal story?

STUDENT A: Such a too personal story may not persuade us.

STUDENT B: But I speak truth. I am serious. This is [pointing at the guideline] Authentic.

In these two short replies to student A, student B attempted to update their shared understanding of authentic deliberation by suggesting that the narration of personal stories be incorporated as a key additional element. Although I, as a facilitator, did not intervene in their interaction, this meta-deliberative moment might have been more fruitful if I had implemented some supplementary interventions. For instance, I should have asked the students questions such as "If a personal story successfully persuades everyone, do you think it is an authentic claim?" "Why does this personal story not persuade you? What is the problem of a personal story?" and "What is a nonpersonal story? Will it become an authentic claim?" These questions can interrupt the deliberation on the subject in question (having a pet). However, these interruptive questions can be an important resource for children to critically scrutinize how they deliberate and realize the underlying assumptions of their deliberative behavior.

Nonetheless, I sometimes engaged in interruptive questioning when a meta-deliberative moment occurred. On day 4, for instance, the students in my group deliberated as follows:

STUDENT C: As I asked you guys, who should look after pets during summer vacation?

STUDENT D: Well, so why don't we take our turn to look after our pets at home during summer vacation?

STUDENT E: Only boys have been talking since a short while ago. Why not ask opinions to girls?

AUTHOR: Okay, good point. Can you tell us more about what the key point of your suggestion is?

STUDENT E: We do not want to be biased.

AUTHOR: Why is such bias wrong?

STUDENT E: Because if I get many kinds of opinions, I might have new ideas.

During this short interaction with the facilitator, student E implicitly problematized that their deliberation was thus far grounded on the inequality between male and female students and attempted to alleviate the situation by connecting some norms they had made (e.g., Listen and Everyone's Included). As a result of student E's meta-deliberative contribution to the group, other participants realized that they had engaged in a male-centric deliberative practice and therefore tried to change it. By the end of this session, more female students had been given a chance to share their thoughts.

In each case, a meta-deliberative moment arose when children disagreed with each other about the communicative norm that each of them had in mind. A meta-deliberative moment, when considered seriously, interrupts students' deliberation about the topic in a way that shifts their attention toward a re-examination of the degree to which each student's communicative norm can be shared. If necessary, students must reach a consensus about the improved version of the communication norm, which is not about the deliberation topic but rather a sort of meta-consensus (see Niemeyer and Dryzek 2007) about how they communicate together.

Anteroom Deliberation

A facilitator or teacher can practice meta-deliberation *outside* the class-room. Although students did not participate in such a meta-deliberative practice, meta-deliberation of this kind allowed facilitators and teachers to collaboratively address the communicative dysfunctions that students faced during deliberation, which are hardly to be resolved solely by them. I call this *anteroom deliberation*. Anteroom deliberation is not merely an exchange of evaluative opinions about the quality of students' deliberation; rather, it is a collective analysis of students' deliberation to identify the problem, a collaborative consideration of ways to move forward, and a reflective preparation for the next session so that the facilitator can create a supportive condition under which students' deliberation and meta-deliberation become more effective.

In our project, this anteroom deliberation occurred mostly in the reflection stage of our action research. After finishing each deliberative session of each day, our research group held a debriefing with teachers and observers. Afterwards, our research group went to a café and conducted a more intensive meta-deliberative session for one to two hours. These meta-deliberations were structured mainly by the following six core questions, with each facilitator sharing their opinions and perspectives to identify and resolve the problems students would encounter during classroom deliberation:

- How did we feel the session went overall? What went well? What didn't go so well? (with teacher/s)

- How did the children respond? Which activities engaged them? Was anything surprising? What do we need to think about for future sessions?

- How did the lesson plan go? How was the timing? Were there any obstacles to the activities? Logistical problems?

- How was our facilitation? What did we do well? How could we improve?

- What did we learn today about deliberation in schools?

- What research questions are suggested by today's session?

In the anteroom deliberation after the classroom deliberation on the second day, one of the facilitators shared two types of communicative issues she observed during the deliberative session. On the one hand, some "low-attention children who had difficulty focusing for long were very engaged with the ideas for the topic, but it was hard to get them to go into much depth (they did a bit)" (debrief note: August 17, 2018). On the other hand, some Asian students who did not speak native English suffered from a linguistic disadvantage compared with native students and might have felt that our deliberation was rapid and excessively focused on native speakers, running the risk of accelerating their marginalization. The facilitators considered this issue and therefore decided to deliberate on the possible logistics that would allow these marginalized students to engage in a (meta-)deliberative practice in the classroom. As a result of our one-hour meta-deliberation about the communicative inclusion of these students, we decided to include a visual practice. On the third day, we provided one group a large piece of paper and encouraged them to freely draw their thoughts about democratic schools. This activity neutralized the language barrier to some extent, and some "low-attention" students were allowed to engage in this collective visual reason-giving practice at their convenience. Figure 3.3 presents an overview of a "democratic school as a fun place" as expressed by the children. The aforementioned Asian students and low-attention children were also able to participate in this process more actively than before. By creating this deliberative structure based on anteroom deliberation, we encouraged students to become aware of the different ways of reason-giving (e.g., drawing a picture) that were not limited to a verbal practice (see also chapter 4).

On another day, we held an anteroom deliberation about the role of one classroom teacher who monitored students' deliberation and attempted to steer it toward a "desirable" consequence. We thought that such behavior ran the risk of preventing children's effective reason exchange, which then led us to reexamine what the ideal role of a teacher as an observer must be (e.g., when should a teacher intervene in a process and when should they not, whether a teacher as an observer should share their opinion and under what condition it can be useful) and share our meta-deliberation contents with the teacher. Consequently, anteroom deliberation not only added a more facilitative element to children's reason-giving but also subtracted some inhibiting elements (e.g., the power of the teacher) from deliberation in an indirect but significant way.

Figure 3.3. Democratic school as a fun space. *Source*: Photo by the author.

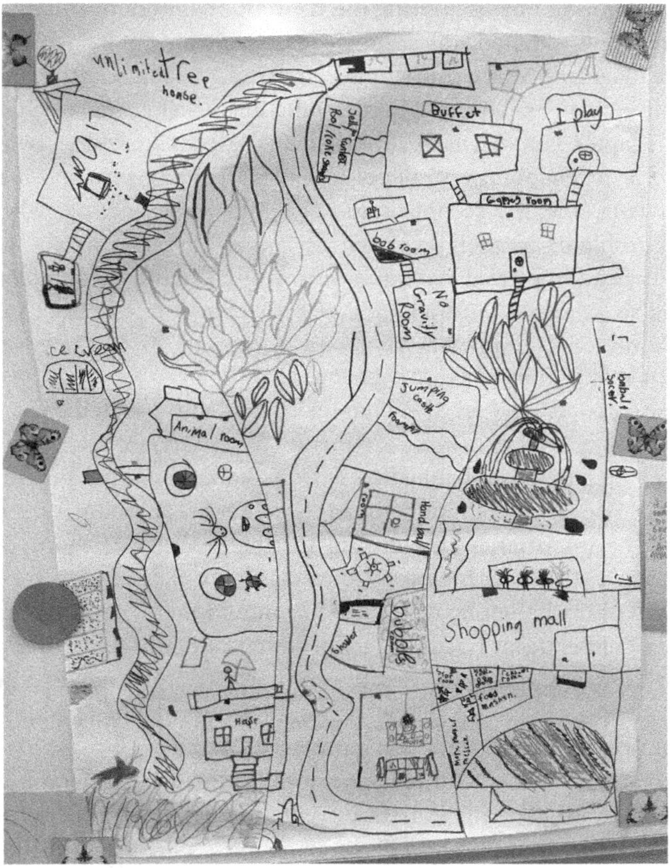

Conclusion

Expecting students to deliberate in accordance with predetermined, strict, and fixed norms of deliberative reason-giving is important in its own right. However, the chapter reveals that the differences between two trends in reason-giving (*reason*-giving and reason-*giving*) blur the boundaries between what we consider deliberative, nondeliberative, and anti-deliberative reason-giving. This in turn gives rise to the question of how democratic education situates reason-giving as an epistemic anchor while also accommodating various ways of reason-giving. The chapter responds to this question not by examining the conventional understandings of top-down and adult-initiated education for reason-giving, but by demonstrating the value of a more revolutionary, grassroots, and student-centric practice of deliberative norm-making and implementation—that is, meta-deliberation. As this chapter has discussed, meta-deliberation consists of two stages. The first is to encourage students to experimentally practice their own reason-*giving*, and the second is to engage in *reason*-giving, where they identify problems in their experiences and deliberative habits, consider and theorize an improved version of reason-giving, and then implement it. By doing so, students can make use of their own communally recognized means of reason-giving, while *simultaneously* recognizing the existence of other possible modes of reason-giving.

The second half of the chapter also demonstrated that relying solely on a single form of meta-deliberation may ignore or even facilitate structural inequality and injustice within the deliberative process itself. Here, the case of deliberation in an Australian classroom was used to illustrate the importance of allowing for the creation of multiple meta-deliberation pathways. This case shows that meta-deliberation takes place not only within the context of a session intentionally designed to facilitate meta-deliberation, but also in the context of contingent interactions between students (meta-deliberative moments) and even in situations entirely outside classroom deliberation (anteroom deliberation). What is important here is not to ask, "Which meta-deliberation is most ideal?" but to consider ways that maximize opportunities for these different forms of meta-deliberation. The more meta-deliberation can help students examine their experiences, habits, and norms of reason-giving, the more they can act as deliberative democratic agents in the classroom who continuously transform the meaning of reason-giving in a revolutionary way.

This chapter has paid close attention to the "talk" aspect of deliberation. However, if there is no listener, our reason-giving, regardless of its variations, may end in emptiness. If reason-giving is one key face of deliberation, we need to take another face—listening—into account. The next chapter shall discuss this point in more detail.

Chapter 4

Listening in the Classroom

Often, listening[1] is treated as a passive, nonverbal practice that happens after a speech activity. According to Gemma Fiumara, the logocentric Western culture in which "the bearers of the world are predominantly active in speaking, molding and informing" left behind a tendency to prioritize speaking over listening (Fiumara 1990, 23). Whether implicitly or explicitly, such assumptions used to be held by the deliberative democracy side.[2] For instance, Jacobs, Cook, and Delli Carpini (2009) researched how Americans engage in political discourse-making and make decisions about it. However, their book title, *Talking Together*, shows that their key measurement criteria were talk-focused and paid less attention to how American citizens *listen* together.

The talk-centric trend in deliberative democracy has been altering recently. A rising number of theoretical as well as empirical research about deliberative listening has been published one after another (e.g., Dobson 2014; Hendriks, Ercan, and Duss 2019; Hendriks, Ercan, and Boswell 2020; Eveland, Appiah, and Bullock 2020; Scudder 2020). Today's majority of deliberate thinkers agree that listening skills have a substantial influence on the quality of speech. Michael Morrell (2018, 242–46) investigates how we might effectively include listening in public deliberation, such as using a skilled facilitator for enabling citizens' mutual listening and designing a more listening-centered structure of public deliberation.[3] Then he lists important traits that listeners who identify as democratic ought to possess.

Similar to Morrell, political theorists have offered a variety of theoretical suggestions for listening instruction and have explained why and how learning listening is important for healthy public deliberation (e.g.,

Dobson 2014, 187; Scudder 2020, 120–22). But how can we be certain that students are listening well and developing into good, thoughtful, and democratic listeners? Indeed, judging the quality of listening is hard work, because it is an internal process and the difference between "good" and "bad" listening is difficult to make through mere observation. Even if a listener claims to listen well, there is a possibility that he merely pretends to listen or, worse, that he is listening with prejudiced and biased ears. Hence, judging the quality of listening needs a tool that allows us to approach and examine both subjective and objective experiences of listening.

In light of this, the chapter will focus on Mary Scudder's (2021, 2022) novel normative framework for assessing the quality of listening, called the Listening Quality Index (LQI), which consists of a combination of the listener's self-report, speaker's satisfaction, and the observer's report. As will be addressed in this chapter, the LQI can be an optimal method for *researchers* to evaluate the value of listening in *public deliberation* (such as listening in a citizens' assembly). However, I contend that the LQI is more taxing for *teachers* and less context-responsive for *students* if it is employed during *classroom deliberation*. For teachers, the LQI is scarcely suitable, because it requires many additional research activities, such as participant surveys before, during, and after deliberation, and writing an observation report. These may even be an unwelcome addition for teachers who already have a packed schedule and a complex curriculum to manage. For students, the LQI does not accurately reflect their life-world in connection to their experience of listening. For some students, a specific form of listening ranked high on the LQI may not necessarily be meaningful in their deliberative practice because they know from their experience that what is regarded as a minimum threshold on the LQI is sometimes more essential than anything else in their everyday context.

Against this backdrop, the chapter will propose a less onerous and more context-responsive form of the quasi-LQI, or what I call the uncapitalized *lqi*, whose normative core is reconstructed based on students' thoroughly examined lifeworld. With the help of a facilitator, students create a list of their listening norms by collectively reconstructing and co-constructing their listening experiences and habits. This list is always open to meta-deliberation, where students revise and edit their list to make it more normatively desirable. Using this list as a guide, facilitators need to concentrate on observing how students adhere to the listening norms they have created and make any required adjustments, which ultimately enables a more context-responsive assessment and is less burdensome than the LQI. Drawing on my action research in a Japanese classroom, I demonstrate how such meta-deliberation about listening lessens the LQI's practical and intrinsic obstacles.

Deliberation, Listening, and Education

Philosophers have discussed the importance of listening ever since the days of ancient Greece. In *Nicomachean Ethics*, Aristotle noted the value of "listening to reason" intended to set a baseline for separating rational from irrational behavior (Aristotle 1985, 1149a25). In contemporary political theory, Susan Bickford sparked the expansion of conversation on listening. Drawing on Hannah Arendt's writing, Bickford makes the case that political listening is more than just a receptive and cognitive effort. Nor is it merely an interpretive practice focusing on perspective-taking and imagination of the different situations. Instead, she views political listening as a focused and imaginative activity in which "a plurality of voices, faces, and languages can be heard and seen and spoken" (Bickford 1996, 129). Andrew Dobson's *Listening for Democracy* is a pathbreaking work that explicitly situates listening at the heart of deliberative democracy, which is defined as the recognition of differences and empowerment of both speaker and listener. Dobson argued that listening should be practiced in an "apophatic" way that "involves a *temporary* suspension of the listener's categories in order to make room for the speaker's voice and to help it arrive in its 'authentic' form" (Dobson 2014, 68; original emphasis). This type of listening endeavors to give speakers space to express their views in their terms; but an apophatic listener does so to learn how and in what sense the speakers differ from one another rather than to discover their points in common.

In response to this trend, some deliberative listening proponents urge for listening instruction in educational settings as their conclusion to their argument (e.g., Morrell 2010; Dobson 2014). For example, Scudder argues that listening should be incorporated into a civic education initiative, because "for a listening approach to democratic deliberation to work, people have to be prepared and willing to accept continued misunderstanding and disagreement even after their best efforts to engage" (Scudder 2020, 128).

In the face of a widespread discussion and debate boom, however, many students have been made to believe that those who talk are considered more talented than those who listen.[4] Listening-related attitudes in discussions are still rated in today's talk-centric school environment not as an indication of democratic practice but rather as a sign of "no opinion." In *Speech and Debate as Civic Education* (Hogan et al. 2017), most contributors place listening at the heart of the deliberative form of civic education, but attention was rarely paid to (the ethics of) listening. Hess and McAvoy (2015) provided some examples of how an atmosphere of free dialogue in the classroom climate encourages attentive listening before group decision-making. While their study successfully revealed how students discuss together in the classroom with an open climate, it is still unknown *in what sense* and *to what extent* students were able to listen in a better way. Some fundamental ideas in democratic education, such as empathy (Molnar-Main 2017), acceptance of diversity and disagreement (Hess 2009), or reflective and caring thinking (Lipman 2003), can potentially be relevant to the value of listening, but their connection has not yet been fully explored. Overall, listening, despite the fact that its relevance in deliberative democracy is widely acknowledged, does not hold a significant role in democratic education. Much ink has been used for exploring "how we talk" or "how we express ourselves," while "how we listen" receives little attention.

Listening constitutes the majority of communication, but why have democratic education studies been less likely to concern listening? Perhaps some scholars have previously attempted to address this issue (e.g., Parker 2010), but they immediately face the standard pedagogical obstacle of *assessment* right away. After all, there is an absence of a shared view on what indicators practitioners should use to assess the level of listening. In many cases, "good (or bad) speech" or "good (or bad) ways of expression" involve visible and audible speech acts, and there are diverse methods for objective assessment, such as the Discourse Quality Index (Steiner 2012). Comparatively, assessing listening requires significant effort, because "listening is an internal act and can only be measured indirectly by looking for observable behaviors that we might expect to correspond with listening" (Scudder 2022, 115).

Perhaps, one of the easiest approaches that can come to our mind would be to rely on *self-report* as a source of information. As we shall see below, we can benefit from some epistemic and ethical contributions from self-report: nonetheless, self-report also faces epistemic and ethical obstacles. Moreover, it is also crucial to take into account two related queries. Firstly, whose self-report should be considered for assessment? Secondly, what standards are used for assessment when we employ self-report? In my view, the answer to the first question affects the second question.

One possible strategy for assessment is to rely on the *listener's* self-report. Here, we question listeners on the extent to which they believe they listen well throughout their deliberation, and then use their self-report to interpret the quality of their listening. If one person reports "I move slowly, taking care not to report every thought that comes to my mind," and "I am not denying or dismissing the validity of the speaker's point of view or manner of talking" (Parker 2010, 2830), we can conclude that she or he is a cautious and engaged listener. This strategy can take up the deliberative participation of those who often abstain from participating in discussions. In classroom deliberation, some students remain silent throughout the whole process of deliberation. They frequently receive unreasonably low evaluations or are viewed as invisible persons. However, some of them may intentionally keep silent to concentrate on reason-exchange between other students and thereby deepen their understanding of the topic in question. Using listener's self-report can free such people from speech-centric assessments and recognize their varieties of forms of "participation" in a deliberative process.

Having said that, relying too heavily on the listener's self-report carries the risk of ignoring listeners' prejudices. Even if one reports good listening, she possibly pretends to do so. Alternatively, she may genuinely think she is listening very well but, in fact, just hears what she wants to hear. Children in the public sphere often suffer from such pretended listening. Adults preoccupied with prejudice (e.g., children are too young; children lack knowledge and experience) appear to listen to children on the surface but, in reality, they do not listen at all (Murris 2013). Even if adults insist that "we are listening!" we must question the reliability of such self-report if there is a major power disparity and structural inequality between adults and children *before* deliberation takes place.

In contemporary epistemology, Miranda Fricker calls this sort of unfair listening referred to as *epistemic injustice*. Fricker unpacks how a socially, politically, historically, and culturally constructed unjust situation wrongs particular identity groups in their role as subjects of knowledge (Fricker 2007, 20). Epistemic injustice is a particular practice of listening by which the credibility of a certain speaker's words is significantly deflated by an individual or collective level of prejudicial listening. One of the core features of epistemic injustice that Fricker herself has long worked to address is what she calls *testimonial* injustice. "Testimony" refers to an effort by the speaker to transfer his or her own knowledge. Listeners find the speaker's knowledge credible if the speaker is capable of offering sufficient reason to believe that the shared knowledge is true. The speaker suffers testimonial injustice when the credibility of the speaker's knowledge is questioned. It is not because there is not enough evidence to support the testimony; rather, it is due to biases or prejudices held by the listeners toward a particular identity. Speakers are allowed to testify their knowledge, and in this sense testimonial injustice is different from explicit exclusion from a communicative process. However, when testimonial injustice happens, a speaker is epistemically marginalized precisely because the audience did not trust their testimony *before* the communication starts. In this regard, Fricker contends that testimonial injustice is harmful to the speaker both epistemically and ethically. Due to the listener's biased and prejudiced listening, testimonial injustice deprives the speaker of the opportunity and, as a result, "they are degraded *qua* knower, and they are symbolically degraded *qua* human" (44). Fricker's original contribution is that she theorized how a specific group of people is excluded from the public sphere neither through explicit harassment nor hate speech, but through the very process of listening.

Testimonial injustice is the matter happening not only in the broader public sphere but also in students' communicative interactions in the classroom.[5] Practitioners of postcolonial theory have warned about the continued situation where, in a white-dominant classroom, talking about race is considered a "no go area," thereby maintaining "whiteness" or "the white as dominant knower" in educational settings for a long time. Even though a marginalized student believes that his or her voice is not taken in the classroom due to preexisting prejudicial listening, it is the dominant knowers who have the power to judge and report whether they listen well or not (hooks 1994; Chetty and Suissa 2017). In such situations, uncritical acceptance of a dominant knower's self-report risks leaving injustice unchecked and even perpetuated. In other words, the fact that epistemic injustice happens in the classroom cautions that overreliance on the listener's self-report offers unmunificent ground for understanding the quality of listening.

So, what about focusing on the *speaker's* self-report? For instance, we can ask a speaker whether she feels that other participants listen to her sincerely. When someone nods, gestures, or asks a question, the speaker may feel satisfied. Bickford claims that a questioning response "probes, extends, or gives new meaning to speaker's remarks" and thus "we can imagine a question designed primarily to evade or obscure those remarks" (Bickford 1996, 157). In this sense, asking a question is a sign of listening that allows a speaker to feel that "we have in the world" (Bickford 1996, 157). As discussed above, giving full ownership for assessing the quality of listening only to listeners may have the risk of perpetuating marginalization of the speaker. In contrast, the speaker's satisfaction can reveal whether they genuinely experience testimonial injustice in the process of deliberation.

This speaker-centric strategy is, however, not without a problem. Imagine a situation where a speaker says that she does not feel she is being listened to during deliberation. Sometimes, this can be the listener's fault. This can, however, be occasionally the speaker's fault if the listener intentionally refuses to listen or dares to take a disinterest in the speaker because the speaker expresses a lot of discriminative statements. Scudder also notes that "a person might interpret other's continued disagreement as a sign that they did not listen when, in reality, his or her arguments simply failed to convince" (Scudder 2022, 117). This strategic denial of listening or persistent disagreement should be recognized not as mere failed listening but as nonlistening with justifiable intention or a sort of epistemic resistance. Therefore, overreliance on the speaker's satisfaction could pass over the speaker's or the deliberative group's own problem.

Furthermore, speakers who experience testimonial injustice sometimes purposefully distorts the truth or make up statements to gain the attention of the privileged listeners. Kamili Posey (2021, 39–40) uses the actual story of Marie, an 18-year-old sexual assault survivor, to illustrate this. Marie reported her rape surviving experience to the police officer, but he did not find her statement credible because she gave contradictory information. As Posey points out, such inconsistency is prevalent among sexual assault survivors due to the deep trauma they have, and yet no one (including the police officer, and Marie's foster parents) trusted Marie's testimony and even criticized it as an exaggerated statement. Many people saw her as a liar. Following a string of accusations against Marie, including a police officer's pressure to recant her statement, she was compelled to declare in front of the public that she had lied (and even paid her court fees). The police officer "listened" to Marie's statement and then at this point accepted her "testimony" that she is a liar even though she was aware that she had not told a lie.[6] She was "being listened to" at the end. Yet, to be "listened," she had to downplay the significance of her evidence, refute her assertion, and consciously tell a lie. By doing so, she became more vulnerable and marginalized epistemically and ethically. Posey refers to the speaker's strategy for avoiding further public accusation and stigmatization as epistemic labor. Although there are many different types of epistemic labor, Posey contends that Marie's tactic was the most extreme one, because "it includes being coerced into making the type of calculated risk that no individual should have to make, to disavow yourself as a knower due to the material threats and harms that a dominant knower, or dominant institution, puts before you" (40–41). As a result, even though a speaker reports "being listened to" as it turned out, we should be cautious about the possibility that they were forced to say so.

Listening Quality Index and Some Practical Challenges

As we have seen, both listener's self-report and the speaker's satisfaction report have advantages, but they could downplay strong ethical and epistemic issues. In this case, Scudder's most recent creative framework, the Listening Quality Index (LQI) (Scudder 2021, 2022) merits attention. Key takeaways we can draw out from the LQI are that the listener's self-report and speaker's satisfaction report are either-or types of issues and in addition to the listener's and speaker's perspective, the observer's (or third person's) perspective is important to include to enable a more equitable and multilateral assessment of listening.

The LQI places a priority on several forms of responsiveness as evidence of listening. Several deliberative democracy scholars advocate this strategy (Steiner 2012; Dobson 2014). Yet Scudder believes that the shortcoming of the standard method is its overreliance on observable responsiveness. Scudder argues that "encouraging listeners to always respond might undermine quality listening" (Scudder 2021, 4). Scudder thus tries to reconcile responsiveness reported by the observer with the self-report of both listener and speaker, thereby implying an overarching framework as follows (Scudder 2021, 2022; see also Scudder 2020, 139).

1. *No listening:* The listener reports not listening to the speaker.

2. *Failed listening:* The speaker is interrupted to the point of being silenced, while the listener reports listening to the speaker.

3. *Passive listening*: The listener does not interrupt to the point of silencing the speaker. The listener allows the speaker to speak.

4. *Attentive listening*: The listener can recall what the speaker said.

5. *Active listening*: The listener responds to the speaker. The response can be verbal and nonverbal.

6. *Responsive listening*: The listener responds to the speaker in a substantive and relevant way.

7. *Performative listening*: The speaker reports being satisfied with the sincerity of the listener's listening.

As displayed, LQI 1, 2, and 4 pertain to the listener's self-report, which is the most fundamental component of the LQI and serves as its foundation. LQI 3, 5, and 6 are observable responsiveness (or observer's perspective). And LQI 7 represents a speaker's satisfaction. Listening becomes most democratic when the listener's, the observer's, and the speaker's perspectives all indicate good listening from various perspectives.[7] One distinctive aspect of the LQI is that it combines the observer's perspective with the perspective of the listener and speaker. With the LQI, it is anticipated that we can assess the degree to which listeners engage in listening or are willing to listen to others without bias on a variety of levels.

Another core feature of the LQI is that these seven steps are arranged in lexical order. Drawing on Rawls's "two principles of justice," Scudder observes that the stages from LQI 1 to 7 are ordered normatively and deductively, and each earlier stage must be satisfied to go to the next stage. For instance, a person's LQI score is 3 if she achieves LQI 1, 2, and 3. If one achieves LQI 1, 2, 4, and 5, her LQI score is 2, because she failed to achieve 3. Each participant reports their perspective and experience of listening on the LQI scorecard. If the circumstances call for it, participants in the deliberation will be interviewed, or we can ask observers to give comments about their observation. Thus, the LQI is an attempt to use the scoresheet, to link participants' self-report with third persons' observations, and to obtain a broad-based, multifaceted picture of the quality of listening.

Is the LQI then a possibility for assessing the quality of listening in classroom deliberation? Obviously, the LQI provides valuable insights into how we overcome a traditional educational gridlock (assessment). Additionally, teachers may have a clearer, more specific understanding of both the deliberative process that needs to be addressed and how much students listen well in classroom deliberation. In particular, the LQI's multiangle examination of listening can potentially contribute to identifying students' (unconscious) engagement in or suffering from testimonial injustice. Despite possible advantages, I assert that there are at least three types of difficulties we would encounter when implementing the LQI in classroom deliberation.

When using the LQI in classroom deliberation, the first barrier is straightforward and likely one that many people will face right away: being too busy to use it. Scudder's LQI would be quite useful for assessing listening in *public deliberation*, which means that its primary user is a *researcher*, not a teacher. Most teachers do not have the resources to allow students to complete all the tasks necessary for using the LQI, such as facilitating deliberation about a specific topic in the classroom, explaining the LQI and its significance, having each student complete the scoresheet, conducting interviews, and so forth. The LQI itself may be seen as even an unwelcome addition by those who find themselves bogged down in numerous curriculum-related activities. Importantly, I am not claiming that the LQI per se is problematic. I assert that it would be practically impossible for the LQI to be used outside of the context for which it was initially intended.

So, given that there is "the most desirable environment," where the teacher can work in a team of other assistant teachers, observers, coders, motivated students, will the practical application of the LQI to classroom deliberation be more realistic? Possibly not, regrettably. To consider this point, let us think about the following circumstance:

> *Student A recently spent an entire day worrying about her gender identity, but she was unable to talk to anyone about it. One day, she participated in a classroom deliberation, and its topic was gender equality. Sadly, during the discussion, several students kept using stereotypical and prejudiced language, and she started to feel attacked. Suddenly, student B told a story about his bisexual brother and made the argument that we should stop discriminating against people based on their gender identity and instead be more receptive to various forms of gender recognition. Student A felt relieved by student B's assertion. She remained*

mute for the remainder of the discussion, carefully considered student B's statement thoroughly, and paid little attention to what other students had to say. She reasoned that it would be risky for her to say something during deliberation, so she decided to speak with student B after the deliberative session.

We can interpret this communicative process using the LQI in the manner shown below. Student A would affirm that she paid attention without being distracted (LQI 2 and 3). But she would also report that she listened only to student B's claim and ignored the claims of the other students (LQI 1). She remembered every aspect of student B's statement but could not remember what the other students had to say (LQI 4). Although she responded to student B after the deliberative session, observers claim that student A did not offer any substantial responses during the process (LQI 5 and 6). Except for student B, speakers and observers might have the impression that student A was not engaged in the subject of the discussion, at least not within the context of a deliberative process (LQI 7). Together, student A would not meet most of the criteria of the LQI and, as a result, her LQI scores may be 1 (no listening—because she did not listen to most speakers except for student B) or at best 3. Should we then give the "no listening" or "passive listening" score to student A, who is seriously contemplating the issue (perhaps much more seriously than other students)? Should we give a low score to student A, who concentrated on thinking about student B's claim, on the basis just of not making a substantive response to speakers? Did student A fail to listen?

This situation, in my view, demonstrates the issue with lexical order in the practical application of the LQI to classroom deliberation. The LQI assumes that the best listeners are all-rounders who pay close attention, retain what is said, and provide thoughtful, satisfying responses. When seen from this perspective, student A is far from being an all-rounder. However, participants like student A are not particularly rare while deliberating in the real world. They are less chatty and prefer to remain silent, becoming fully engaged in and reflecting on a particular participant's statement. They believe that listening to and taking into consideration one crucial statement during the course of a lengthy discussion is more significant than listening to 100 average statements. For them, a normative presumption that "substantive response" is more important than "no response" occasionally makes it difficult to focus on this type of contemplative listening. Listeners are put under an epistemic burden if we expect them to react to speakers. The lexical order of the LQI undervalues the reality that, for certain individuals deliberating on an existentially fundamental issue, no response is sometimes more important than a substantive response.

Let's now examine student B's point of view to think about the third challenge with LQI applied to classroom deliberation—that is, students' fixed relationship:

> *Student B had known student A for more than 10 years and was somehow aware that she has concerns about her gender identity these days. In classroom deliberation, therefore, student B chose to emphasize the significance of openness for gender identities by giving the example of his brother. For him, whether or if other students paid attention to him did not matter all that much. He was more interested in whether student A listened to him.*

For better or worse, relationships between participants in classroom deliberation are more fixed than those in public deliberation such as minipublics. Most of the student's time during the week is spent with other students, so they get to know who has what kind of ideas, who has (and does not have) power, who is talkative, and who prefers to listen. Even the expert facilitator might struggle to quickly intervene and alter such a fixed relationship in a short space of time. In such a situation, not all students want everyone to listen or make a substantive response. Instead, they can choose their intended audience *in advance* because they are aware of each other's knowledge, identities, and types of opinions before they deliberate. Student B just wanted student A to listen to him and did not expect a meaningful response from everyone. Even though he did not receive any substantive response from student A, he might still feel that all aspects of the LQI were met because he was confident that his message reached her.

In response to these examples, some may contend that this is an exceptional case occurring only in a specific context. Yet I argue that the context matters. Unlike an artificially designed deliberative space, a classroom is embedded within a social, political, historic, and cultural context, and various contextualized factors fix students' relationships. Some students like to focus on a certain speaker's speech, thus becoming perfect listeners is not as appealing to them. LQI's normative standards are less sensitive to contextualized meaning and value of listening, which is ultimately its shortcoming when applied to classroom deliberation. Especially in the context of classroom deliberation, where individuals entrenched in various contexts converge for discussions, "what is substantive," "what is meaningful," and "what is failed" forms of listening should be defined and implemented not only in a deductive/normative fashion but also in an inductive/grassroots way. In other words, when the LQI is applied directly to the discussion in the classroom, students' various lifeworld can be neglected.

From LQI to lqi

Again, the above challenges do not discredit the LQI itself. However, my point is that a practical application of the LQI to *classroom deliberation* is not so straightforward because of its limited context-responsiveness. Uncritical use of the LQI to evaluate listening skills in the classroom may miss the extent to which students value each component of the LQI, endangering their actual practice of listening in that environment. With this, how can we redesign the LQI and apply it to a contextualized practice of classroom deliberation without missing its normative anchor? More specifically, how can we combine the idea of the LQI with the lifeworld of students with respect to listening? Also, how can we reconstruct it in a way that helps to reduce the burden on teachers?

I believe that we can respond to these questions not by abandoning the LQI and seeking for alternatives but by redesigning the LQI in a way that can be more context-responsive. In my view, this may be possible when we enable students to actively redesign the LQI through a critical and reflective examination of the contexts in which they are embedded. This is a kind of meta-deliberation, but it can be practiced in a different way from meta-deliberation about reason-giving. As we have seen in chapter 3, meta-deliberation is mostly used *during or after* classroom deliberation. In contrast, listening norm-making may require meta-deliberation *prior* to the beginning of deliberation, making time for students to elaborate and establish their own context-responsive LQI by examining their listening habits from various perspectives. Students can then start main deliberation, committed to listening in accordance with their own agreed-upon norms. The objective of such meta-deliberation is not only to let students to construct their own deliberative norms but also to engage in continuous reflection on and development of their own listening practice so that they exercise their revolutionary agency. This will in turn motivate them to be self-reflective and self-corrective about their own more democratic listening habits. Although such LQI-inspired practice is less stringent than Scudder's original idea, its objective is not to present ideal assessment criteria prior to actual deliberation, but *to let students themselves act as norm-makers and norm-improvers*. In contrast to Scudder's normative concept of the capitalized LQI, I will hereafter refer to such student-centric norm-making of listening as the uncapitalized *lqi*.

There may be two ways of implementing the lqi. One is to present Scudder's LQI to students and then let them deliberate about the relevance of each criterion (1 to 7) and reconstruct its contents. Another approach is to allow students to participate in the conceptual analysis of listening based on their experiences and then set up their own model of listening. Regardless of the approach we take, meta-deliberation is designed in a way that (1) enables students to examine their listening habits and experiences (listeners' perspective), (2) shares experiences of and opinions on how listening (dis)advantages specific groups of students (speaker's perspective), and (3) provides possible indicators for observers to assess their listening in a meaningful way (observer's perspective). Based on meta-deliberation that includes multiple perspectives, students reconstruct the LQI from "no listening" to "good listening." The facilitator's job is not to demand them to create normatively rigorous assessment criteria of listening, but to assist students in exploring listening in a balanced way—that is, that sufficiently includes the listener's, observer's, and speaker's perspective. *Students* take the primary ownership of deciding whether, how, and to what degree the lqi shall be enhanced in this activity, even though their original proposal for their lqi is normatively less rigorous than Scudder's LQI.

There are some noteworthy advantages of situating the lqi at the heart of classroom deliberation. First, similar to the LQI, the lqi integrates three distinct viewpoints (listeners, observers, and speakers) for norm-making. Unlike LQI, however, the extent to which these views are integrated can primarily be defined by students. While a facilitator must get involved in students' meta-deliberation so that they can fairly consider these viewpoints, she should not exercise paternalistic control over the entire process of deliberation. Second, students construct the lqi inductively by sharing their lifeworld in order to make the lqi more context-responsive. Third, a facilitator can learn from students' lqi what they actually value in listening and how they perceive good/bad listening more sensitively. Fourth, the lqi makes it easier for teachers to evaluate students' listening skills. As previously mentioned, the LQI's requirement that a team of researchers conducts observation, coding, and interviews is particularly onerous for teachers who are already extremely busy in general. Instead of grading students according to predetermined standards, the lqi expects teachers to organize meta-deliberative sessions (see chapter 3) that allow students to self-evaluate their listening based on the norms they have developed for themselves. There, students consider how they listen during deliberation and collectively probe the disparity between their own norms and reality, thereby, if needed, modifying the norm. Such meta-deliberation and norm modification are subject to assessment, and thus teachers need not spend considerable time transcribing or coding as expected by the LQI.

Lessons from the Field: A Praxis Story

With a help of the teacher (Mr. Taiji Ogawa) with whom I have been working for more than 5 years and his teaching assistants at a technical school (called *Kosen*[8]), I undertook action research with students (16 years old) to put the idea of the lqi into practice. Ogawa regularly practiced deliberative sessions in his civics class. I and Ogawa had two online meetings (2 hours in total) to elaborate on the idea of the lqi and determine how we would apply it in the real classroom. We finally agreed on the following steps, which we then practiced in the classroom (1.5 hours in total). Students discussed their everyday experiences of "poor listening" as an icebreaker during the first stage of the lesson. To determine how and whether these examples are "bad," we asked students to role-play situations in which they felt like "someone did not listen to me."[9] The second step is a combination of individual practice with group practice. Students were divided into five or six groups, and everyone engaged in brainstorming about "good listening" and "bad listening." We encouraged students to provide examples and personal stories of good/bad listening. We prepared two types of Post-its, using a red Post-it for writing "bad listening" (e.g., using a smartphone while listening, not making eye contact) and a blue Post-it for illustrating "good listening" (e.g., no interruption, asking questions). Each student shared their Post-it with group members 20 minutes later. In this sharing process, we gave students a worksheet that was designed based on the LQI but also reorganized by considering the students' context (e.g., level of content comprehension). The worksheet contains five steps of listening that were reworded by Ogawa in a more student-friendly way, and they are as follows:

Step 0: Prohibited listening
Step 1: Minimum listening
Step 2: Good listening (easy to achieve) or bad listening (easy to stop)
Step 3: Good listening 2 (difficult to achieve but essential for democratic listening) or bad listening 2 (a key challenge for democratic listening)
Step 4: God of listening

Students shared and described their experience written in the Post-its and then considered where the content of each Post-it fits into the above steps. Importantly, the lifeworld of students who could be affected by testimonial injustice could be dismissed as "trivial," if there was a situation where a certain Post-it is ignored or taken less seriously by the dominant students. To obtain all shared experiences (including seemingly "trivial" ones) out on the table of deliberation, we set a rule that group members must incorporate all Post-its into the step and continue to deliberate about where they placed each Post-it until everyone agreed on it, so that all students' experiences and perspectives (including those suggested from relatively "powerless" students) were shared and taken seriously. Some groups discussed where to place a single Post-it for longer than 5 minutes, giving typically "silent" students the chance to share their views and add to the process of norm-making. Different normative criteria for "good/bad" listening were presented by each group, and there was discussion about which of these elements were sharable and how their interpretation of "good/bad" listening differed. Students sometimes found some friction about their interpretation of listening. As an illustration, the majority of the group supported "casual responses" (such as nodding) as an indication of listening, but they disagreed on where such "casual responses" may be found in the aforementioned steps, as will be explored later. Students exchanged reasons and negotiated with each other to sophisticate their collective norm of listening. Figure 4.1 is one example of students' agreed norms of listening steps.[10]

Students' lqi, in contrast to LQI, did not clearly distinguish between the perspectives of the listener, speaker, and observer. Rather, each level of their lqi incorporated these three views. As previously mentioned, students primarily took the initiative over where, how, and to what degree these three perspectives should be included in their lqi, even while we facilitators encouraged students to consider their habits, experiences, and perspectives. Here is an illustration.

Figure 4.1. Students' deliberative norm-making. *Source*: Photo by the author. *Note*: See note 10 for English translation.

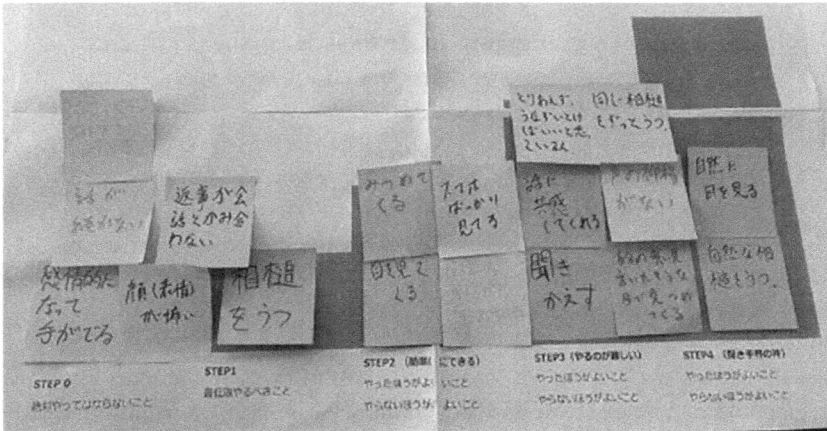

Observer's Viewpoint

Some students in one group, where I facilitated, told stories of their English teacher. According to the students, the teacher is viewed as an overreactor who "makes seemingly needless overreactions on a regular basis." When students noticed her exaggerated gestures, bombastic tone of voice, and hyperbolic facial expressions for the first time, they saw that "many students felt irritated" because they did not think that she listened seriously. But as time passed, they began to see her differently, and some of them even stated that many students now considered her overreaction as a sign of her good listening.

> Author: Well . . . as I heard what you are saying, the teacher's overreaction was very stagy. Why can you now feel that the teacher listens to you?

> Student A: Of course, for the first time, I had unpleasant feelings. But now that we've established a certain amount of rapport with her, I can already tell that she is such a kind of person. So, even though her response seems out of character, I believe it to be as usual. So I can feel that she listens to me.

AUTHOR: Alright. Any more opinions?

STUDENT B: What is important is to think about each situation. If she behaves accordingly outside the school, she is just crazy. But she overreacts to us only in our school, so we can feel that this is part of her educational strategy.

STUDENT C: Also, I believe we must be already familiar with the repertoires of her reactions. We are all aware of how she reacts to us and how she behaves in the classroom. So even though her reaction seems strange, we know that this is from her repertoire of reaction. No issue.

We then distilled a tentative "core" of listening from the above story and decided that overreaction can be justified as a sign of listening under the following conditions: (1) the relationship between a speaker and a listener is already established to some extent, (2) communication (and overreaction) occurs only within a restricted setting, such as a school and classroom where "unnatural" communication can be justified under the name of education, (3) speakers know a specific listener's repertoire of responses. A student who wrote "overreaction" initially placed his Post-it on step 1 (minimum listening). However, after this meta-deliberation, he changed it to step 2 (good listening—easy to achieve), arguing that a specific sign of listening (such as overreaction) is meaningful only under the specific situation, and, in this sense, such contextually practiced listening is different from "minimum listening"—and everyone agreed with him.

SPEAKER'S VIEWPOINT

Sympathy was one of the most dominant topics, assessed from the speaker's point of view. Students shared their experience of "being listened to" by drawing on instances such as receiving a sympathetic response from listeners or seeing the listener's sympathetic physical reactions (e.g., nodding, clapping one's hand in delight). Still, several students queried this argument, asking about the degree of sympathy. In one group, a student used his personal experience in which a listener who did not concur with the student posed as sympathetic superficially. The student said that while a listener of this type might be able to appease the speaker, what the listener did was to engage in superficial listening rather than genuinely and honestly seeking out the speaker's opinion. However, another student offered a rebuttal, saying that "superficial listening is not necessarily harmful. Even if you initially appear sympathetic in a superficial fashion, you will eventually get interested in what the speaker has to say as long as you continue to pay some attention." The student continued, "unlike ignoring, adopting a [superficial] sympathetic pose indicates that you are at least listening to something. You can potentially understand others if you keep doing this." Immediately after this statement, another student questioned the term "understand." The student stressed that he did not want even his best friends to show complete sympathy. He contended that it is impossible to perfectly understand others and, thus, that those who sympathetically behave as if they perfectly understand someone should realize that this is hubris or a behavior that must be altered.[11] As a result, the group initially shared the view that sympathy can be placed on step 4 (God of listening), but ultimately they all agreed to replace it in step 3 (see figure 4.1).

Physical activities were also the popular subjects of deliberation in many small groups. Scudder (2022) admits that her LQI is somewhat a voice-centric standard,[12] while students proposed different physical or nonverbal practices as primary indicators for assessing listening. Students attempted to take the speaker's perspective and considered which physical responses of listeners can be helpful (or not) for better speech. As figure 4.1 demonstrates, examples suggested by students varied, and included "blink," "nodding," "facial expression," "direction of eyes," and so forth. Other students focused on the discomfort they experienced while talking to explain how each physical response may be situated (e.g., yawning while talking, sighing while talking, using a smartphone).

LISTENER'S VIEWPOINT

Many students cited casual response (in particular, nodding) as a crucial attitude for successful listening when considering the viewpoint of listeners. They believed that casual responses from the audience allow the speaker to continue talking and, more importantly, such casual responses are objectively observable. One student suddenly intervened in this talk by offering a counterargument that "some casual responses can be a sign of no-listening." She supported her assertion with two examples: one is over-nodding, which can make a speaker feel mocked, and another is pretending to nod while not caring what the speaker has to say. This intervention helped in shifting our attention to the difference between nodding being used when one listens and nodding being used for refusing to listen. Students shared experiences and stories of the circumstances under which they pretend to listen by nodding or they use "good nodding." As exemplified in figure 4.1, this deliberation resulted in students' agreement on placing "casual response" on both steps 1 and 4. They shared the opinion that expressing (regardless of its underlying intention) any kind of response is preferable to prohibited listening because one cannot respond to speakers if they do not listen, and because responding means that a speaker and a listener are discussing on the same thing. According to the students, even a poor type of casual response may be able to pique the attention of the listener in the speaker's topic, therefore such a response is, in their own terms, "better than nothing." In step 4, however, they added the phrase "natural response."

This type of answer is not meant to mock the speaker or to express disinterest. Instead, such a response happens organically when a listener is engaged in the speaker's presentation and earnest in their desire to learn more about them. Given that this is a natural response, which is rarely practiced on purpose, a student brought up the idea that creating an occasion where such a response naturally occurs is a sign that a listener and a speaker are developing democratic relations.

Conclusion

Deliberative democracy experts have recently focused on the deliberative value of listening, because the quality of listening influences how we speak, what we speak, and when we speak. As the chapter has illustrated, however, democratic education that incorporates deliberative theory still tends to fall into a pitfall of talk-centricity. One reason for this is because listening is hard to assess. Listening is an interdependent practice happening within interactions between speakers, listeners, and observers rather than being an isolated activity carried out by a single person. Therefore, we need to think more carefully about the question of perspective when assessing listening—this is the guiding question that anchors the empirical argument of this chapter.

To respond to this question, the chapter examined Scudder's LQI as a pathbreaking model that provides valuable insights into how we assess listening in *public deliberation*. Scudder's LQI has value as a specific toolkit that informs how and in what order we should combine and implement multiple perspectives in assessing listening. Nonetheless, the chapter also discussed the ways in which the practical application of the LQI to *class-room deliberation* presents difficulties, insofar as the classroom is more contextualized than public deliberation and because many teachers find the LQI too demanding to be practical. To fill such a theory-practice gap, the chapter drew on the idea of meta-deliberation from the previous chapter and then suggested the uncapitalized lqi as a more student-centric and context-responsive version of the LQI. In using the lqi, students themselves are encouraged to take primary ownership of defining, reconstructing, and co-constructing their shared norms of democratic listening. As the second half of the chapter demonstrated, the lqi in practice meaningfully incorporates multiple perspectives (speaker, listener, and observer) and contributes to students' revolutionary learning.

The empirical part of the chapter demonstrated that students created their own normative model of listening by interweaving the perspective of observers, speakers, and listeners. As already revealed, this may not be a perfect list, nor is it normatively rigorous criteria for listening. For instance, the student's list depicted in figure 4.1 lacks elements of what Scudder's LQI calls attentive listening (the listener can recall what the speaker said). Even so, the value of students' lqi is its context-responsiveness, inclusiveness, and openness. Because the norm-making process puts the students' lifeworld at its center and attempts to incorporate their experi-ences and stories through meta-deliberation, it is context-responsive and inclusive. It is also open, since the list is, ideally, open to reinterpretation and revision. Students are asked to assume responsibility for using the list and making appropriate decisions as creators of their own listening norms. They must amend the list's contents through meta-deliberation if they believe it could be improved. Possibly, they can generate an idea that is closer to Scudder's LQI, or potentially they can suggest a novel idea that goes beyond the LQI. It is crucial to encourage students to exercise their deliberative agency as a deliberative norm maker with the support of the teacher or facilitator, rather than imposing "someone's norm" unilaterally at the beginning of a deliberative session and making learners follow it accordingly, so that they can continue to engage in the revolutionary process of meaning-making during classroom deliberation. The role of adults is not to assess the quality of individualized listening based on predetermined norms, but to help students collectively engage in meaning-making practice.

Thus far, chapters 3 and 4 have discussed the different faces of deliberation. Moving beyond the traditional top-down deliberative practice in the classroom, both chapters, with the support of empirical insights, have made a case for the value of more grassroots and meta-deliberative meaning-making practice in classroom deliberation. However, these chapters did not claim that such deliberative practices are possible without any adult help or support. Even if deliberative democratic learning is critical of adult's paternalistic intervention, this does not mean that we should exclude adults from an entire process of deliberation. As the next chapter illustrates, deliberative democratic learning becomes more realistic and effective when people become more aware of the ethics of facilitation.

Chapter 5

Ethics of Facilitation

Diana Hess and Paula McAvoy noted that "democratic education requires teachers to create a political classroom in which young people develop the skills, knowledge and dispositions that allow them to collectively make decisions about how we ought to live together" (Hess and McAvoy 2015, 11). Much evidence shows that there is a greater possibility for classroom deliberation to be effectively galvanized and vividly democratized if a teacher serves as a skilled and experienced facilitator (Hess 2009; Journell 2017; Molnar-Main 2017). Of course, facilitation is hard work, because a facilitator has to flexibly select and implement various communicative strategies and toolkits by putting themselves in conversation simultaneous with the changing situation. Therefore, facilitation is sometimes described as a jazzy work (Escobar 2019).

Having said that, a facilitator is not a miracle person who can realize all deliberative ideals anywhere and anytime. In chapters 3 and 4, a theory and cases of reason-giving and listening in classroom deliberation have been presented, and the second half of each chapter extensively highlighted the "success" case analysis. From the perspective of the facilitators, however, these experiences can be understood differently. As will be examined in this chapter, I as a facilitator confronted various challenges ranging from the relatively simple to the complicated. To show some degree of the generalizability of my experience, I frame each example as (1) structurally embedded power imbalance between a facilitator and students, (2) disagreement-averse attitude, and (3) testimonial injustice.

In light of these challenges, what can and should a facilitator do? To respond to this question, this chapter examines three possible theoretical models of the ethics of facilitation: involved facilitation, passive facilitation, and task-sharing. The chapter shows that both involved facilitation (informed by Paulo Freire's banking concept of education) and passive facilitation (informed by Jacques Rancière's ignorant schoolmaster) are theoretically valid approaches that outline ways to address, or at least mitigate, the above three challenges. From a practical perspective, however, these approaches fail to do what they promise and sometimes even make matters worse. While both forms of facilitation rely almost exclusively on facilitator's own techniques and attitudes, these challenges are caused by collective and structural factors that a single individual's efforts will almost certainly fail to encompass. I argue that the third approach, the facilitator as a task-sharer (informed by John Dewey's theory of inquiry), gives a more effective and concrete solution: it democratizes the facilitation by shifting our attention from individualized facilitative techniques toward what I call *facilitation by design*, or reconceiving facilitation as a series of acts that alter the deliberative environment in order to provide further deliberative structure.

Unlike the previous two chapters, this chapter begins with "Lessons from the Field," which is a self-reflective analysis of what I experienced as a facilitator intended to examine three key challenges of facilitation of classroom deliberation. Then we examine three models of ethics of facilitation.

Lessons from the Field

FACILITATOR'S POWER

> *Vignette A*: In each session, we asked the students to form a circle and sit so that they can pay attention to the speaker, and, at the same time, the speaker can see the face of each listener. Despite our intention, many students chose to face toward the adults (teachers and facilitators) rather than toward the other students. It seemed to me that the students put much value on the response from the adults rather than from their classmates.

Facilitators in deliberative minipublics are expected to be as neutral as possible or, at least, less active and involved than the participants (Hendriks

2005). In classroom deliberation, however, it would be difficult for teachers to become a neutral facilitator. Generally speaking, schools and classrooms are spaces where the power of the adults is more privileged than that of the children in a way that legitimizes the power imbalances in the guise of education.

The types of power imbalances vary across schools, cultures, time, and individual teachers with administrative (e.g., teachers mark students' work, meet with parents), authoritative (e.g., teachers have authority in relation to knowledge), and normative (e.g., teachers police norms of communication and behavior in the classroom) roles (Nishiyama et al. 2023). In particular, vignette A illustrates the typical asymmetrical power imbalance between the teacher and the student that is embedded in the school system being inseparable from administrative power. In most of our meta-deliberation (anteroom deliberation) and debrief meeting with the schoolteachers, the curriculum and the school's requirements were questioned. The administrative role of schools and teachers is largely evaluation oriented: a mark must be generated from activities. While this mark serves as an essential core of the existing school system, it tends to restrain the deliberative capacity of the group and individual students by limiting the students in their behavior and expression as they focus on the mark and judgement from teachers. Insofar as deliberation is practiced in the classroom, students are aware, whether intuitively or empirically, that the teacher's eyes are everywhere, even in "free" deliberation. As long as the adults serve as facilitators, the students inevitably have to cope with a power imbalance that is strongly intertwined with the school system.

Such an asymmetrical power imbalance may also pose the risk of biased and unfair treatment of a teacher toward a specific group of students. Facilitators normally have the power to determine which students are given stronger privileges in a deliberative community. For example, in an Australian primary school, a classroom teacher regularly identifies a male student who raises his hand and confidently speaks up like a key person. Said teacher often asks the student to share his thoughts in order to trigger further deliberation with other students. As a result, the student becomes more outspoken. However, this becomes an indirect cause of another power imbalance among students. Such a situation may get worse if a teacher who belongs to the dominant community consciously or unconsciously gives the students from the same community a greater opportunity, unlike the minority students.

DISAGREEMENT

> *Vignette B*: One day, we noticed that the deliberation ended
> with a "peaceful" atmosphere. There was neither controversy
> nor disagreement. At the end of the session, we had a meta-
> deliberative session, and one of my colleagues asked, "Why
> was there a little disagreement in today's deliberative session?"
> One male student answered, "We wouldn't expect to disagree
> because we share similar backgrounds, and we share a lot of
> things in common. We don't need to disagree with each other."

Vignette B describes the collective strategy of the students behind the
seemingly "harmonious" and "peaceful" deliberation. During deliberation, the students made a huge effort in maintaining their friendship and
avoiding "unnecessary" conflict and disagreement. Their deliberation was
characterized by "harmony," and, as they expected, there was literally no
disagreement during the session.

Is deliberation without disagreement a sign of healthy and desirable
democratic practice? Deliberative thinkers may oppose because they have
long contended that disagreement is an essential factor of a healthy deliberation (Gutmann and Thompson 1996; Young 1997). Disagreement is
supposed to reveal various dilemmas and contradictions that allow further
reflective and critical deliberation among participants. Precisely because
there is disagreement about opinion, value, belief, and communication
norm, students engage in a dialectical, revolutionary, and creative process of
meaning-making through deliberative democratic learning (see chapter 2).

Yet students in vignette B believed that deliberation without disagreement is a sign of mutual respect and good quality of listening. However,
as we have seen in the previous chapter, this kind of listening may reduce
the democratic quality of deliberation. When students intentionally avoid
disagreement, they are less likely to listen deeply to what the other students
say. From the facilitator's point of view, this is problematic, because the
students are not engaging with each other's views, neither exchanging reasons nor reflecting on their differences and their deliberative styles. Instead,
they are *pretending* to deliberate. Such listening may prevent people from
knowing their differences and taking position of others. Moreover, such
listening is unjust because, firstly, it leads to reinforcement or neglect of
the ignorance and bias of the majority toward minorities and, secondly, it
deprives the minorities of the opportunity to challenge the majority and
may result in instilling a state of disempowerment.

Furthermore, the intentional avoidance of disagreement would run the risk of depriving students of an opportunity for their critical and creative engagement in meta-deliberation. In chapter 3, I demonstrated the value of allowing students to share the ownership of (re)defining the difference between deliberative, nondeliberative and anti-deliberative reason-giving and improving their habits of reason-giving. This argument is anchored by a premise that students are willing to engage in such a reflective and critical meaning-making activity. However, if students intentionally try to avoid disagreement, not only are students unable to exercise their revolutionary agency, but also some may be further marginalized due to the limited opportunity to counterclaim against a specific form of reason-giving. In short, no disagreement is not a sign of healthy, harmonious, and peaceful deliberation. This is the absence of democracy.

TESTIMONIAL INJUSTICE

> *Vignette C*: A white native English-speaking student displayed his leadership during classroom deliberation. However, he often asked questions when other students shared their opinions. Sometimes, he deliberatively provided counterexamples to stimulate further deliberative interactions. In this sense, he served as a shadow facilitator. However, when an Asian nonnative English-speaking student spoke, the white native English-speaking student neither responded nor made further attempt to deepen the conversation.

In relation to vignette C, I also observed the following scene.

> *Vignette C'*: As the facilitator in one small group, I posed one open-ended question to a nonnative English-speaking Asian student who did not speak much during deliberation. He answered my question with few sentences. In the next breath, a native English-speaking student summarized the Asian student's talk and said to everyone, "What he was going to say was XXX."

Discussing vignette C and C' is complicated. Firstly, there was no explicit exclusion, as the Asian students had indeed opportunities to speak. Secondly, it was possible to interpret both vignettes as the white native English-speaking student knowing the Asian student's limited language ability and so *kindly* deciding not to discuss with him. Put differently, the vignettes can be read as the native English-speaking student's "good intention." Thirdly, the scope of the facilitator's responsibility is unclear, because these interactions happened between students, not between students and the facilitator.

In both vignettes C and C', two Asian students had at least an opportunity to express an opinion, and thus, we might evaluate both cases positively as kind assistance by the white students. However, the question is, Were these Asian students listened to? Put differently, were they treated and respected as epistemic agents? In vignette C, the facilitative student might not see the Asian student as an interlocutor *prior to* deliberation, due to his assumption regarding the latter's behavior: "a deep pursuit of a nonnative English-speaker's statement will not yield meaningful answers." The native English-speaking student did not attempt to discuss further only with the Asian student. In vignette C', the native English-speaking student might have kindly spoke for the Asian student: but he also assumed that language of a nonnative English speaker was difficult to understand. That's why he resorted to *immediately* summarize the Asian student's opinion without any confirmation. This act is disrespectful for the Asian student as the speaker and deprives him of his own words. Despite the opportunity to speak, the Asian student was not heard due to the assumed low credibility of his voice. Even though the majority's "supportive" act was underpinned by their "goodwill," this undervalued the epistemic agency of the minority students, thereby ultimately causing testimonial injustice (see chapter 4). In short, when examined in terms of listening, both vignettes C and C' reveal that the credibility of the words of a specific group of students were judged *prior to* classroom deliberation.

Fricker (2007) argues that a democratic and virtuous listener should be ethically responsible for considering the socioculturally constructed relationship between the listener and the speaker so that the listener can be self-reflective and self-critical about how they listen and how their listening potentially influences the speaker's communicative engagement. If we accept her claim, then the person who should be primarily responsible for testimonial injustice in the vignettes C and C' is not the facilitator, but *the listener,* specifically the native English-speaking student. This is because both vignettes C and C' happened during the communicative interaction between students, not between the student and the facilitator. However, does the facilitator have no role? Some may argue that it is unrealistic to expect the student to be self-critical and self-reflective without any facilitative interventions and supports. Thus, the facilitator's assistance might have been necessary for the student, so that he becomes aware of his own biases and stereotypes and thereby improves the way he listens. But, how is this possible? What kind of facilitative assistance do we need?

The extent to which the facilitator can and should intervene into such structural injustice is indeed unclear. No matter how skillful and experienced the individual facilitator is, the causes of stereotype and prejudice that anchor the students' engagement in testimonial injustice are beyond the control of an individual facilitator.[1] Even though a facilitator can address superficial problems related to testimonial injustice through facilitative intervention, the structural problem per se still persists. If so, should the facilitator be responsible for dealing with all challenges that cause testimonial injustice in classroom deliberation? If yes, the facilitator must put in more effort than just facilitation of classroom deliberation, which can be excessively burdensome. Otherwise, is the facilitator truly ethical?

Models of Ethical Facilitation in Classroom Deliberation

While the facilitators are, in principle, expected to provide the democratic scaffold within which deliberative participants can engage in inclusive and authentic communication, there are still challenges, especially in the classroom setting. Thus, we need to rethink the question, What is the ethics of facilitation in the face of these challenges?

The role of the facilitator in a public deliberation has been increasingly studied, which can be a good starting point to respond to this question. In a public deliberation, there are two types of facilitators: *involved* and *passive*. The involved facilitator has "control over how deliberation happens" (Dillard 2013, 225) by asking various questions, interpreting opinion of participants, or using the devil's advocate responses to enable participants to see things from multiple angles. In contrast, the passive facilitators employ a hands-off and uninvolved approach. Unlike the involved facilitator, the passive facilitator attempts to eschew interventions during deliberation to avoid power imbalances between the participants and the facilitators.

Both involved and passive facilitation in a public deliberation are possible in a classroom setting, to some degree. Nonetheless, we also need to be sensitive about the difference between public deliberation and classroom deliberation in terms of their function in a deliberative system. For example, in some public deliberation, such as citizens' assemblies, a facilitator is expected to draw out citizens to participate in policymaking

(Escobar 2019), whereas, in classroom deliberation, students are expected to engage in a high-quality deliberative democratic learning. Thus, the idea of involved and passive facilitation in classroom deliberation can and should be theorized differently. In the following, I will scrutinize the definitions of involved and passive facilitation in terms of classroom deliberation and consider their ethical implication for the challenges described in the previous section. In the field of philosophy of education, "involved" and "passive" are best described by two theorists: Paulo Freire's banking concept of education and Jacques Rancière's ignorant schoolmaster. Although both theorists did not talk about facilitation itself, their arguments help distil the different constituting elements of the ethics of facilitation. However, it turns out to be clear that both involved and passive facilitation in classroom deliberation is unsuccessful in fully addressing the challenges that I described. Thus, after discussing these two facilitation ideas, we will move our attention to the third idea: John Dewey's theory of task-sharing.

INVOLVED FACILITATION

Some facilitators have strong beliefs about what "right" knowledge is and what (anti-)deliberation is. They tend to play an unneutral role: they disclose their own views and beliefs, call out misinformation or biased views and use various pedagogical strategies (e.g., devil's advocate) to stimulate students' argument. Such a facilitator maintains the deliberative norm by directing the process of deliberation based on the principles of authenticity and inclusiveness.

Theoretically, the involved facilitator of classroom deliberation resonates with the *banking* concept of education coined by Paulo Freire, the Brazilian educator and the earliest thinker of critical pedagogy. In *The Pedagogy of the Oppressed*, he defines this concept as follows: "In the banking concept of education, knowledge is a gift bestowed by those who consider themselves knowledgeable upon those whom they consider to know nothing" (Freire 1970, 58). Using the banking method in educational practice, a teacher sees the learners as empty receptacles and plays the expected role, that is, to fill the emptiness with a package of knowledge as if we save money in an empty bank account one after another. In other words, there is a clear-cut asymmetrical relationship between a teacher and a learner. A teacher should impart wisdom (e.g., knowledge, ideal behaviors) to "empty" learners, thereby assisting their development. In

Freire's words, "The more completely he fills the receptacles, the better a teacher he is" (58).

Freire's banking concept of education would better explain the key features of involved facilitation of classroom deliberation. First, both share the premise that a facilitator must have better, deeper, and clearer knowledge of what good deliberation is than students. To take Freire's words, "The teacher disciplines and the students are disciplined" (54). For proponents of the view, letting the students take ownership of their own deliberation may make deliberation disruptive, and therefore a facilitator should guide their communication through active interventions. Second, it is the facilitator, not students, who must be in charge of monitoring and, if needed, policing the process of deliberation. As Hess and McAvoy pointed out, "A well-informed teacher will be able to correct students who appeal to questionable evidence to defend offensive views" (Hess and McAvoy 2015, 180). Once the students engage in "bad" behavior during deliberation, the facilitator is expected to intervene in the deliberation and explicate why the behavior is problematic. Such pedagogical intervention of an involved facilitator is justified because active interventions improve deliberation.

Freire coined the term "banking concept of education" and used it in his series of works intended to offer critical analysis on the Brazilian society of his time. According to Freire, the banking concept of education was a dominant approach to compel oppressed people in rural regions to be more silent and manipulated by reinforcing their lack of critical consciousness about their lives (Freire 1970, [1974] 2005). For Freire, the banking authority is problematic, because it not only prevents people from being emancipated from the oppressive circumstance but also "inhibits creativity and demonstrates (although it cannot completely destroy) the intentionality of consciousness by isolating from the world, thereby denying men their ontological and historical vocation of becoming more fully human" (1970, 71). How valid is Freire's critical view on the banking authority when we are faced with the issue of the facilitator's power, disagreement, and testimonial injustice in classroom deliberation?

Facilitator's Power

In most cases, involved facilitation anchored by the banking authority reinforces and reproduces an asymmetrical power relation between a facilitator and the students. Freire was deeply concerned about the dehumanized nature of the banking concept of education, because deliberation facilitated by this kind of involved teacher would be at a greater risk of "addiction" or "dependence" by which "students can no longer think for themselves because their thinking is only borrowed from the teacher" (Bingham and Biesta 2010, 65). Thus, with involved facilitation, it is possible to deprive students of their agency by reproducing and reinforcing the existing power structure where the students inevitably depend on the facilitator.

Disagreement

By actively intervening in a process of deliberation, the involved facilitator can initiate a collective analysis of disagreement between students and provide rich opportunities to think about it as a group. The involved facilitator can organize a meta-deliberative session on a regular basis, make explicit the students' disagreement about an opinion or communication norm that each student has, and encourage them to engage in further reflective and critical deliberation. Alternatively, the involved facilitator points out the disagreement between students by asking, for instance, "Why are the opinions of A and B in conflict?" In such a situation, however, only the facilitator has a power to frame the disagreement and assigns students the task of reflective deliberation. The facilitator must explain why and in what sense the disagreement is important to students' deliberation at hand. Otherwise, the students may not be willing to examine *their* disagreement. Ironically, the more the facilitator explicates the value of disagreement framed by himself, the more serious the above power issue becomes.

Testimonial Injustice

The involved facilitator must be self-critical of his or her prejudicial perspective (about gender, race, disability, language, and so forth). Otherwise, the facilitator's active intervention in a deliberative process may accelerate the marginalization of a specific group of students (Kotzee 2017). The involved facilitator also monitors the deliberative process to check for testimonial injustice; in such cases, the facilitator polices the process through various interventions. For instance, when a facilitator notices a testimonial injustice directed toward language-minority students, the facilitator has to take an ethical responsibility for stopping the deliberation and organizing a meta-deliberative session to discuss the fact of injustice. The problem is, however, such meta-deliberative session itself risks strengthening the marginalization of specific students. When discussion about prejudice takes place in contexts where the majority is always privileged (e.g., classrooms), only the majority has the power to define and express "tolerance for difference," and their power and privilege itself is rarely examined (Burbules 2000; Chetty and Suissa 2017). In addition, the majority students sometimes feel they are unfairly charged by the minorities and become overly defensive when discussing race and gender with minority students. All in all, if (meta-)deliberation takes place in an unneutral setting, less privileged students hardly overturn the power structure from the beginning.

PASSIVE FACILITATION

Jacques Rancière is not an education philosopher, yet the idea of an ignorant schoolmaster, elaborated in his book *The Ignorant Schoolmaster* (1991), has been read by a wide range of education researchers (e.g., Bingham and Biesta 2010; Engels-Schwarzpaul 2015; Kohan, Santi, and Wozniak 2017). To summarize the key points of his argument, Rancière suggested the idea of the ignorant schoolmaster not for charging the teacher's lack of knowledge, but for demonstrating how and why "the most important quality of a schoolmaster is the virtue of ignorance" (Rancière 2010, 1).

While the term "ignorance" conjures up Socrates,[2] Rancière took the term from the story of Joseph Jacotot, a French teacher in the post-revolutionary time. Although Jacotot had no knowledge about Flemish, he attempted to teach French to Flemish students, which means that "there was no language in which he could teach them what they sought from him" (Rancière 1991, 1). The strategies he took were, however, quite radical: his pedagogical approach was opposite to the banking form of knowledge transfer. More specifically, he used a bilingual edition of the novel (*Télémaque*) and "taught" French in the following fashion: "He had the book delivered to the students and asked them, through an interpreter, to learn the French text with the help of the translation. When they had made it through the first half of the book, he had them repeat what they had learned over and over, and then told them to read through the rest of the book until they could recite it" (Rancière 1991, 2). With his "teaching," Jacotot's students finally mastered French without Jacotot's teaching. From this experience, Jacotot realized that *"one can teach what one doesn't know if the student is emancipated, that is to say, if he is obliged to use his own intelligence"* (22; emphasis added).

Based on the story, Rancière questioned the traditional aspiration for "good teachers" as knowledge-givers and instead explored a new paradigm of teaching. According to Rancière, what made Jacotot's practice unique and radical was that he split the connection between teaching and explicating. For a long time, Rancière argued that people strongly believe that to know something needs a banking form of knowledge transfer. An "intelligent" teacher is a person who dedicates oneself entirely to transmitting knowledge to knowledgeless students through explication. A teacher with a good explication capacity can "transmit his knowledge by adapting it to the intellectual capacities of the student and this allows him to verify that the student has satisfactorily understood what he learned" (7). For Jacotot, however, what such a model of the good teacher brings to students is *stultification*. Rancière argued that the traditional model of teaching undermines students' intelligence in a way that makes them a person who cannot think without a teacher's explication. Rancière argues, "Explication is not necessary to remedy an incapacity to understand. On the contrary, that very incapacity provides the structuring fiction of the explicative conception of the world. It is the explicator who needs the incapable and not the other way around; it is he who constitutes the incapable as such. To explain something to someone is first of all to show him he cannot understand it by himself" (10).

Importantly, Rancière's intention was not to argue that teachers are totally meaningless, nor does he recommend an uninvolved approach to teaching. Again, the core essence of Jacotot's practice was to liberate teaching from *explication*. The only interaction he engaged in during his practice was to demand his students manifest their intelligence through maieutic interrogations so that the students would gain rich opportunities to use their own capacity, think for themselves, and take responsibility for what they think. Even if the teacher himself does not have a clear answer to the issue in question, Rancière indicated that the "effective" teacher must be an ignorant facilitator whose primary task is not to transmit knowledge, but to ensure equality between learners and teachers by assisting students to know how to think and learn for oneself through interruptions (e.g., Wait, what do you mean by X?) and interventions (e.g., What is your opinion? How is it different from Y's opinion?).[3]

For those who explore passive facilitation in educational settings, Rancière's argument is informative. The ethics of passive facilitation of classroom deliberation can draw out at least two key lessons from Rancière's philosophical take on teaching. The first one is to trust and liberate students' intelligence. The passive facilitator is recognized as a member of a deliberative community, but the facilitator does not engage in paternalistic interventions such as correction of students' opinions and transmission of knowledge, because such intervention can strip students of their active agency by forcing students into the passive position. The facilitator should not control what students argue and how they express their views; instead, they should trust the capacity of the students to shape their own deliberative acts in their own terms. The second core feature of ignorant facilitation is to create meta-deliberative moments as much as possible through *interruptive questioning*. During deliberation in a classroom, the teacher asks questions about what the teacher does not know: for example, the definition of the concept that the student uses, a source of the student's opinion, or the quality of the students' deliberation. Thereby, the students are assisted in shaping their deliberative quality for themselves.

Facilitator's Power

The ignorant approach forces a facilitator to establish authority and power as minimally and invisibly as possible, at least in the classroom. Facilitative intervention (or interruptive questioning) is justified only when it helps with the emancipation of students' creative intelligence (or what I have called agency). Otherwise, the facilitator trusts students' intelligence in shaping their own deliberation. Instead of deceiving oneself and pretending to know everything, the passive facilitator should only continue to ask questions, as Jacotot did, and encourage students to keep thinking and to exert their agency. Doing so also emancipates the facilitator from the burden of explication and ultimately neutralizes the facilitator's power to a greater degree.

However, if a teacher serves as a passive facilitator, the biggest challenge would be the teacher's integrity. Rancière conceptualizes the ignorant schoolmaster not as a mere pedagogical technique but as an *identity*. If one decides to live with the ignorant ideal in the context of classroom deliberation, consistency must be ensured throughout the career, as Jacotot did. Put differently, one cannot be an ignorant schoolmaster at one time and a nonignorant at another, like changing hats. If a teacher tries to be a passive facilitator during classroom deliberation but nonetheless uses authority in other contexts, the students see the teacher's "ignorant" behavior just as a deceptive business practice rather than a sincere one.

Because ignorance is, according to Rancière, an identity guiding one's behavior, a teacher in principle cannot and should not change hats flexibly. The problem here is whether it is realistic for a teacher to maintain integrity in the classroom setting. Quite often, teachers have no option but to exert their authoritative, administrative, or normative powers due to various social, educational, and parental expectations, which inevitably compel them to give up holding the ignorant identity. Overall, Rancière's argument sets a bar too high when it is brought into the real-world educational institution.

Disagreement

If students express their disagreement with each other about a controversial topic, the ignorant facilitator can induce a meta-deliberative moment or a meta-deliberative session to clarify the nature of the disagreement. However, the ignorant facilitator may become just a powerless onlooker when students *intentionally* avoid disagreement. The facilitator may be able to ask questions about why there is no disagreement. However, for many students, this kind of question may not be so attractive, because they strongly believe that disagreement is an obstacle for good deliberation. In such cases, the passive facilitator must continue to ask questions until the students truly understand the value of disagreement in their own terms. As vignette B shows, however, the passive facilitator cannot do anything if the students understand the value of disagreement and nonetheless decide to avoid it.

Testimonial Injustice

The ignorant facilitator is at risk of escalating testimonial injustice. The key question is, "How can people who grow up in the dominant community emancipate themselves?" Rancière presupposes the decontextualized nature of intelligence and agency with little regard for the context-embeddedness of intelligence and agency. If a student grows up in a biased, unneutral, and prejudicial environment, their intelligence and agency are inevitably socialized accordingly, and it is hard for them to be self-corrective without any active intervention (Fricker 2007, 94–95). If the passive facilitator places complete reliance on pure intelligence and agency and deliberates with students with few interventions except for questioning, both students and the facilitator share only a limited opportunity to be self-reflective and self-corrective about their historically cultivated prejudicial habits. We can expect the passive facilitator to continue to ask questions in order to shed light on the prejudicial view that the majority students share. However, as long as deliberation is conducted in the structurally biased classroom, the dominant students would ignore the facilitator's question as something trivial. Kotzee argues that the only way of achieving epistemic justice in an educational institution involves "an attack on elite forms of education that provides the children of some (but not others) with disproportionate cultural influence in our society and that, at the same time, holds up a certain culture as a pinnacle of education and refinement" (Kotzee 2017, 331). He continues, however, that this is possible only by the "institutional change."

FACILITATION AS TASK-SHARING

Both involved and passive facilitations in classroom deliberation provide insufficient ground for addressing power imbalances, disagreement-averse attitude, and testimonial injustice. Both theories focus on whether or not and to what degree a facilitator intervenes in students' deliberative activities. However, the active or passive intervention alone hardly addresses the three challenges, because these problems are caused by collective, cultural, and structural factors that exceed an individual's facilitative technique and identity. Of course, some challenges can be addressed by both facilitation types. Nonetheless, taking the challenges more seriously necessitates a more comprehensive facilitation theory that focuses not only on a deliberative process (as the involved or the passive facilitator would do) but also on a deliberative *structure* or *environment* that induces the challenges. To this end, we now turn our attention to John Dewey's theory of inquiry.

Dewey's philosophy of education is in tandem with his philosophy of science (Dewey 1938). Echoed by pre-Dewey pragmatist philosophers, Dewey argues that the primary purpose of science is the search for truth. Yet, Dewey's main attention is not on the truth itself but on the process in which people arrive at the truth. In various incomprehensible and uncertain situations, we try to obtain tentative knowledge by inquiry, where we hypothesize about the situation and consider the best possible method for analyzing the situation and testing the hypothesis. However, the generated and examined knowledge must be regarded as a falsifiable outcome of inquiry, because a single inquiry cannot give an overarching explanation of the situation. Thus, even when we generate knowledge, the quest for inquiry continues until there is no room for doubt—this is a situation where we finally reach truth, or true knowledge. Dewey argues, "We have no right to call anything knowledge except where our activity has actually produced certain physical changes in things, which agree with and confirm the conception entertained. Short of such specific changes, our beliefs are only hypotheses, theories, suggestions, guesses, and are to be entertained tentatively and to be utilized as indications of experiments to be tried" (Dewey [1916] 2014, 393). As discussed in the introduction, Dewey thinks that genuine inquiry takes place only in a democratic community, rather than in monologue thinking. In the inquiry process of knowledge generation, every single possibility must be scrutinized, and, therefore, everyone must be regarded as an epistemic subject who enriches the shared knowledge pool through dialogue. If a specific person is excluded from the process of inquiry, we would never arrive at the truth. In this dialogue-based community of inquiry, what is important is the idea of *task-sharing*. According to Dzur, the meaning of Dewey's idea of task-sharing is "to share power over tasks and responsibility for problems [people] cannot fully handle on their own" (Dzur 2018, 21). When we face a problem, task-sharing avoids a small number of "powerful" or "competent" individuals having a privileged access to an epistemic community and an interpretation of what the problem is and how it is resolved. Instead, the idea promotes everyone (including teachers and students) having a sense of co-ownership of their grassroots knowledge and lived experiences as their common properties, uses the properties for the purpose of deepening their understanding of the problem they confront, and thereby innovates a better solution. Hence, the idea of task-sharing is the essential assessment criteria of whether the community of inquiry arrives at truth in a democratic way.

From Dewey's perspective, a teacher is neither a knowledge-giver who explicates everything to the students one-sidedly nor someone who merely steps back from the students' activity and trustingly observes. The primary task of the teacher is to be a task-sharer who shares authority with the learners and builds knowledge with them. Both students and teachers must be regarded as subjects in the epistemic community who work together to deepen their understanding of the issue by contributing to its process differently. Unlike the ignorant schoolmaster, the task-sharer can give input if the students demand it to accomplish their common tasks. The task-sharer "should be occupied not with subject matter in itself but in its interaction with the pupil's present needs and capacities" (Dewey [1916] 2014, 215).

At the same time, Dewey argues that it is unwise to assume that a teacher can relinquish power altogether and that the students can do everything without their teacher. For Dewey, a task-sharer engages in community-making through direct and indirect interventions. More specifically, unlike in involved and passive facilitation, a facilitator intervenes not only in the students' communicative interaction itself but also in a *learning environment* where the facilitator and the students deliberate together. Dewey, like William James, rejects the dichotomy between individual and environment and rather points out their inseparable relations. If we wish to achieve a successful inquiry, a teacher should interact with both the individual and the environment. In Dewey's words, "The nature of educators' practice is to 'furnish the *environment* which stimulates responses and direct the learner's course" (Dewey [1916] 2014, 212; emphasis added). As discussed in chapter 2 (figure 2.3), our learning is influenced significantly by various environmental factors, ranging from mediating artifacts to norm, community, division of labor, and subject–object relations. A democratic teacher interacts directly with learners as subjects of knowledge as well as engages in designing and transforming various environmental factors to create a space where learners are more willing to make an epistemic contribution toward the truth.

Task-sharing offers a key insight into facilitation of classroom deliberation. It expands the meaning of intervention in a way that shifts our attention, away from the technique- and identity-based facilitative intervention in an interactive process, and toward *facilitation by design*. Facilitation by design is employed by a facilitator, alongside technique, to provide further discursive scaffolding and structure the task at hand. For example, facilitation by design can intervene in the students' mediating artefact that allows them to engage not only in a traditional speech practice but also in a visual activity. Doing so allows the students to think about various strategies to express their views and about the new norm of the new communication method; sometimes, the students may also reconfigure the structure of their relationships.

Facilitator's Power

The idea of task-sharing and facilitation by design can potentially naturalize the presence of the facilitator during a deliberative process. The facilitator as a task-sharer steps back and follows students' deliberation where it leads by concentrating mainly on the role of a questioner. If the situation requires, the facilitator intervenes in the students' deliberation and provides impetus for further deliberation not through a banking authority but through task-sharing. An example can be found in the deliberative norm-making practice at the Australian primary school (see figure 3.2 in chapter 3). This practice can be read not only as one concrete example of a meta-deliberative session but also as one example that shows how we can introduce task-sharing and facilitative design in classroom deliberation.

For example, during this norm-making, our team facilitated the students' meta-deliberation about deliberative norms in the following manner:

1. From the beginning, our team let students watch the video of debate at the Australian Parliament that was, according to students, a "bad quality of communication."

2. We then asked what good communication is. The students were encouraged to write their opinions with Post-it notes. The Post-it notes were attached to the whiteboard, and each student shared their opinion with others.

3. We worked on condensing the guidelines. A little while later, the facilitators asked additional elements by making full use of their imagination (e.g., What about your everyday life? How do you communicate with your parents and friends in a better way?).

4. After completion of the tentative norm-making, we asked the students to follow the guidelines individually and as a group throughout the project. We printed out the norm and attached it on the wall. We allowed students to revise or add/change the guideline any time if they felt the guideline did not work well for everyone. It was only students who could suggest revise or change the guideline.

5. We used the guideline to evaluate the deliberative process. At the end of each deliberative session, we organized a short *meta-deliberative session* where we asked the students whether they deliberated on their own and encouraged them to evaluate their deliberative quality by themselves.

In the process of deliberative norm-making, we used multiple facilitative strategies for designing and intervening in environments and structures in which students deliberate. For example, we facilitators created a situation that diversifies the students' use of vocal and visual mediating artifacts, including video and Post-it notes. In addition, by designing a process in which the students themselves create the norms and only they have the right to modify the shared norms, we reconstructed a traditional division of labor between a teacher and the students, where the former gives the norms and the latter receives them. Our only direct facilitative interaction occurred in 3, where our primary goal was to think together about the norm. Our team neither drilled students' minds into given deliberative norms (as the banking facilitator does), nor waited until students recognized the significance of deliberative norms (as ignorant facilitator may do). As members of the community of inquiry, we set the environment in which students themselves could reflect, innovate, and transform their deliberative styles and repertoires.

Disagreement

The task-sharing and facilitation by design create a deliberative structure that gets students with conflict-averse minds involved in deliberation in a relatively modest manner. For example, after several anteroom meta-deliberations, our team decided to introduce what we called "deliberative disagreement exercise" as an interventive facilitative structure. This was aimed at eliciting and visualizing students' small but significant disagreements about the issue in question. The exercise consisted of the following four steps. First was topic selection, in which both facilitators selected a controversial question or claim that can generate disagreements. At the school, we selected the claim "Australia is a peaceful society." Second was individual work including thinking and writing, in which the students considered the claim and wrote down their opinions and reasons on Post-it notes (e.g., I agree that Australia is a peaceful society because . . . / I disagree because . . .). Third was visualizing, in which the facilitator prepared a worksheet that had three sections: Agreement A (positive), Agreement B (negative), and Disagreement (figure 5.1.).

Then the participants shared and considered each other's opinion and reasons. If *everyone* agreed with a positive opinion (e.g., Australia is a peaceful society because . . .), the Post-it note was placed in the Agreement A section. If *everyone* agreed with a negative opinion (e.g., Australia is not a peaceful society because . . .), the Post-it note was placed in the Agreement B section. If there is disagreement about the opinion, the Post-it note was placed in the Disagreement section. The final step was

Figure 5.1. Disagreement worksheet. *Source*: Photo by the author.

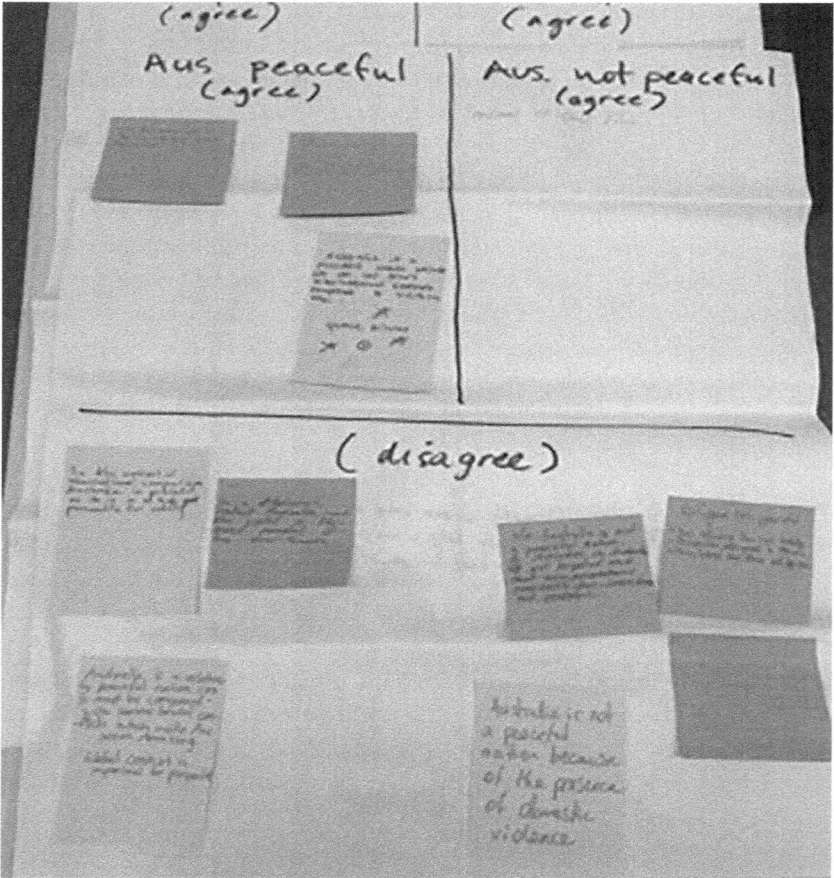

deliberation about disagreement. From the worksheet and with help from the facilitator, the students selected a particular area of disagreement (where disagreement was strong, clear but not too diverse) and then formed two groups with opposing perspectives, but included some "neutral" students in each group who were still undecided. These neutral students listened to the arguments of the opposing sides. Then the groups came together, led by the neutral students, and deliberated (1) the degree to which they could accept each other's opinion and (2) whether there was a common ground. They were then encouraged to express a group position, which might be a consensus or compromise, or may be an explanation of their disagreement. This deliberative disagreement exercise allowed students to visually recognize their disagreement and to be located at the situation where they inevitably took their disagreement into account seriously. The exercise was also beneficial for facilitators, as it gave an opportunity to analyze and understand the degree of disagreement together with students.

Testimonial Injustice

Rather than taking all responsibilities for addressing testimonial injustice through involved or passive intervention, we facilitators attempted to intervene or create a design against the structural and environmental factors that cause testimonial injustice, thereby encouraging minorities to resist the culture and actions of the majority in ways that are not the way of the majority. Different situations may require different facilitative interventions in a deliberative environment. As described in chapter 3, in an Australian primary school, we intervened in the mediating artifact of students' spoken language and offered them the option of drawing a collective claim-making picture, so that language-minority students could make an epistemic contribution to the shared knowledge of a democratic school (see figure 3.3 in chapter 3).

This seemingly simple practice gives some implications for how a facilitator and students share the responsibility to create a space for inclusive expression. Pens were given to all students in a group, and we encouraged them to express their views at any time of their convenience. The students were also advised that they could draw from any angle, no matter where they sat. This advice allowed linguistic minority students to contribute to the sharing of knowledge without being deprived of their own expression. As linguistic minority students had a chance to express and to be heard like majority students, a chain of communication emerged. For example, when a minority student drew a picture of one building, one majority student asked "What is this?," which began a conversation. A native English-speaking student also had the opportunity to hear an Asian student's opinions of what to build in the blank space and which colors to use. As noted in chapter 3, this picture per se shows an unrealistic blueprint of the democratic school and therefore does not make a substantive contribution to moving our deliberation forward. Nonetheless, the collective picture served as a mediator for generating the common purpose and experience of different students, allowing them to share responsibility for completing their common task. The facilitator sometimes gave comments on students' drawings (e.g., What is this? Why is the building important?), but many communications occurred in a horizontal, not vertical, way.

The idea of the facilitator as a task-sharer provides a framework for mitigating deliberative challenges that are difficult to address with an individual's facilitative technique or identity. An ethical facilitator is, therefore, neither an individual who attempts to address deliberative challenges on one's own nor an individual who puts his 100 percent trust in students' autonomous agency for addressing the challenges. Rather, an ethical facilitator takes the responsibility for intervening and designing a deliberative environment to enable both the facilitator and students to collaboratively engage in a better quality of deliberation.

Importantly, facilitation by design may not be generated out of nowhere. The abovementioned facilitative designs were indeed products of our anteroom meta-deliberations with collaborators and teachers that took place before and after the deliberative practice. When we were confronted with the deliberative challenges, we initially tried to solve them individually, but we soon realized that this does not work. We shared these challenges in an anteroom meta-deliberation, discussed the creation of the most appropriate deliberation environment, and implemented it. Therefore, for task-sharing and facilitative design, meta-deliberation plays an important role in discussing what tasks need to be solved, which environmental factors cause challenges, and the degree to which the facilitator's individual efforts and facilitative design contribute to addressing the challenges. Meta-deliberation is not only the basis for students to define and practice the nature of reason-giving and listening but also creates an important foundation for how facilitators behave ethically.

Conclusion

Scholars in democratic education studies believe that facilitation can help to establish and maintain deliberative norms, assist students in deliberating meaningfully, and enable goals of deliberation. And, indeed, facilitated deliberation sometimes achieves this goal. However, a facilitator is not a miracle-person who is always capable of enabling productive and meaningful deliberation. In particular, deliberative and democratic facilitation is hard to achieve in a classroom beset by structural problems. Even when a facilitator proceeds with deliberation "successfully," this chapter cautioned that such "success" may potentially be anchored by the facilitator's authoritative power, students' intentional avoidance of disagreement, or the exclusion of a specific group of students from the epistemic community. This is why deliberative democratic learning that situates students' deliberative agency at its heart calls for a reconsideration of the ethics of facilitation.

Guided by Freire and Rancière, we first considered the possible contributions of the involved and passive facilitation models. We concluded that the implications of both theories regarding facilitation are meaningful to some degree, but nonetheless fail to deal with collective and structural challenges because they understand "facilitative intervention" only in terms of the facilitator's individualized technique of (non)participation in the students' interactions, overlooking the possibility that these interactions are themselves embedded in a problematic environment. Thus, I suggested learning from Dewey's focus on task-sharing, which in turn provides a theoretical foundation for the idea of facilitation by design or facilitation as the active transformation of deliberative structures. Given Dewey's view of education as a shared community of inquiry, the ethical facilitator is one who is neither too involved nor too passive, and does not rely on their own facilitative technique for (non)intervention. Rather, an ethical facilitator is a person who intervenes in the deliberative environment in which students are embedded in order to design optimal conditions under which students are more willing to engage in continuous and collaborative meaning-making. The final part of this chapter drew on my field stories to illustrate how Dewey's task-sharing and facilitation by design can work in the face of various challenges and mitigate the risk of disrupting classroom deliberation.

Throughout part 2(chapters 3–5), we have been giving a concrete shape to the theory of deliberative democratic learning and outlining how it can be brought into complex classroom contexts. However, some questions still remain. As discussed in chapter 1, the classroom is not the only space capable of enabling deliberative democratic learning. Limiting opportunities for deliberative democratic learning to within the classroom may mask the fact that children learn deliberation by participating in various parts of the deliberative system. What and how do children learn deliberation outside the classroom? Unlike the classroom, many spaces of deliberation do not have a facilitator. Thus, what and who facilitates their learning? Part 3 shall respond to these remaining questions with a specific focus on school and activist groups.

Part III

Beyond the Classroom

Part 3 will expand the scope of deliberative democratic learning by focusing on schools and activist groups and demonstrating how deliberative democratic learning occurs in these spaces in a different way from classrooms.

While mainstream studies on democratic education typically equate schools and classrooms uncritically, chapter 6 suggests distinguishing students' deliberative engagement in schools from those in classrooms and then explores schools' deliberative capacity. Such distinction is important because students' experiences in the classroom are spatially, conceptually, and qualitatively different from their experiences in school. Even if students have only limited opportunities to engage in classroom deliberation, their school can provide different pathways that allow them to engage in a variety of deliberative practices across deliberative systems. To theorize the notion of the democratic school from a deliberative system's point of view, we need to avoid the all-too-common assumption that the democratic schools is by definition always equipped with a well-designed deliberative curriculum for classroom deliberation. In order to undermine the assumption, however, we must return to the basic question, What does the idea of the democratic school mean? Chapter 6 responds to this question in the following manner. First, it identifies the key functions of the democratic school (educational, political, and social functions) in deliberative systems, using the story of a well-known democratic school, the Byrd Community Academy in Chicago. Subsequently, it suggests the integrative concept of the democratic school as a mediating space that contributes to the growth of deliberative systems by connecting children's everyday experiences and wider public spaces. To identify conditions under which schools provide opportunities for a more naturalized deliberative democratic learning process than classrooms while simultaneously functioning as mediating spaces, chapter 6 discusses empirical findings from two case studies of Japanese junior high schools. These cases unpack the significance of the democratic school's horizontal and vertical connections of various actors.

Chapter 7 focuses on children's democratic engagement and learning in the broader public sphere, namely, in an activist group. Unlike classrooms, youth activist groups normally do not have a well-designed deliberative curriculum, nor do they have a teacher or skilled facilitator. Due to this fact, youth activists have more freedom to design, reinterpret, and implement their own democratic practice in the broader public sphere than do students in the classroom. Chapter 7 draws on my ethnographic fieldwork with youth climate activists (Fridays for Future Kyoto, or FFF Kyoto) to make a case for how deliberative democratic learning occurs beyond traditional educational settings (i.e., classrooms and schools). In thinking about the link between participation in activism and one's own development, we have to pay attention to how activists make meaning of their collective actions in the face of various changing and unforeseeable contextual challenges and requirements, such as climate change and the COVID-19 pandemic. Members of FFF Kyoto have continued to redefine the movement's raison d'être and the nature of their protest activities through meta-deliberations, thereby firmly establishing a place for themselves in spite of ever-changing contexts. To show how this has happened, chapter 7 in particular sheds light on how their regular protest activity on the street (called the standing protest) has transformed its nature through deliberative meaning-making via in-group deliberation. The story reveals that the leader of FFF Kyoto at that time played a significant role in facilitating the transformation of the nature of the standing protest; yet it is notable that she did so not by exercising her strong leadership but by designing deliberative environments within the group and sharing tasks with other members so as to facilitate further collaboration. Such facilitative leadership serves as a key for triggering youth activists' deliberative meaning-making and their revolutionary learning outside the classroom.

Chapter 6

The Democratic School as a Mediating Space

On Monday, January 19, 2015, students at the Langata Road Primary School in Nairobi, Kenya, gathered on the school playground carrying placards "Occupy Playground." A month previously, during the December school holidays, a powerful politician and a private developer had seized the playground of the Langata Road Primary School without showing adequate justification and hired gangs to guard construction workers as they worked. At the beginning of the new school term, students were surprised to discover that their playground was no longer available. They protested the illegal seizure and destruction of their playground. Students were prevented from entering by police officers who had accepted bribes, but students, carrying sticks and shouting *Haki yetu!* (It's our right!) broke down the newly constructed wall, ran onto the playground, and began playing football as they usually did. Suddenly, the police fired teargas at the students' feet. Some students were injured, some adult activists were arrested, and some ran, while many students continued to stay on school ground and chanted "Shame! Shame! It's our field!" The use of teargas and the illegal seizure were criticized domestically and internationally. As a result, Joseph Ole Nkaissery, the interior minister, visited Langata Road Primary School to apologize to the students officially.[1]

This Occupy movement, known as Occupy Playground, shows one way in which schools shape children's experience of democracy beyond the classroom. In part 2, especially in chapters 3 and 4, we focused on deliberation in the classroom to examine optimal means of enabling and facilitating students' deliberative reason-giving and listening. I intentionally distinguish classrooms from schools at large precisely because the two are spatially, conceptually, and qualitatively distinct, and thus students' learning experience at the level of the school might be qualitatively and quantitatively different from their learning in a classroom. For example, the Occupy movement described above shows that the playground, as a constituent part of the school served as a political and pedagogical hub through which students learned how to be critical of authority through protesting peacefully and making effective use of media to gather public recognition of their issue. Generally speaking, this can rarely be learned within the curriculum activity.

This chapter examines the deliberative democratic role of schools. Readers might take the conceptual difference between classrooms and schools for granted, but, surprisingly, the difference between the two rarely becomes part of debate in democratic education. Of course, classrooms are key constituents of a school, and it would be difficult to imagine a school without a classroom. However, as the Occupy protest clearly illustrates, Langata Road Primary School encouraged students' engagement in protesting, bypassing normal classroom activities. As is discussed in this chapter, unpacking the work and functions of schools can have profound implications for broadening the scope and potential of democratic education.

Another reason for spotlighting schools in this chapter is to reconsider the meaning of the democratic school. For many thinkers on democracy, a school is normally considered to be a democratic institution only when it sufficiently embodies all democratic ideals, including deliberative-minded teachers, well-functioning school councils, well-designed deliberative curricula, an open and reciprocal climate shared between students and teachers, and a seamless connection between students, parents, teachers, and broader communities, among other aspects (Youniss 2011; Noddings 2013; Rietmulder 2019). Realists, however, problematize these desires, pointing out the oxymoronic nature of the term "democratic school." On their account, schools by their nature have anti-democratic features, including internal (e.g., discrimination, bullying, authoritative teachers, and prioritization of the majority's knowledge and language code over that of the minority) and external gridlock (e.g., students' poverty and lack of sufficient financial support from the government) (Schultz 2007, 2018; Thornberg and Elvstrand 2012). While the democratic school movement has grown in many countries (Apple and Beane 2007; Rietmulder 2019), this movement has had success not because schools have developed a fully supportive democratic structure but largely because a few passionate and dedicated teachers in isolation have been making a tremendous effort and sacrificing their time to instill a democratic ideal in an undemocratic school.

However, if the realization of the democratic school must rely on such saviors alone, it might remain a pie in the sky. To make the idea of the democratic school more realistic while maintaining its normative anchor, we need to identify the minimum conditions under which schools can function democratically. A clue taken from the deliberative system framework, coupled with the findings obtained in my fieldwork, offers a possible account that focuses on the concept of the functional division of labor. As discussed in chapter 1, a deliberative system pinpoints the significance of the comprehensive realization of deliberative ideals through a functional division of labor with other deliberative sites and practices rather than the perfect functioning of a single site and practice. Even if a school lacks a particular deliberative component of the kind envisioned by normative theorists (e.g., it does not have a deliberative curriculum), we should not immediately jump to the conclusion that this school cannot afford to educate its students in democracy, as the democratic quality of schools in a deliberative system should be considered with respect to their particular function within the broader system.

These two concerns (contributions of school to democratic education and ways of making the democratic school realistic) invite us to examine specific democratic functions of schools from multiple angles, and, as we shall see, our discussion leads to the same conclusion: it is of utmost importance to pay sufficient attention to the school's *mediating* function. Schools coordinate their educational, political, and social functions and then act as a hub for students' various deliberative activities both within and beyond the walls of school. This mediating function makes a significant contribution to a deliberative system that bridges children's deliberation happening across different constituent parts of a deliberative system and, equally important, enhances the inclusive quality of the public sphere by providing ordinary students with the first step to act as deliberators in a wider society. Even though students do not fully enjoy deliberative opportunities *inside* their schools, a deliberative system recognizes the democratic value of the school if its mediating function develops human and institutional connectivity and discursive linkages, thereby creating a new deliberative learning opportunity for children *outside* of the school.

The next section indicates the necessity of conceptually distinguishing classrooms from schools. Then schools' three democratic functions are investigated using the story of a well-known case of the democratic school, the Byrd Community Academy in Chicago (Schultz 2007, 2018), followed the suggestion of a conceptualization of schools as a mediating space. Findings from my fieldwork will be used to illustrate and develop this concept. From these arguments, the concluding section lays out some key implications for making the democratic school realistic.

Unblurring the Conceptual Difference

Heidi Benneckenstein, a teenager who grew up in a neo-Nazi family and was herself an active member of a neo-Nazi group until the age of 18, wrote in an autobiographical essay that she behaved as a "good girl" in the classroom, and thus her teachers thought about her quite positively. However, outside the classroom she behaved badly, such as smoking cigarettes and wearing neo-Nazi clothes (Benneckenstein 2019, ch. 2). This experience provides one simple lesson: a student's behavior in the classroom is different from what it is elsewhere outside the classroom. Because students like Benneckenstein can act quite differently in and outside the classroom, the ways in which we democratize the classroom and the school require different strategies and foci. Even though they act as democratic citizens in the classroom, this does not always guarantee that they behave in the same fashion outside the classroom.

In *The School and Society*, John Dewey carefully distinguished the terms "classrooms" and "schools," employing them for different purposes. By classrooms, he referred to spaces where students engage in specific curricular activities and "everything is arranged for handling as large numbers of children as possible; for dealing with children *en masse*, as an aggregate of units; involving, again, that they be treated passively" (Dewey [1915] 2001, 22). On the other hand, Dewey defined schools more broadly: this was where "the child should really live, and get a life-experience in its own sake" (37). When Dewey illustrated using his experiences at the experimental school at the University of Chicago, his argument was structured around the concept of schools, not classrooms. Moreover, in *Schools of To-morrow* (Dewey and Dewey [1915] 2002), which Dewey coauthored with his daughter Evelyn Dewey, this conceptual distinction became more obvious. In their analysis of students' learning of curricular content, the term "schoolroom" was more likely to be used than "classroom."

This conceptual distinction between the school and classroom can also be seen in other, more recent literature on democratic education. For scholars, classrooms are recognized as an indispensable component of a school, but they argue that the democratization of schools necessitates shifting the focus away from classroom practices (e.g., learning democratic curriculum contents) toward school-wide ones (e.g., those relating to classrooms, student council, playground, corridors, and empty rooms). Peter Senge (2012), for example, argues that it is key for realizing the democratic reformation of schools to reconceptualize the school as a nested system that consists of classrooms, schools, and broader communities and then explore the seamless connections between them.

Where democratic education meets deliberative democracy, things become more complicated. When advocates of education for deliberative democracy scholars use the term "classroom," the school-classroom distinction is rarely relevant. Scholars fall into the pitfall of a category mistake where the difference of classrooms and schools is blurred. This happens in particular when the term "school" is used but nevertheless curriculum contents and specific pedagogical techniques and design are discussed. An example of this is found in Luskin and his colleagues' experimental research on the practical application of Fishkin's Deliberative Poll to citizenship education or what they called "Deliberation in the School." Although they concluded that "deliberating policy issues in *school* appears from our experiment to produce significant increases in civic engagement" (Luskin et al. 2007, 11; emphasis added), the study focused intensively on students' performance and deliberative engagement within the confines of the classroom. Likewise, Sorial and Peterson's (2019) theoretical review of the deliberative democratization of Australian schools focused on the democratic quality of Australian *schools*, but the suggested coping strategies were limited to the deliberative pedagogy that takes place within the classroom.

Note that I am not criticizing the intrinsic value of the above studies. They are seminal works par excellence, making a significant contribution to developing deliberative education one step further. What I question, rather, is the implicit presupposition that equates what students learn in a *classroom* with what they do at a *school*.[2] This presupposition masks the particular deliberative functions of a school and its unique contribution to students' deliberative learning. We are now at the stage of expanding the scope of democratic education at a systemic level to unpack the latent learning opportunities.

Functions of the Democratic School

Classrooms and schools have some overlapping features, but the latter may have more diverse functions than those of the former, so what is the core feature of school with respect to deliberative democracy? To understand the key functions of the democratic school, we now turn our attention to a well-known story of Byrd Community Academy[3] in Chicago and its teacher Brian Schultz (2007, 2018). I do so not because the case provides specific insight into the representative sample of the democratic school, but because it offers a practically grounded source of knowledge, inductively offering us a clue that we can use to unpack what the key functions of the democratic school are. According to the editors' note in *Democratic Schools*, despite a number of internal as well as external challenges, the case of the Byrd Community Academy shows "examples of what happens when young people are committed to a genuinely democratic project and integrate a variety of content and skills into it" (Apple and Beane 2007, 62).

The Byrd Community Academy is now known as a distinct and particular case of the democratic school, but the school was not orig- inally blessed by the goddess of democracy. Rather, the school was in trouble, inside and out. According to Schultz, Cabrini Green, where the Byrd Community Academy is located, was known as an example of the large-scale failure of the public housing policy and urban development in the United States. From the 1970s to the 1980s, a large number of low-income people had no option but to live in deteriorating high-density buildings, and the area soon became among of the most dangerous public housing areas, becoming a "haven for drugs and murder, gangbanging, misery and mayhem" (Schultz 2018, 17). This led to many children and young people having various life and learning handicaps, and what made matters worse was that Byrd Community Academy reproduced and even reinforced such handicaps. The harsh conditions under which students spent their time created troublesome learning circumstances, including the broken stall doors and toilets leaking foul odors, cold wind coming in broken windows, lack of heating in the extremely cold winter, and no lunchroom, forcing students to eat lunch in the corridor, among other issues. Due to these challenging circumstances, many students were less motivated to learn, and both students and teachers had to live with the school with a feeling of resignation. Schultz returned his memory of the first few weeks at the Byrd Community Academy, recalling that many students were testing him to see whether he could survive at the Byrd Community Academy, and he wrote, "More than once I contemplated quitting and never returning" (Schultz 2018, 31).

Schultz taught his fifth-grade students in room 405. Initially, he employed undemocratic strategies, foregrounding his authority intended to "educate" his apathetic and hostile students, but he later came to realize that the traditional one-sided and unilateral teaching method would never help his students out of their current predicament. Instead, he reorganized the curriculum so that the students would be enabled to work on their shared problems and implement constructive actions to change the situation. In his classroom, he launched the student-directed educational workshop for learning citizenship, which he called Project Citizen. Schultz encouraged his students to brainstorm the problems of their school and their community to determine which problems should be solved immediately and to implement concrete actions to address these on their own. In the deliberation in the classroom, the students suggested various problems that needed immediate resolution, including repairing the broken windows, reducing littering, and picking up trash, among others.

The students were then asked to find an appropriate method and approach to address the problems they identified. The students suggested various possibilities, including interviews with legislators, creating a video documentary about the Byrd Community Academy, conducting surveys, making a petition, doing fund-raising activities, and so forth. From their planning, the students steered their project, inviting activists, media representatives, and local legislators. To attract attention from the broader public and attract further public support to their activities, students also made effective use of the connective power of media, inviting journalists who wrote about the students' project at the Byrd Community Academy, and setting up their own website.

During this period, his classroom "turned into a headquarters for the fifth graders' efforts and was the place to make important decisions about who we [Schultz and his students] should bring in to help us get the job done" (Schultz 2007, 79). At the same time, the students were engaged in the range of activities noted above. Their longitudinal out-of-classroom effort finally attracted local legislators to visit the Byrd Community Academy, and it brought more and more people to lobby on behalf of the students. One day, the students heard directly from the US Department of Education, meaning that their democratic endeavor was receiving official recognition by decision-makers. Despite their extensive achievements, including gaining broader public support, receiving awards, being the object of media attention, and leading to decision-makers' recognition of the problem the Byrd Community Academy was facing, the Chicago school superintendent and the board of education decided to close the school. However, the students did not stop working on Project Citizen, continuing to invite media and activists until the school finally closed.[4]

We can draw three main lessons from this story. A school has an *educational* function. As Schultz illustrates, the classroom (room 405) was the headquarters that provided learning opportunities. In the classroom, students brainstormed, discussed, pursued Socratic inquiry, interviewed visitors, and so forth. However, Schultz's project provided students with the impetus for further out-of-classroom learning engagements, harnessing the rich connections of his classroom with the wider society. Students gained a rich trove of knowledge concerning the problems that their school and community faced through participating in school-wide and out-of-school activities, including working with teachers, writing to decision-makers and the board of education, surveying other students, learning how to set up their own website, and negotiating with media or other political agents. Thanks to the facilitation of their teachers, students gained knowledge, skills, and experience in pursuing their objectives.

This story also demonstrates the ways in which the democratic school harnessed its *political* function. The school became a political space that mirrored the political problems of the community and compelled students to cope with them. Indeed, students' learning experiences at Byrd Community Academy were by no means for simulation but were instead something driven by their own strong desire to address the realpolitik problems drawn from their community (e.g., poverty and inequality in and outside the school). This sort of political function of school is a topic of discussion in the literature. For example, Hess (2009) reveals that the classroom condition, as part of the school, reflects the political ideologies and political disagreements of the community. McAvoy and Hess (2013) also demonstrated that high levels of polarization among citizens have a dramatic influence on how schools function and how students behave in their school. Thomas also describes how students bring the identity politics of their community into the school, drawing on her observation of her students: "When a teen enters into a racial-ethnic territory that she is seen to not properly embody, she is met with stares, verbal assault, or is quickly and sometimes silently encouraged to leave" (Thomas 2009, 12). All in all, the more political that the community is, the more frequently and inevitably the students face the same political problems in their school. In these conditions, they challenge dominant discourses or "question, contest, and reinterpret dominant narratives and in the process, build the foundations of social change" (Flanagan 2013, 22).

Schools are often treated as an isolated space, "charged with primary responsibility for the tasks of preparing children and young people for adult's roles in society" (Bottrell and Goodwin 2011, 4); along these lines, advocates for education for deliberative democracy conceptualize schools as merely spaces for preparation and rehearsal (Gutmann and Thompson 2004). However, this type of go-it-alone logic can only have a loose grip on one of the most important functions of the Byrd Community Academy—the *social* function that kept the educational and political functions connected and brought vitality to the school. The term "social" refers to the collaborative capacity of school and community that can be employed to change society and bind together people who are differently situated.[5] As this story shows, the Byrd Community Academy was a hub for society at large. Even if some connections with the wider society (e.g., newspapers, magazines, other schools, local legislators, and activists) were immediately neither available nor accessible for students alone, the school at large could make these meetings possible through the connections it had to a variety of other entities, through parents, the board of education, new and old media, local government, and civil society groups. Thus, Schultz recollecting his experience with students at the Byrd Community Academy, concluded that "if there are few barriers to true democratic participation, students often choose to make their curriculum one of *social* action . . . they choose to focus their energies on larger social issues important to them" (Schultz 2018, 152; emphasis added).

The Democratic School as a Mediating Space

The story of the Byrd Community Academy tells us the three key functions (educational, political, and social) that make a school democratic, but it should be noted that these three functions are intertwined with each other—this is equally important. For instance, if the community has a specific political problem (e.g., conflict among students in different ethnic groups), the school's various connections with the community enables students to bring the problem into their school. Collective learning activities, such as those in Byrd Community Academy, can help students consider the ways in which they address their common problem and thereby contribute to the democratization of their school and their community. Thus, the interactions among the school's educational, political, and social functions can *mediate* students' diversity of experience across their lives (including their everyday lives, school lives, and public lives).

Dewey was aware of the mediating function of the school. In *The School and Society*, he problematized the classrooms of his time, which were often isolated from a school and wider society as a whole. Building upon his experience at the experimental school at the University of Chicago, he suggested that schools be redesigned to naturalize the connections among traditionally separated venues and events both inside and outside of school. A school of this kind emphasizes student-centric practices of learning by doing and the creation of environments that facilitate students' access to a range of sources of information both inside and outside the school to allow students to be exposed to a variety of knowledge resources. For example, Dewey identified institutions and individuals outside the school (e.g., those of the home, business, public facilities such as parks, laboratory, university, and museum) and designed each room inside the school in a way that connects directly to an out-of-school institution. In this connection, Dewey argues that the school must "get out of its isolation and secure the organic connection with social life" (Dewey [1915] 2001, 49).[6]

In such schools, students necessarily enter with an array of shared political problems drawing on their everyday lives at home or in other spaces in society. The school is a hub through which students share their common tasks, examine them collaboratively, engage in various experiments to consider how the task should be addressed, and, if necessary, bring the insight they receive back into out-of-school settings. From Dewey's normative point of view, a well-functioning school in a democratic society is characterized as follows: "The child can carry over what he learns in the home and utilize it in the school; and the things learned in the school he applies at home. These are the two great things in breaking down isolation, in getting connection—to have the child come to school with all the experience he has got outside the school, and to leave it with something to be immediately used in his everyday life" (Dewey [1915] 2001, 50). Drawing on the discussion of the educational, political, and social function of schools, coupled with Dewey's connective understanding of schools, I suggest understanding the democratic school as a *mediating space* (Nishiyama 2019). A mediating space is neither a well-designed deliberative forum (e.g., deliberative minipublics) nor an ordinary space where small-scale political action takes place. Conceptually, a mediating space falls in between these two spaces. Such a space is characterized in terms of its connective capacity, providing individuals—especially those who have limited access to wider public spaces—with an initial first step to allow them to be engaged in public action.[7]

Conceptualizing schools as a mediating space is not only beneficial for elucidating their ability to build bridges between students' in-school democratic experiences and their activities in a wider society, but also for remedying a general weakness of deliberative system thinking. Hendriks, Ercan, and Boswell summarize the problem of systemic thinking in deliberative democracy as its overreliance on a "communicative miracle," grounded in the assumption that "well-designed institutional mechanisms and governing practices will allow claims and ideas to move seamlessly across spaces of opinion and will formation" (Hendriks, Ercan, and Boswell 2020, 11). For these authors, the assumption is problematic not only because the question of how a systemic connection and transmission occur comes to be put into a black box, but also because it masks the fact that systemic interactions are messier than deliberative democrats expect them to be. Against this backdrop, Hendriks and her colleagues make the case for the importance of highlighting the *connective* function of a deliberative system by taking ordinary people's political agency and practice into account. While their practice (e.g., knitting in the activist group) may seem apolitical, their creative action can serve a connective function by increasing previously fragmented people's solidarity and reinvigorating the critical public sphere.

Here, the concept of mediating space is a type of crystallization of this connective element of a deliberative system. As we have seen in the case of the Byrd Community Academy, a school, as a mediating space, repairs disconnections between students' own lives and the broader public sphere by harnessing the multiple functions of the school. For instance, students experienced political problems, including the injustices and various sufferings that occur in their everyday lives, although these students generally had almost no chance to be heard by people in public sphere (e.g., authorities, decision-makers, journalists, members of the board of education, activists, parents, teachers, and students at other schools). Against this backdrop, a range of human and institutional connections and school networks created a new linkage through which their harsh experiences in their school lives and their out-of-school lives and their educational practices within and outside the school were bridged. The political and educational functions of the school also encouraged students to examine the environment they were embedded in more closely, thereby allowing them to develop maneuvers they could use to gain more public recognition of their experiences. Seen through the lens of the deliberative system, this process can be paraphrased in the following manner: the Byrd Community Academy, understood as a mediating space, (1) stands between the components of the system, such as the private space and the public space and even as the empowered space, and (2) enhances the inclusive and connective capacity of the system in a way that empowers students through deliberative practices in and outside the school and encourages them to work with diversity of agents and institutions across the system. Students' mediated deliberative engagements repair the disconnection of students from the wider public, reinvigorate the solidarity of previously separated, or even hostile, groups of citizens, thereby creating a democratic foundation for social change. Figure 6.1 presents a visual conceptual summary exhibiting how the Byrd Community Academy and the democratic school more broadly act as a mediating space.

Figure 6.1. School as a mediating space. *Source*: Created by the author.

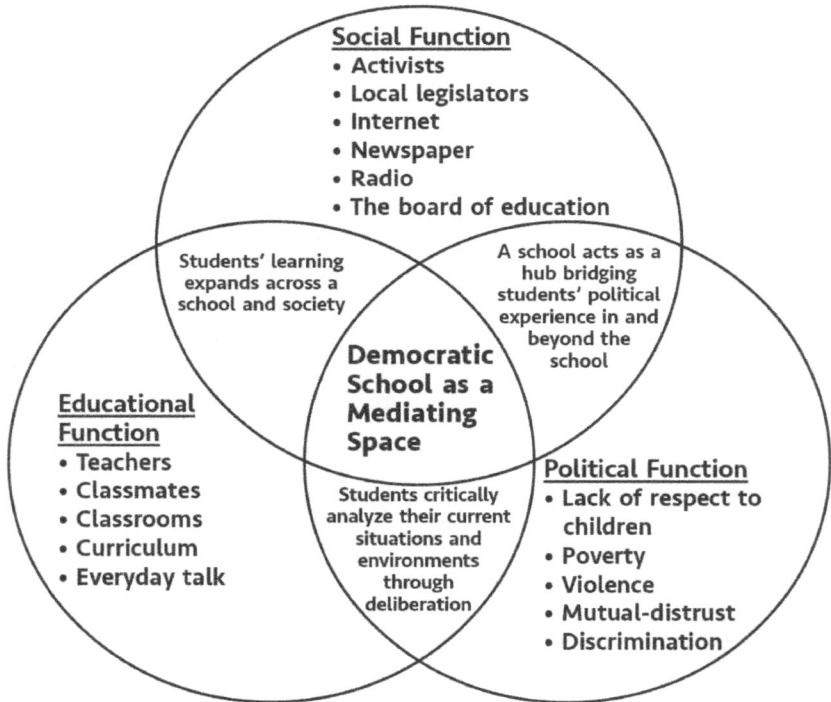

Lessons from the Field: Unpacking Conducive Conditions

However, in reality, not all schools are capable of serving as a well-functioning mediating space. There are many inhibiting factors that diminish a school's mediating capacity. For example, Ed Cairns (1996) indicates that during wartime, schools may tend to be an incubator of students' out-of-school commitment to guerrilla or terrorist activities. Here students may harness their school's educational (e.g., indoctrination), political (e.g., war situation), and social (e.g., connection with adult guerrillas and terrorists) functions, but this may obviously lead to anti-humanistic consequences (e.g., exploitation or early death). We should not take it for granted that students' educational, political, and social experience in their school will seamlessly produce a democratically desirable consequence.

Moreover, as schools can function as a mediating space, what are the implications for democratic education? The discussions in previous chapters have shown that classroom deliberation needs to be enabled with the intentional design of a deliberative process (e.g., meta-deliberation on reason-giving and listening, and facilitation as design). On the other hand, many questions are left hanging with reference to schools: What enables students' deliberative activities within and beyond the school? What role do teachers have in the democratic school? Attaining deeper insight into how schools function as a mediating space and how they contribute to democratic education necessitates bringing together the theoretical trajectory of the previous sections with further empirical inquiry.

From September to December 2016, I undertook fieldwork, including participant observation, at K School,[8] a private school in Japan. I selected this school because the school incorporates a deliberative approach to moral education as part of its official curriculum. My initial aim was to explore the relationship between the in-classroom deliberative practice and students' out-of-classroom activities; however, as my fieldwork continued, my attention shifted beyond my limited focus on students' classroom activities to those activities' link to their out-of-classroom practice, the deliberative potential of the school.

K School has two types of classrooms that have different educational aims. In the "advanced" classrooms, Socratic deliberative practice, known as Philosophy for Children, shortened to P4C, was part of the moral education curriculum. P4C is a Socratic form of dialogue, where students discuss their own common ethical, political, and philosophical questions that were generated from their everyday lives (Lipman 2003). In P4C, students sit in a circle in the classroom with a teacher as facilitator. In P4C, students who have different perspectives or opinions supply reasoning, assisting each other in drawing inferences from unsupported opinions and from what has already been said, helping them identify one another's assumption, allowing them to challenge dominant or taken-for-granted discourses and social norms. The first case, Ari to Pla, to be described below emerged from the practice of P4C in the advanced classroom. Ari to Pla is a student-led monthly deliberative group that takes place outside of school, organized and managed by students themselves (Burgh and Thornton 2022). The school also has "general" classrooms that put their focus on students' basic capacity-building in a traditional knowledge-transfer. Although no deliberative curriculum was available for this type of classroom, one student in the general classroom organized a deliberative event called "The Future Talk" (TFT), which is worth paying attention to, as it can help us examine the conditions under which the school serves as an effective mediating space.[9]

In the following, I briefly outline the two cases (Ari to Pla and TFT) based on their observations and in-depth interviews. The subsequent section shall discuss the conditions under which the school served as a mediating space and consider its implications for democratic education and the democratic school.

Ari to Pla

One day, a P4C teacher asked some of his students (students G to O) who had been engaging more actively in the P4C session than others whether they were interested in holding a dialogue event at their school festival. The students immediately agreed. The students invited their friends and some adults (e.g., parents and local community members) to the festival to speak together about the philosophical questions that students had. The students, however, did not consider that the event went well. There were many adult participants who were neither ready to listen to students' voices nor willing to engage collaboratively in a philosophical discussion with students. Many adult participants forced their beliefs and opinions onto the students one-sidedly or talked nonstop about their own stories, thereby preventing students from expressing their views. During the interview, all students whom I interviewed complained about these adults. For example:

I think it may be inevitable that adults have fixed beliefs and opinions because they are adults. But what I wanted them to do was just to listen to our opinions. We of course know adults have opinion like us. But we wanted them to be more open to our opinion. (interview with student F, November 21, 2016)

As I predicted, adults had a fixed image of children. They underestimate our opinion because we are children. (interview with student O, November 21, 2016)

The main message I received from adults was "children should study, not state an opinion." (interview with student M, November 21, 2016)

Student G expressed her outright displeasure about the adult participants. However, she also had a strong desire to continue the philosophical dialogue practice with her friends. She asked her teacher to prepare an out-of-school space for a monthly deliberative event, called Ari to Pla (named after Aristotle and Plato—*to* means "and" in Japanese). In Ari to Pla, participants deliberate about the common philosophical concerns that arise in the course of their lives (e.g., friendship, schooling, and love) by applying the P4C method that they studied in the classroom. According to student G, the unique characteristic of Ari to Pla was that only teenagers are allowed the group to prevent adults from bringing their paternalistic manipulation to it. She said, "I think adults tend to have a lot more experiences than us, and for better or worse, these experiences force them to refuse to change their ideas or to accept new opinions. So, they often dominate dialogue by speaking about their fixed beliefs and opinions. But we students usually do not have so much experience like adults do, and that's why we can accept various opinions" (interview with Student G, November 21, 2016).

One student participant appreciated the absence of adults in Ari to Pla, saying, "I can concentrate on dialogue because there is no adult like a teacher or parent who makes me feel rushed when I consider my opinion slowly. So I can enjoy the time for keeping on thinking deeply and slowly" (interview with student C, December 6, 2016). After conducting the deliberations in Ari to Pla, however, student G gradually observed the value of listening to adults' opinions, as they can provide different perspectives that the students alone usually did not possess. Thus, while Ari to Pla is in principle a teenager-only group, after deliberation with student L, another core organizer of Ari to Pla, they decided to allow adults to participate in the group on the condition that the participating adults must be ready to see students as equals and treat them with respect. This rule provided the student participants with a sense of safety during their deliberation. According to student L, "There are a lot of educators who are trying to instill their moral values when we discuss together. I don't like that kind of thing. There is no freedom. It's not interesting. . . . If we do dialogue together, we need a consensus. I mean, consensus on the attitude for understanding each other, creating a safe space. I don't like the attitude of teachers and adults who don't care about the importance of this consensus" (interview with student L, November 24, 2016).

Students attempted to overcome the adult-centric unwritten deliberative habit by which adults, whether implicitly or explicitly, privileged their own presence and opinion over those of the students. Students found that a shared adult-centered habit of dialogue was far from the principle of free and open dialogue. For the students, therefore, Ari to Pla was a counterstrategy to challenge and overcome the unequal relationship between adults and students in deliberation, which resonates somewhat with what Fraser calls the *subaltern counterpublics*, that is, "parallel discursive arenas where members of subordinated social groups invent and circulate counter-discourses, which in turn permit them to formulate oppositional interpretations of their identities, interests and needs" (Fraser 1990, 67). In Ari to Pla, students invented and formulated various counterstrategies for their deliberation together and to form different interpretations regarding what students can do. After the adults' domination of students' dialogue during the school festival, for instance, the students formulated their own communicative norms as part of their counterstrategy. By applying their own deliberative experience in the classroom to Ari to Pla, students created their own space where the conventional asymmetric relationship between adults and children was mitigated by compelling adults to see students as equals. Importantly, Ari to Pla was a space wherein students could have a relatively safe and protected deliberation without requiring them to be greatly concerned about domination by adults. By doing so, Ari to Pla enabled students to design, initiate, and organize their own deliberative activities and sometimes connect its participants with the wider public sphere (see the story of "The Future Talk" below). Ari to Pla itself was a group designed neither to exert substantive political influence nor to offer any constructive resolution to political gridlock. The reflective experience of organizing their own deliberative group reconstructed a traditional relationship between adults and students in a deliberative practice by empowering them through deliberative norm-making and offering a freer and more open communication space, where their voices are meaningfully heard.

The Future Talk

The story of student T (13 years old) in the general classroom at the K School, who was not involved with P4C or any other deliberative curriculum, also sheds light on the democratic role of the school, only in a different fashion. When he was a primary school student, student T was selected to be a child interviewer in a nonprofit organization's project. He visited the Philippines to interview Filipino kids suffering in the wake of Typhoon Haiyan in 2013. After this point, he became interested in dialogue practices. After he entered K School, he hoped to share his experience in the Philippines publicly. However, student T did not have sufficient resources to achieve his goal. He had no friend interested in his project plan, nor did his classroom teacher share useful information to make it possible. He had no chance to learn methods, ideas, and strategies to make his aspirations real. One day, he heard about P4C by chance from a friend in the advanced classroom. He then became interested in P4C:

> STUDENT T: After getting back from the Philippines, I thought about what I can do. But I had no answer when I thought alone about it. That's why I wanted to think with others. If we exchange opinions and discuss over and over, I think it may be possible for us to get a better idea. Then I got to know P4C and I found it really interesting and useful.
>
> AUTHOR: Sounds great. But why P4C?
>
> STUDENT T: Well . . . the biggest reason was simply because my friends did it in their class. I then collected information about P4C and participated in Ari to Pla, which was very nice. In P4C everyone can express their own opinion freely. Sometimes they are sympathetic to my opinion, and sometimes they value what I say. These experiences helped me to produce more and more new ideas. (interview with student T, December 16, 2016)

He then asked his teacher to support his new project for a deliberative workshop called "The Future Talk," in which both students and adult citizens spoke about controversial social, political, and philosophical questions. Then the same teacher contacted a professor at the University of Tokyo Center for Philosophy (UTCP) to ask for the support of the Center for student T's project. Student T and UTCP announced the TFT project to the broader public, and they finally held the TFT at the University of Tokyo in August 2015, where around 30 participants gathered. At the beginning of the TFT, student T reported his experiences and some of the findings from his interviews with Filipino children. Then, the participants deliberated together, asking questions on global poverty and global cooperation using the P4C method. TFT eventually enabled adult participants to become interested in hearing the voice of a youth.

While designing and implementing TFT, student T also developed his own deliberative norms. Before TFT, he thought that a key to sharing his experience with a wide range of audiences was to speak as logically and clearly as possible. However, his experience of TFT transformed the way he thought in the following manner: "What I value now is listening and thinking. And the most important for good listening and thinking is not to overemphasize only my opinion. I used to make judgments based only on my own experiences and my fixed opinion. But now I ask audiences, 'This is my opinion, and what do you think?' Doing this will, I think, help people to get more interested in my activity and to be more sympathetic" (interview with student T, December 16, 2016). By contrast with Ari to Pla, TFT was not motivated by a desire to run contrary to adult-centricity. Instead, student T used TFT as an opportunity to gain further public recognition of his practice and seek further opportunities for collaboration. He said, "I foreground my identity as a junior high school student. When I do so, many people recognize me, and they become more willing to support my project. I want them to be surprised by what I say and what I do." Here, his opinion resonates with what Arendt called *a space of appearance*, where "I appear to others as others appear to me, where men exist not merely like other living or inanimate things but make their appearance explicitly" (Arendt 1958, 198–99). A space of appearance is a temporary and fragile public space that only emerges when speakers and spectators jointly encounter each other and recognize the unreplaceable oneness and otherness of each other. In a space of appearance, individuals who are differently situated bring their identities and uniqueness to the fore during communicative interactions with each other to forge a connective public space.

Neither Ari to Pla nor TFT produced a tangible and immediate influence over social change. These groups were also small, informal, grassroots, and temporary. Nonetheless, they made a crucial contribution to empowerment of students in the public sphere, which provided them with rich connective pathways through which they took advantage of their school's educational, political, and social functions in conjunction with their everyday experiences and their out-of-school activities. For Ari to Pla, P4C in the classroom, and the school festival increased students' motivation to organize the deliberative group outside of the school context. For TFT, teacher-provided connections and networks helped student T bring his ideas into practice, although the student himself did not have any experience of deliberation in the classroom. Both cases expanded the students' deliberative opportunities, encouraging them to innovate their own deliberative norms and practices through iterated analysis, design, implementation, and reflection.

Horizontal and Vertical Connections as Mediating Factors

The lived experience thus observed from the fieldwork helps elucidate a key factor in school functioning as a mediating space. As demonstrated in part 2, meta-deliberation is a key factor for enabling deliberative democratic learning, while the stories of Ari to Pla and TFT demonstrate the significance of (at least two types of) connectivity—*horizontal* and *vertical*.[10]

Horizontal connectivity is a face-to-face type of informal human connection, created and sustained within schools. Generally, human connections that are created within and across school settings, in-class curricular activities, peer/friends-based communities, and relationship with teachers, are seedbeds for creating this kind of network (Hayward 2012; Senge 2012). This connects activities and experiences of different students (and teachers, if necessary), thereby allowing them to engage in collective and collaborative action and projects. Classroom deliberation can induce such horizontal connectivity. The presence and availability of deliberative activity in the classroom can allow students to share their own common knowledge regarding deliberation and sometimes provide a certain collaborative opportunity. For Byrd Community Academy, rich

184 | Children, Democracy, and Education

deliberative opportunities within the classroom of room 405 created a common experience among students, enabling students who previously did not respect each other to come to know each other, thereby motivating them to collaborate further. Alternatively, in the case of Ari to Pla, P4C in the classroom produced opportunities for deliberation lovers and induced a key impetus for them to apply their classroom experience to their deliberative event for the school festival. Without classroom deliberation, this type of horizontal connection is only available with difficulty. Needless to say, classroom deliberation is not the only element that can be used to induce horizontal connectivity. As the cases of student T and TFT illustrate, the school's institutional structure can help induce varieties in horizontal connection, such as the teacher-student relationship or classmates.

However, as discussed in chapter 2, the idea of deliberative democratic learning is founded upon the theoretical premise that the development of learners' deliberative competencies occurs within the organic connections of their environments (Bronfenbrenner 1979; Engeström 2015). The sequence of students' self-reflective deliberative activities, including questioning, analysis, modeling, examination of the model, implementation of the model, and reflection, do not need to be conducted only within the classroom. As the case of Ari to Pla illustrates, students examined, applied, and reconstructed their own deliberative norms and models, formulated not in the classroom but in other, extraclassroom settings. This means that, although horizontal connectivity is a key element in making schools function as a mediating space, horizontal connectivity *alone* is not sufficient for elevating students' established connectivity at the out-of-classroom level.

For this reason, I emphasize the significance of another connectivity, a vertical one, made up of a wider set of human and institutional connections (e.g., parents, universities, businesses, media, and politicians). For instance, Ari to Pla may not be established without a set of vertical connectivity, including the school's provision of out-of-school connections such as public space for organizing Ari to Pla, which were otherwise hard for students alone to possess and utilize. These vertical connections offered students pathways for scaling up their experiences in their schools or classrooms outside of school. Likewise, although the horizontal connection that student T shared with his friend offered him knowledge of the details of P4C, this connection alone may not be able to make his desire realistic. For him to scale up his plan, chains of vertical connections provided by K School played an essential role, including the group Ari to Pla, where student T could experience and learn how to organize deliberative practice; a teacher who regularly supported student T's plan of TFT by introducing him to others; a professor at the University of Tokyo; and the University of Tokyo Center for Philosophy.

A whole-school event is an important factor that produces both horizontal and vertical connectivity, thereby facilitating students' school-level deliberative practices. Although the event itself is not designed in relation to deliberative democratic ideals, it can nurture various connections and then create seedbeds for students' future democratic engagement inside and outside the school. Ari to Pla derived from students' experience in a school festival, and forming it in turn helped students to establish new relationship with students in other classrooms or with students of different ages, which in turn enabled them to organize their own deliberative groups. As such, Ari to Pla is a typical example, in the sense that it shows how the deliberative curriculum in the shape of P4C and the whole-school event of the school festival worked together for allowing students to harness various vertical and horizontal connections. K School itself is not designed to be the democratic school, but, nevertheless, it has served as a mediating space in a broader deliberative system.

The deliberative importance of the school's horizontal and vertical connectivity may not be specific to K School. As the in case of the Byrd Community Academy or the case of Occupy Playground, schools often mirror the political problems of their community (e.g., corruption, low respect for children's human rights, and poverty), and their horizontal connections bring these problems into the school and the classroom context. The vertical connections are an integral part of scaling up students' experience within the school at the deliberative systemic level.

Theoretical Implications and Some Defenses

The most important theoretical implication that we can draw from the above argument may be that there is no one-size-fits-all ideal for the democratic school. Put differently, the degree to which horizontal and vertical connectivity are necessary and useful is contextually determined. For instance, Ari to Pla and TFT are contrasting cases in several ways: in Ari to Pla, the horizontal connectivity formed by P4C and school festivals had a synergistic effect with vertical connectivity, thereby elevating students' deliberative experiences at the out-of-school level. In TFT, on the other hand, student T used only a very limited horizontal connectivity (with his friend), while most of his deliberative project was made possible by vertical connectivity. The conditions for a democratically functioning mediating space are not necessarily limited to environments that can provide a perfect set of horizontal and vertical connectivity. Rather, the key condition for a democratic mediating space is the capacity to provide an appropriate degree and type of connectivity in relation to the particular challenges and contradictions that students actually face.

The creation and provision of horizontal and vertical connectivity depends significantly on the presence and role of teachers, although I contend that their expected role is different from their role in classroom deliberation—this is the second theoretical implication. In the context of classroom deliberation, teachers are, as discussed in chapter 5, expected to be facilitative agents who engage in an interplay of facilitative techniques and designs to increase reflection and inclusiveness. At the school level, however, teachers themselves did not need to be deliberative anywhere or at any time; nor do they always need to directly intervene in students' deliberation as a facilitator. Their role would be more *entrepreneurial* that of an individual who takes "it upon themselves to provide invitations and opportunities for others to engage in reflection and deliberation on the topic of common concern" (Barvosa 2018, 43). Teachers as deliberative entrepreneurs do not have to be involved directly in students' deliberative experience. Instead, their primary work and responsibility is to assist students to find or utilize their school's connective capacity. For instance, in the case of Ari to Pla, the teacher did not participate in students' deliberative experience itself but instead simply provided an out-of-school connection for students who faced a challenge of adult presence in deliberation. In addition, the teacher provided a method and external opportunity for deliberation with students who wished to deliberate but had no idea about how to do so. Importantly, the mere use of the school's connective capacity does not guarantee a democratic consequence. What is important is that teachers should make use of the school's connective capacity in a way that motivates students to engage in further deliberation outside the classroom or school. School's connective capacity without such *deliberative orientation* fails to function well in a *deliberative* system or even isolates the school itself from a deliberative system. Both school and teacher per se do not always need to be deliberative, but if we situate them in a deliberative system, they always have to be deliberative-oriented.

Critics may disagree with these theoretical implications on the grounds that, first, I underestimate the value of classroom deliberation, and, second, I am optimistic about the realization of the democratic school in the real world. Regarding the first point, I acknowledge the fact that democratic education theorists usually underscore the deliberative curriculum as an indispensable component of the democratic school (Gutmann 1999; Hess 2009; Youniss 2011; Noddings 2013; Sorial and Peterson 2019). Importantly, I am not claiming that the deliberative curriculum is meaningless. Rather, my empirical findings show among other things that the deliberative curriculum can provide an important step closer to the realization of making school function as a democratic mediating space. However, what I note here with respect to the role of school is twofold: (1) such a deliberative curriculum becomes meaningful and democratically desirable at the *school* level when it induces students' horizontal connectivity or meaningfully bridges between students' various experiences inside and outside of the school, and (2) schools at large have a broader potential for deliberative democratic learning than classrooms not only because students can form horizontal and vertical connectivity *without* classroom deliberation (e.g., TFT), but also because classroom *alone* cannot provide vertical connectivity. As observed in part 2 classroom deliberation is an integral element of deliberative democratic learning, but this is not the only way that school functioning can be realized as a mediating space. If we wish to use classroom deliberation for realizing the democratic *school*, classroom deliberation without horizontal or vertical connective capacity is simply isolated from a broader deliberative system, and this may lead to what Dewey calls a "great waste" that increases a student's inability "to utilize the experiences he gets outside the school in any complete and free way within the school itself; while on the other hand, he is unable to apply in daily life what he is learning at school" (Dewey [1915] 2001, 46).[11] In the context of deliberative democracy, the democratic school, or a systemic account of it, is not a school that embodies all deliberative norms within it. Rather, it is expected to function as one constituting part of the system, the core role of which is to mediate the everyday, school, and public political/pedagogical experiences of students through its vertical and horizontal networks. The democratic school of this kind is therefore not a discrete, independent and peripheral space but is a relational and connective one.

I can also defend my argument from the second skepticism. Critics might contend that the idea of school as a mediating space is important but that this is different from the democratic school per se. For them, the democratic school should be something like the Byrd Community Academy that makes a substantial political influence. Of course, if all schools could become like the Byrd Community School that would be very pleasing news—but is it realistic? My key concern is that existing normative and empirical requirements for the democratic school tend to set the bar too high, and only a "lucky" school could have fulfilled the requirements for this. Many schools in the real world do not always have a brave, dedicated, and democratically spirited teacher like Schultz, and instead many contemporary schools are instead conditioned by their deliberation-averse orientation (Journell 2017). In many countries, schools are reluctant to allow or even strongly disagree with students' classroom deliberation on controversial political questions. Some may be concerned about a case where deliberating politically controversial question (e.g., marriage equality) may compel marginalized students to be forced to listen to the offensive, discriminatory, and stereotyping opinions of other students (Hess and McAvoy 2015). Alternatively, others assume that introducing deliberative curriculum is almost impossible because a limited time is allocated to it or where lack of practice or financial support prohibit it from being tried. For a long time, such schools without sufficient deliberative opportunities in the classroom have rarely been considered to be the democratic school. My argument in this chapter opposed this assumption, making the case for how a school can, despite the *absence* of the deliberative curriculum, function as a mediating space in a deliberative system if its weakness (e.g., no deliberative curriculum) can be compensated by other deliberative practice (e.g., out-of-school deliberative opportunity) or if a teacher as deliberative entrepreneur can understand the contextual problems that students face and provide a sufficient degree of connectivity.

Conclusion

This chapter has explored two main topics: deliberative democratic learning at the school level and the meaning of the democratic school. For the first topic, the chapter both theoretically and empirically illustrates how deliberation occurs at the school level and how it differs from deliberation in the classroom. Both the classroom and the school are capable of inducing students to practice learning-by-doing deliberative experiences, but they do so in a different way. While meta-deliberation is a key constitutive element in deliberative democratic learning in *classroom* settings, connectivity is an essential component for scaling up students' deliberative experience at school to outside of it. The TFT case demonstrates how the school enabled student T to reflectively examine possible methods for sharing his experience with the wider publics, connecting him with the out-of-school deliberative group (Ari to Pla) and educational institutions that possessed a wide range of human and institutional connections (University of Tokyo), thereby enabling the student to develop his own best possible deliberative practice. In some cases, such as the Byrd Community Academy and Ari to Pla, the experience of in-class deliberative activities played a powerful role, although it should be noted that the in-class deliberative practice provided students with impetus for further deliberative activities in and beyond the school. In Ari to Pla, students' reflective examination and learning about how to deliberate with others took place outside the classroom, including modeling (the first deliberative practice in the school festival) and the examination and implementation of the model in conjunction with reflection (Ari to Pla).

This chapter has also called for rethinking the meaning of the democratic school. The movementization of the democratic school is under way, but it faces a bumpy road ahead (Apple and Beane 2007). This may be because of the pitfall of imagining the myth of the "perfect" democratic school as a potential reality. Scholars often dream of the democratic school as something in which all deliberative democratic norms are deeply immersed across the whole school, otherwise people might contend that one school or another does not count "as democratic schools in my meaning" (Rietmulder 2019, 12). An influential democratic education theorist Nel Noddings (2013, ch. 1) also defines the aim of democratic education as the creation of productive deliberators and argues that, to this end, the normative standard of the democratic school should include the presence of accountable teachers, a well-designed student-centric curriculum inducing students' critical thinking, collaboration, fair opportunities for learning, and so forth. Granted, schools of this kind are undoubtedly deserving of being called democratic. On the other hand, skeptics may argue that the normative claim is too demanding, in the sense that these democratic principles can, in reality, only be injected into schools that already have an array of democratic features. Indeed, teachers, educators, and scholars, even including Noddings herself, concede that such normative requirements set the bar too high. Noddings laments the problem of today's school, saying, "Teaching for deliberative participation is not easy in even supportive situations; in our schools today, with so many forces opposing such teaching, it is very difficult" (22). In short, the ideal and the reality of the democratic school are not yet bridged. However, the pessimistic take on modern schools does not always hollow out the ideal of the democratic school itself. The empirical clue to be taken from the story of the Byrd Community Academy and my fieldwork at the School K is that it is too early to conclude that the democratic school is infeasible as a project. Taking a systemic view on deliberative democracy, this chapter has spelled out how and why schools ought to be understood as a space creating a new deliberative connection and providing a *first step* in students' various actions across a broader deliberative system.

Schools are, of course, not the only space capable of providing students an opportunity to take this first step. There are in fact various out-of-school opportunities that create new channels through which children become involved in deliberative activities and learn about democracy. Moving beyond the traditional learning spaces (classrooms and schools) that this chapter and previous chapters have focused on, the next chapter sheds light on the role of self-organized associations in the wider public sphere, more specifically activist groups and their qualitatively different capacity for facilitating children's experiences of deliberative democratic learning.

Chapter 7

Deliberative Activism

Every Friday early evening, after the couple of lectures at my university and before going home, I take the train to the Shijo Ohashi Bridge in Kyoto city. The bridge connects two popular sightseeing spots where a lot of tourists come and go even during the COVID-19 pandemic. At around 5:30 p.m., several young people (normally three to six people) gather at a small space near the end of the bridge. They take out cardboard placards from their bag, place them on the ground, or hold them in their hands and then continue to stand there. This is what they call *the standing* (or the standing protest). Many and various types of messages are written on the placards, including themes of consciousness-raising about the coming climate crisis, criticism of the government, encouragement of veganism, a serious flood in Pakistan, and so forth.

When I arrive at the space, the young people greet me as usual. I stand next to them holding one of the placards up as they do. While doing so, I switch my identity from a university lecturer to a climate activist. Quite often, our conversation starts with a causal talk about the day's weather ("Hey, very hot day today, isn't it?" "It's really crazy cold today. Winter will come earlier than last year!"), but this is about almost all we talk about in relation to the climate. Actually, we talk about many things that are not limited to the issue of climate change. Some start talking about philosophical issues ("What and who should define minority?" "What is the meaning of social change? What is society? What is change?"), while others discuss future plans for their protests. Alternatively, some of them talk about nature and the animals they saw on their recent travels.

Figure 7.1. Standing. *Source*: Photo by the author. *Note*: The author sits in the middle of the photo.

We do not talk to passers-by. We rarely hand out flyers. Perhaps, and I feel, people may see us as a strange group because what we do is just to stand around (chatting and laughing), holding up placards. Several people ask what we are doing, but most people look at us for a moment and immediately look away. Thirty minutes later, we finish the standing and go home. This has been my, and our, routine for the past couple of years.

Fridays for Future Kyoto (FFF Kyoto) is one of the local groups of the FFF movement (see chapter 1), which was organized in mid-2019. FFF Tokyo was the first group formed in Japan, and FFF Kyoto became active soon after that. FFF Kyoto has around 10 young climate activists, including junior high, high school, and university students, as core members who organize various climate actions such as the abovementioned standing protest every Friday, climate marches, and climate workshops, among others. I started my ethnographic study with FFF Kyoto in February 2021, participating in the standing protest, climate march, and regular meetings, and undertaking formal as well as casual interviews.

In the second half of chapter 1, I discussed how the FFF movement can be situated within the macro-scale deliberative system of global climate governance. In contrast, the focus of this chapter is on a more micro perspective of the FFF movement, with a specific focus on the lived experience of youth climate activists of FFF Kyoto. Members of FFF Kyoto engage in the standing almost every week. In that respect, it is easy to conclude that they have been repeating the same activity, keeping the same identity, and holding on to the same emotions over several years. As we shall see in this chapter, however, the meaning FFF Kyoto's members find in their standing, the reasons for their participation in the movement, and the meaning of each action they perform in their protesting activities are continuously questioned, reinterpreted, and reconstructed. Focusing on their collective action in the public sphere per se is important, but I contend that ignoring or underestimating the *self-transformative* nature of social movement allows us to engage only in a superficial observation of the phenomenon while preventing us from deeply approaching the rich experience each activist has.

That the internal process of meaning-making and reflection (and self-transformation as a result of these) ground the foundation of social movements has widely been discussed by the scholars in the new social movement camp. As Alberto Melucci, a key scholar of the field, notes, "A social movement is not a unified subject but always a composite action system" (Melucci 1989, 28). Interestingly, Melucci may be the first person who indicates that a movement's self-transformation and learning are inseparable. He writes, "The organizational form of movements becomes a field of investments, a self-reflexive set of relationships which can be modeled and remodeled according to the learning process of its acting members. . . . The excess of available resources and cultural possibilities in the system enables the *learning of learning among actors, that is, a self-reflexive action upon action itself*" (61; emphasis added).

Existing research on learning in new social movements is more likely to pay attention to the "What is achieved?" type of question with a specific focus on knowledge gain and skill-building as a result of participating in protesting activities (e.g., Lee 2015; Laguarta 2019). In contrast, Melucci's sharp eyes call for further attention to the "What is happening?" type of question whose core focus is on the rich opportunities for learning in the internal process of self-transformation of the movement. However, he did not dig into this topic in more detail, and therefore some questions remain (e.g., what such learning in social movements looks like and what makes it possible). As we have seen in the previous chapters, learning does not occur from nowhere. Rather, it is triggered by a complex combination of varieties of dilemma, internal as well as external conflict, facilitative individuals and designs, and reflective (meta-)deliberation. How are these elements crystalized in social movements, and how are they different from deliberative democratic learning in traditional educational settings such as the classroom? In this chapter, I draw on the ethnographic story of FFF Kyoto with a view to deepening the idea of deliberative democratic learning in an out-of-classroom context. Before going into the main story, let me begin with a brief review of the existing research on the FFF movement and then justify the rationale for my ethnographic approach.

FFF Revisited

One of the mainstream research missions of social movement studies is to elucidate the mechanism of collective action, exploring why social movement occurs and why people participate in it (Tarrow 1998). Questions of this sort are predominantly found when it comes to the study of the FFF movement due to its novelty. Many children and young people across the globe who were previously considered "politically uninterested" or "politically uninfluential" started school strikes and protested on the streets against the climate crisis without their parents or guardians. There are also many children and young people who reported that FFF was their first experience with activism (Wahlström et al. 2019). Hence, it is natural that researchers are interested in what drives children and young people to participate in climate activism.

A dominant approach for explaining the motivation for collective action is to distil variables from the activities and statements of Greta Thunberg and apply them to each context. This sort of approach has a shared assumption that "Greta Thunberg represents children's resistance" (Holmberg and Alvinius 2020, 79), and so understanding Greta enables us to know and explain more detail about the FFF movement. Leading research by Anandita Sabherwal et al. (2021) statistically unpacks that a high group efficacy tends to be formed among those who express higher empathy for Greta, and such group efficacy has served as a driving force for enabling young people to continue to participate in climate activism, which Sabherwal and colleagues call the Greta Thunberg effect. Marika Kettunen's (2020) research also indicates that Greta serves as a role model for the high participation of young female students in FFF around the world.

Another approach is to derive a master frame from Greta's emotion, which Greta has expressed in her public speeches, and superimpose her emotional status on the motivation of the FFF participants. This approach helps elucidate why differently situated children and young people share the sense of "us" when participating in the FFF movement. Psychological counsellor Linda Goldman, for example, attempts to explain the motivation for participation by connecting it with Greta's various emotions such as eco-anxiety, climate grief, and resentment against politicians and adults. Her emotional statuses are, on Goldman's account, more or less, shared by many participants of climate activism, which ultimately generates a sense of shared collective identity. She argues, "Greta Thunberg, teenage activist, has warned 'Our Earth is on fire!' When kids hear this, they become afraid. Some wonder, why should I go to school, do my homework, or play sports if we are not going to live?" (Goldman 2022, 100). This sort of interpretation has formed the dominant image of the FFF movement such that young climate activists who feel strong eco-anxiety and climate grief express a high level of concern for the coming climate crisis, which in turn motivates them to feel a sense of duty and responsibility and fight against political elites (Hayward 2021). Grounded on such images, some researchers analyze Greta's public speeches in order to understand how her narratives and storytelling represent many other youth climate activists' motivations for participation in the movement and, ultimately, their political agency (Holmberg and Alvinius 2020).

Such research has contributed to giving an explanatory shape of the FFF movement and its novelty. However, several researchers have questioned the research trends, arguing that the interpretive approach puts too much focus on Greta as the icon of the movement. Neas, Ward, and Bowman (2022, 9) are leading researchers who critically review such research trends as *Greta framing*. Although it is true that Greta's school strike sparked the worldwide FFF movement, Greta framing sometimes nails our eyes down to the universality of the movement at the expense of the context-dependent story and lived experience of how the movement's spirit is introduced, (re)interpreted, and implemented in each local context. Moreover, a top-down interpretation and description of the FFF movement as a sudden and instantaneous practice motivated by Greta-represented emotions such as anger, anxiety, or grief would run the risk of overlooking youth climate activists' grassroots efforts in designing and managing the movement. In short, Greta framing may create an understandable and acceptable public story while simplifying rich and diverse experiences of activists within the movement by treating them as if they are just a copy of Greta.

In light of methodology, one problem with Greta framing is that it turns researcher's spotlight solely onto publicly visible mass mobilization. The framing offers a superficial interpretive framework of the movement but fails to capture the internal dynamics that help people to organize and sustain the movement. Even some research known as "in-depth" studies of the FFF movement fall into this pitfall. For instance, Kettunen (2020) and Christian Haugestad et al. (2021) describe their studies as "ethnographic," yet they are not ethnographic enough, precisely because participant observations focus intensively on protest marches, with little attention to the publicly invisible experiences and activities of the youth climate activists who make huge efforts to underpin the marches. In short, with the presumption that a majority of youth participants in the FFF movement are inspired significantly by Greta, the analytical perspective of these studies tends to be limited to scenes where FFF participants behave like Greta in the public sphere (e.g., doing a school strike, expressing emotions). As many social movement scholars have already revealed, "participation in the movement" should not be reduced only to participation in protest activities on the street because such publicly visible activities are anchored significantly by the rich and deep participatory experience of designing that protest, creating signifié to give legitimacy to the activity, and planning the activity to gain mass support. As Sidney Tarrow (1998) rightly notes, "contentious collective action is the basis of social movements," and yet "this does not mean that movements do nothing else but contend" (3).[1] All in all, many existing studies on the FFF movement to date fail to take into account the classic theme of social movement studies, the close relationship and interplay between a movement's democratic dynamics in the public sphere and activists' in-group experience of meaning-making.

Certainly, many activists call their movement FFF, but that does not mean that they are mere copies of Greta. To capture the nuanced experience of youth climate activists in the FFF movement, it is not enough to observe the surface of their contentious and protestive actions in the public sphere or to analyze their actions using the Greta-related variable. Instead, what should be taken into account is a deeper understanding of the interplay between their publicly visible and publicly invisible experiences and the way in which such interplay gives shape to the activists' own FFF movement. As long as we see FFF as a standardized movement that can be practiced in the same way in any place, we will never understand what it truly is, because the perspective greatly misses youth climate activists' *contextualized* beliefs, values, efforts, and even failures that anchor the movement. In contrast, by closely observing how the original meaning of the FFF movement is continuously (re)interpreted, reconstructed, and implemented by youth climate activists of different contexts, we will realize how the Western-centric and simplified interpretation of the FFF movement like Greta framing ignores the self-transformative nature of the movement. This is why I decided to engage in ethnography.

While many people become involved in FFF Kyoto's activities, my research puts much focus on the experiences of its *core members*. Mainstream research tends to conduct simple surveys or impromptu conversations with randomly selected participants during the FFF's protest march (Wahlström et al. 2019; Martiskainen et al. 2020) or in-depth interviews with those who have previously participated in the protest march (Kettunen 2020; Haugestad et al. 2021).[2] However, in my view, these approaches pay little attention to the diverse meanings and experiences of "participants" (Melucci 1989) in social movements. While there are organizers or core members who take ownership of defining the meaning of the movement and shaping it in a way that adapts to the specific context, there are also people who normally cannot do so (e.g., ordinary people). Even if a movement publicly emphasizes its structurelessnes or lack of hierarchy, there is in reality no social movement without what Paolo Gerbaudo (2012) calls a choreographer or megaphone holder who has substantial decision-making authority.[3]

Scholars who employ Greta framing may believe that Greta plays an important role as a designing authority, mostly in the global context, but this should not be interpreted as that she always plays the same role in all local contexts. Rather, specific movement themes, policies, directions, and goals of local movements are significantly influenced by core members' contextualized and collective experiences, values, beliefs, and interpretations of the FFF movement. Random selection and random conversation fail to capture the power relations and dynamics within the movement. Therefore, to understand the meaning of FFF in a specific context, we should be more sensitive to different types of membership and focus more on the experiences of core members.

Since February 2021, I have immersed myself in the activities of FFF Kyoto on a regular basis, which include (1) participation in the standing protest on the street every Friday, holding placards and talking with other members and participants, (2) participation in protest marches, (3) attendance at FFF Kyoto's regular meeting if needed,[4] (4) in-depth interviews with core members, and (5) casual conversations outside the movement (e.g., my office, café, public events). I wrote fieldnotes every time. My positionality in FFF Kyoto is located in-between insider and outsider. When one becomes a core member, they are invited to the communication platform (currently, Slack), and in this sense I am not an official member because I am not included in this online community. However, when the group made significant decisions, I was frequently invited to their meetings and became part of their decision-making process. Alternatively, when they organized an important event (e.g., protest march, workshop), they asked me to help (e.g., being a photographer) and they gave me FFF Kyoto's armband, a membership symbol. In this sense, I call myself a "part-time" member of FFF Kyoto.[5] When M and K, main characters of this chapter, confronted various challenges and barriers, they often visited my university office and I talked with them as a sort of trusted counsellor. In this way, as a part-time member as well as an adult researcher, I engage in learning-by-doing research in order not only to study the group but also study with them and support them.

It is of course next to impossible to write everything about my two-year ethnographic experience within a single chapter; so to write this chapter, I inevitably (and somewhat regrettably) had to sort out[6] data, especially the focused period, focused individuals, and focused activities. First, the chapter presents the story of FFF Kyoto observed from February to December 2021. This is a period when M, who played a central role in FFF Kyoto, was an official leader of the group. M's varying attempts at meaning-making for FFF Kyoto amid the COVID-19 pandemic offer important insights into how the self-transformation of the movement occurs. The chapter also focuses on K, who initiated and shaped FFF Kyoto in collaboration with M. Finally, the chapter's story plot is structured around the practice of standing, which, as mentioned, is a central activity of FFF Kyoto. The self-transformative nature of FFF Kyoto will be highlighted by looking at the ways in which M, K, and the other members reinterpreted and implemented the meaning of the standing. With this information taken together, I illustrate how youth climate activists grow into deliberative and revolutionary activists.

Lessons from the Field: A Story of FFF Kyoto (February–December 2021)

Two "Leaders" in a Single Group

Describing FFF Kyoto without M is almost impossible. She initiated group activities as one of the core members and as its official leader. M became a climate activist when she was a high school student. One day, her teacher invited a member of FFF Kyoto as a guest speaker, which inspired M to participate in FFF Kyoto's climate protests. In late 2020, the leader at that time asked her to take over his position, and she accepted. She then *worked* as an official leader of FFF Kyoto, serving up until the end of 2021. Here, I used the term "work" precisely because it fits perfectly to describe what she did as the official leader. She was in charge of recruiting new members, communicating with old and new members on a regular basis to manage the group, and, together with K (to be described later), shaping and defining what FFF Kyoto should look like. She has a strong sense of responsibility, so she sometimes worked until midnight to create information materials for the upcoming group meetings even though she had many homework assignments. No matter how busy M was, she almost always participated in the standing in 2021, holding a handmade placard with a white bear on it (figure 7.2). I usually did not know who would come to the standing on Friday before it started, but I felt sure that M would come, because she was always there before I arrived.[7]

Figure 7.2. M's placard. *Source*: Photo by the author.

Doing such extraordinary works (as both a leader of FFF Kyoto and a university student) was so challenging that another key person, K, usually supported M's work. While M had been asked directly to take over the position of the official leader of FFF Kyoto by the previous leader, many members recognized K's informal leadership within the group, from which he became another key person. K used to be a university student in the Tokyo area, but he dropped out of university and had been attending university abroad since mid-2021, as his first university experience amid COVID-19 gave him far less intellectual curiosity than he had expected. Compared to other core members, K had various unique experiences when it came to the environment and politics. For instance, he was the only person who had participated in a climate march in an overseas country (UK), his grandmother lived in an area surrounded by rich nature, and he used to be a core member of FFF Japan.[8]

One of K's key "works" within FFF Kyoto was to communicate regularly and closely with M to manage the group effectively. They worked at the same part-time workplace and discussed plans and concerns for their regular FFF Kyoto meetings during lunch breaks. Both M and K were dedicated to group management partially because they had shared the same negative experience when they initially joined FFF Kyoto. According to M, when she had first attended an FFF Kyoto meeting, she felt uneasy and uncomfortable because, from her point of view, there was no room for dialogue. She said, "We . . . original members were not so friendly. There were only four members at that time. They had different personalities and different ways of thinking. They were all very smart, but I felt pressured because they thought that we had to only say the right thing. I felt very nervous. They were logical, and their answers were usually correct. But such logical conversation made me feel a bit tired" (interview, March 30, 2021).[9] This experience prodded M to create a safe space within the group where other members could feel comfortable during communication.[10] If M failed to deal with a problem in the group, K tried to address it. For example, when M facilitated the regular meeting, K worked as a shadow facilitator pointing out overlooked comments made by other members or asking questions of members who did not talk much. K's assistive contribution was recognized by other members, particularly newcomers, which established the base of his leadership in the group. One of the members, R, recalled a story about the role K played during the meeting as follows:

Just up until a few months ago, when we introduced ourselves during the meeting, we said how long we had belonged to the group. This was our habit. But we stopped it because K said we shouldn't do this. This habit might create an atmosphere that "longer membership is better." He said we are equal regardless of how long or short we have belonged to FFF. . . . Well, he notices a lot of things that we don't, and he really can see things from multiple angles. He is very sensitive and has a broader perspective. (interview, April 15, 2021)

Thanks to M and K's efforts for creating a safe space in the group, the number of members of FFF Kyoto increased, which fueled their collective motivation for further political and protestive actions in the public sphere. From mid-2020 to the beginning of 2021, while still doing the standing protest each week, they organized and participated in an official meeting with the mayor of Kyoto city and held a series of online activities such as the digital march and youth meeting (Generation Z's Kyoto Conference), where more than 20 high school and university students gathered and deliberated.

Interestingly, and in contrast to the assumption of researchers who apply Greta framing, most new members joined FFF Kyoto at this time with reasons that had nothing to do with Greta. I interviewed members about their motivation for participation, and what they explained in common was their apolitical school experience. They said that even though they were interested in political issues, they had to avoid political conversations with their friends because they often felt that talking about politics in school was a kind of unspoken taboo. T, one of the core members, for example, said, "My friends aren't interested in politics, so we don't talk about it. They like talking about pop singers rather than politics. But I don't like talking about pop singers, because I feel this is a waste of time. But I often feel that there is an atmosphere where you aren't allowed to talk about politics unless you are knowledgeable" (interview, May 12, 2021).

When T participated in FFF Kyoto activities, he felt that he had finally found a space for political talk. T continued, "In FFF, our conversation begins with a topic about ourselves. We share recent updates, what we have thought about, what we have experienced these days. . . . Then someone reinterprets the experiences from a political perspective, saying, 'Maybe your experience can be reworded as this and that political issue.'"

Like T, many members joined FFF Kyoto around this period with a wide range of political concerns that did not directly relate to climate change, including veganism, animal rights, gender, poverty, or refugee problems.[11] They nurtured their political concerns and interests in their everyday settings and then decided to join FFF Kyoto in order to find a space for deepening their understanding of the topics and exchanging political opinions. This means that, unlike the general expectation of researchers, Greta-like emotions such as anger, grief, and anxiety were not a key driving force in their activism engagement. This by no means implies that they did not care about climate change issues at all. They took climate change into account and always situated it at the heart of their activity, but they did so because, for many of them, the term "climate change" served as an umbrella term encapsulating their diversity of political concerns and creating their common ground. For many members, FFF Kyoto enabled them to continue to deepen their individual political concerns and practices through their active involvement in discussion of climate change. FFF Kyoto was a kind of sanctuary they had been seeking.

THE STANDING

Because, as noted above, many members joined FFF Kyoto with different political interests and concerns, they brought a variety of signs to the standing. One participant held a sign with a message calling for more veganism, another participant questioned the government's COVID-19 policy, and more recently some members brought a signboard about floods in developing countries for the purpose of consciousness-raising. Some signs had a QR code so that passer-by could learn more details about FFF Kyoto. Other signs featured a message encouraging young people to vote (figure 7.3). Regardless of these different messages, M and K (and other members) respected members' varieties of political interests and even encouraged them to bring their own political concerns and interests to the fore in the standing.

Social media platforms, especially Twitter and Instagram, were important means for seeing how the standing went every Friday. Every time after the standing, FFF Kyoto's social media team posted their group photo on the social media platform with the text "Week X" (X refers to the number of weeks they continued to engage in the standing) coupled with some hashtags (e.g., #COP26, #SaveOurPlanet). In my observations

Figure 7.3. Various types of cardboard placard. *Source*: Photo by the author.

of the social media posts from mid-2019 to early 2020, there were 4–10 young people who participated in the standing on a regular basis.

Among more than 30 local groups of FFF in Japan, only FFF Kyoto has continued the standing every week. M and K's effort is obviously a key factor. With their efforts to create a space and opportunities for members to exchange opinions and talk about politics freely, other members were able to feel connected even in the pandemic situation, thereby sustaining their solidarity. They acted as climate activists; but unlike the general pervasive image of youth climate activism represented by Greta, what characterized their daily and weekly political action was mostly laughter and enjoyment, rather than anger or anxiety.[12] At least until mid-April 2021, there were more than 15 young people and students (including several junior high school students) who joined the standing. M often described this period as "the best atmosphere in which we felt that we were on the right track."

CLIMATE MARCH UNDER THE STATE OF EMERGENCY

On April 22, 2021, the US president Joe Biden convened 40 world leaders in the online Leaders' Summit on Climate. They discussed how to find a way to collaboratively deal with the coming climate crisis and announced their vision for emission reduction, called the Nationally Determined Contribution (NDC). Many environmental activist groups in Japan, including local FFFs, demanded that the Japanese government cut emissions at least 62 percent below 2013 levels by 2030.[13] To pressure the Japanese government into accepting this target goal, it was decided in FFF Japan's regular meeting that local FFF groups would hold a simultaneous protesting action on the same day of the Leaders' Summit. Echoing this decision, members of FFF Kyoto decided to organize a massive climate protest march in Kyoto city, planning to mobilize more than 300 people. For M, the value of this climate march was more than putting political pressure on the government. M said that the climate march could strengthen solidarity among members of FFF Kyoto. Because, as mentioned above, many members at that time shared the feeling that "we were on the right track," M thought that the experience of organizing the climate march could provide members greater confidence and inspire them to engage in further protest actions in the future. She planned to organize the climate march and then step down from her position as a leader of FFF so that other members could shape the movement more freely and actively.

A day before the climate march, I was invited to FFF Kyoto's regular meeting on Zoom starting at 8:00 p.m. There were 13 high school and university students, along with three invited adult citizens (including myself) who supported FFF Kyoto. As usual, we introduced ourselves and did a check-in (see note 10). Then we started a discussion focused on a "safe climate march in the COVID-19 situation," including topics such as whether we would use a megaphone, how to keep social distance, who would bring antiseptic, and so forth.

In the middle of the meeting, K screamed out, interrupting our discussion in dismay: "Wait . . . oh . . . what!? Oh no. The government just declared a state of emergency!" A state of emergency is neither a legal restriction on going outside nor a hard lockdown. It puts restrictions on "nonessential" activities such as traveling or dining out. Many members felt that they were back to square one, because they needed to define whether the climate march could be "essential." K suggested that we should continue the discussion, and everyone agreed. However, the discussion was more challenging and controversial than K expected, because members were divided with respect to their interpretation of the meaning of "essential" and "nonessential." Some members including the other two adult citizens were afraid of receiving unnecessary public criticism. They pointed out that going on the climate march as originally planned under the state of emergency might fuel citizens' feeling of opposition, because many citizens would see the protest as "unnecessary" and "nonessential." These members thought that it might be difficult to hold other actions in the future if many citizens developed a feeling of opposition to FFF Kyoto. Their suggestion was postponement of the march.

A few members, however, expressed a strong objection to this suggestion. For instance, one said, "FFF is a movement that should not be influenced by how the public thinks and feels. I personally want to do the climate march and express our claim even in the state of emergency without worrying about the eyes of the public." M and K struggled to find a way to reconcile the two opposite opinions. They continued to collect opinions and concrete suggestions from the members. Some suggested a photo-based visual march (e.g., each participant takes a photo that represents their claim and posts it on social media with a hashtag), and others proposed using umbrellas to ensure the appropriate social distance between each participant during the march. Still, M and K were not able to find a better solution, and finally K muttered in a quiet voice as if he had given up, "Well . . . we may have to postpone it."

However, the pro-march members held onto the idea of doing the climate march and asked K to continue the discussion and find a better way forward. Around 20 minutes later, one member proposed the idea of a two-person march. In her opinion, a march consisting of only two persons would not be much different from going for a walk. It would be less likely to be criticized by the public and would still constitute the climate march as scheduled. This suggestion, albeit less perfect than the original marching plan, struck many members as convincing idea as it could be located in-between the two sides. Hence, everyone agreed to the two-person march, which could be one of the smallest protest marches in the history of social movements in Japan.

The matter of who would carry out the two-person march was uncontroversial. It was decided quickly and naturally without any candidates except for M and K. K then asked other members to share their thoughts about ways for making the two-person march as inclusive as possible. One member suggested bringing one of FFF Kyoto's banners featuring images of many handprints representing the support of nonpresent members, and everyone agreed. We then circulated tweets and messages to potential participants announcing the two-person march.

On next afternoon, we gathered in front of the Kyoto prefectural head office building. Some other activists, mostly senior activists, gathered as well, because they had missed the announcement that the march would be done by two representatives. M and K explained that the march would be conducted with two persons, and some expressed a strong objection (although a majority accepted it). K and M asked me to be a photographer during the march, so, while writing fieldnotes, I took more than 300 photos before, during, and after the march. What follows is an excerpt from my fieldnotes:

> A few minutes before the march, a group of police[14] began to gather. Because FFF had originally planned to organize a rather massive protest march (N = 300+), there were more than 10 police officers ready to make sure the protestors walked the predetermined route. They seemed a bit surprised when M and K let them know that the march would be done by two persons. A senior police officer said, "Are you really sure? You can do the march with more people." Police officers rarely speak to protestors in such a gentle manner because, for many of them, such security tasks are an unwelcome addition to their already packed schedules. Even though they wore a mask, I sensed a somewhat pitying sentiment from the police officer's eyes and tone of voice.
>
> . . . The march started. M and K started walking slowly. No laughter. No smiles. No chants or rallies. No conversation between them. They just walked. Six police officers in front of M and K, four behind them, and six newspaper reporters (one of whom had brought a stepladder) followed the march. It seemed like a small protest march because the "real" protestors were just M and K. A passerby asked me, "What's this?" Both M and K did not express emotion, stared straight ahead, and continued to walk, very slowly. . . . We finally reached the destination, Yasaka Shrine.
>
> The police officers went back to their office once their job was finished. Only one newspaper reporter walked with us (I was not sure when the others came back). A young

man wearing a black shirt also followed us from the middle of the march, and he said that "the government has just set a 46 percent reduction target."[15] K just said "alright" in a small voice, then quietly wept, without speaking. (fieldnotes, April 22, 2021; see also figure 7.4)

While the climate march took place as planned, for members (especially for M and K), the process and outcome were by no means satisfactory. After the march, we went back to the Kyoto prefectural head office building to pick up our bicycles. I observed dark expressions on the students' faces and their silence. Yes, they had done the march—but it was very different from what they had envisaged 24 hours earlier.

AFTER THE MARCH

The state of emergency continued for around three months. To avoid some risks (including criticism by the public), the members decided not to do the standing protest during the state of emergency. Thus, FFF Kyoto's

Figure 7.4. Two-person climate protest march and a banner with handprint images. *Source*: Photo by the author.

activities amid the state of emergency were confined only to their online-based regular meeting. Some members were, however, less motivated to participate even in the meeting in part because they felt that the power M and K held was so consolidated that they hesitated to give opinions freely or displayed a reserved attitude.

Between May and June, M and K visited my office separately and expressed their worries about FFF Kyoto. For example, I recorded the following in my field notes:

> M was worried about the future of FFF Kyoto. She often said that "I should have retired from the leader position immediately after the march," but she thought that she messed up its timing. She asked herself whether it would be desirable for FFF Kyoto for her to continue to be its leader. She was especially worried that, after the march, her presence and her continued leadership inevitably boosted her influence within the group. This was far from what she had expected. (fieldnotes, May 19, 2021)

K shared a similar anxiety when he visited my office in June. His concern was the power he inevitably owned within the group. It was almost always either K or M who started the discussion. Also, when K spoke in the meeting, his opinion influenced the way other members thought. They always agreed with him, and no one offered a counteropinion. He said that this was acceptable in its own right, but their conversation became inevitably centralized and uncritical.[16] Before the two-person climate march, M and K took the initiative to schedule and implement their regular meetings. At that time, their meetings functioned quite well precisely because M and K supported each other and tried to connect the group's meetings with their concrete actions in the public sphere. In short, members could feel a kind of efficacy in that their opinions were used for vitalizing their collective action. After the march, however, members temporarily lost opportunities to take concrete action in the public sphere, and the only activity they could do was to join the regular meeting. Gradually, their motivation decreased, while M and K's presence at the meetings grew. As a result, M and K felt strong anxiety about their power and presence when the meetings took place, because they thought that their presence per se accelerated the disfunction of the meeting.

As one misfortune followed another, M confronted a significant challenge: K left Japan to study abroad. In August, K entered an overseas university and had to concentrate on his first-year experience. As a result, M had to cope with a lot of "work," including group management and meeting organizing without K's support. As indicated, she was quite a responsible person, so she tried to generate conversations with other members in a more active way than before. When the state of emergency ended, she participated in the standing almost every week and tried to reestablish solidarity within the group. Nonetheless, she worried about her power potentially preventing other members from deliberating freely and meaningfully.

As a result of the faltering atmosphere within the group, some members gradually became less involved in FFF Kyoto's activities. This was exemplified in the standing. Before the march, there were more than 15 members who participated in the standing on Fridays. When the standing was held for the first time after the state of emergency, there were only four participants. On October 1, only M (and myself) attended the standing, and, moreover, on October 8, there were no participants except for me. When I had an online conversation with M and K, they said that many of the members had gradually lost motivation for their involvement in FFF Kyoto's activities, as the stagnation of activities had prevented them from maintaining a concrete vision of what FFF Kyoto should do now and in the future.

Connecting Again

LIt became obvious from M's point of view that the ties between members of FFF Kyoto were becoming weaker, and M herself felt pressured by this. When she visited my office on October 5, she showed an ambivalent attitude toward FFF Kyoto, saying, "I recently felt double identities: 'me in FFF Kyoto' and 'me and FFF Kyoto.'" On one hand, she felt that she should be responsible for managing FFF Kyoto as its leader (otherwise, she thought that the group was not working out), but on the other hand, she wanted to distance herself mentally and physically because she felt that her engagement was too burdensome.[17] For M, therefore, regaining members' connection was an urgent task. She thought that the key to changing the atmosphere within the group was to recreate a space where members could hold discussions together with few restrictions, like they had during the active deliberations of the pre-march period. Particularly because FFF Kyoto's activities were stagnated by members' low motivation, M believed that having conversations together and defining their common terms and concepts would help members to create a common and shared foundation, thereby building a sense of togetherness.

One day, during a text chat with M, I mentioned a dialogue event (called a philosophical dialogue workshop) that I planned to organize a few weeks later. Philosophical dialogue is a dialogue method in which the purpose is neither to make a final agreement nor to determine a winner/loser but to deepen our understanding of an open-ended philosophical question (e.g., What is a friend? What is the purpose of life?) through a dialogue anchored by reason-exchange and mutual-questioning.[18] Participants do not need to decide a specific plan for action or reach a particular conclusion. Instead, in philosophical dialogue, the core purpose is the process of thinking itself, so participants do not need to feel decision-making pressure. M was interested in philosophical dialogue, because the method was different from what FFF Kyoto's members did in their weekly meetings. M found such free dialogue attractive, because she thought that it had the potential to neutralize her power within the group and, at the same time, free her from the leadership pressure.

Soon after our text chat, M decided to organize FFF Kyoto's first in-group philosophical dialogue workshop at their meeting and asked some members to participate in it (I served as a facilitator). I asked the members to share their own philosophical questions, and we selected one from the question pool. I initially assumed that they would select a climate-related question, but they did not. Many members voted for the question "What is a human?" We spent more than two hours in deliberation on this question, mainly examining the differences between animate and inanimate beings, subjective and objective understanding of humans, humans and society, humans and humanity, and a human in a society and a human on a desert island. Interestingly, the most active speaker that day was a female member (N) who normally did not actively engage in their regular meetings.

Because both M and other members found the philosophical dialogue interesting and enjoyable, they decided to organize a second philosophical dialogue workshop the following week. The question they selected was "What is education for social change?" and they also discussed this question for more than two hours. More interestingly, the experience of dialogue influenced their concrete movement design and plan. During the Global Days for Climate Action (October 2021) in which many FFF groups across the world engage in simultaneous protesting actions for climate justice, many Japanese local FFFs planned to conduct a specific form of protesting action in the public sphere (e.g., standing, climate march). However, FFF Kyoto decided not to be in line with this trend and instead organized its third philosophical dialogue workshop, named Philosophy for Future, to which it invited nonmembers. On social media, they emphasized the significance of not conducting a substantive political action like the other local groups, noting that "in order to continue the movement, we now need to establish solidarity through open dialogue by bringing different values, ways of thinking, and attitudes about climate change."

At the workshop, T (one of the core members and a leader of FFF Kyoto since 2022), not M, facilitated the dialogue, which enabled participants to feel the special nature of the meeting. After the event, members continued to run the philosophical dialogue workshop on a regular basis, and it was utilized as a social space where members (and nonmembers) could communicate together. Again, in these workshops, the participants did not make any decisions. They just talked together.

In addition to the philosophical dialogue workshops, FFF Kyoto's regular in-group activities began to include more dialogue opportunities. The integration of multiple meetings is one example of this. FFF Kyoto originally had two types of weekly meeting: a preparatory meeting in which a few core members (normally four members) reported on each other's work and plans for what to discuss in the general meeting, and the general meeting in which all members (10+) participated in the discussion and made decisions about the group's actions. Around October, M unified key functions of the preparatory meeting and the general meeting and renamed the integrated meeting the "management meeting." One day, I asked M about why she had done this. She answered, "Well . . . we need more management than preparation. I mean . . . what we need at this point is not to prepare for substantive climate action but to make our group comfortable so that each member can become more connected" (fieldnotes, January 27, 2022).

Unifying the two meetings also contributed to democratization of the decision-making process within the group. In the past, the meeting agenda was mostly determined in the preparatory meeting, whereas now all members were allowed to bring their desires, expectations, and demands to the discussion table. As a result, all members had a chance to have a say about shaping the movement, and previously less engaged members gradually came back to the meetings and gave suggestions. One suggestion that was made and accepted in the new-style meeting was to reduce the time for the standing protest. For some high school and university students, taking time out of their packed schedule to regularly attend the one-hour standing was not a high priority, and therefore one member proposed to reduce the time for standing so that more members (and nonmembers) would find it easier to participate. All members including M accepted this proposal, and they decided to do the standing for 30 minutes starting the following week. What was important not only for M but also for other members was to revitalize (or "reactivate" in K's terms) FFF Kyoto in a way that created an environment for members' reconnection.

FRONTSTAGE, BACKSTAGE, AND WINGS OF THE STAGE

With the gradual change of members' relationships, the standing protest also changed its meaning and nature. The most immediate change was the quality of conversation during the standing. When I started my ethnographic research with FFF Kyoto in February 2021, what characterized their standing protest was its critical character, where more than 10 participants exchanged up-to-date ideas on political topics (e.g., each country's situation concerning climate policy) and discussed a variety of political themes such as the climate crisis or global injustice. Eight months later, however, this critical aspect of the standing had become relatively dormant, and instead they engaged in more social as well as everyday forms of conversation:

> Today, members still had casual conversation topics, such as stories about their school or information about a café they had recently been to. Two high schoolers bought a stuffed fish and brought it to the standing. They and T took a photo of the stuffed fish holding their sign. When they took the photos, they even turned their backs on passer-by. . . . Their sign showed a critical message, but probably, unlike the message, "fun" and "enjoyment" might be the best words that characterized what they did during the standing. (fieldnotes, December 10, 2021)

As explained, the standing originally started by Greta is a symbolic activity for many FFFs. Many people create and justify a widely shared narrative of "activists who feel strong anxiety about their future and get angry with political elites' inaction" *because* youth climate activists do the standing (Goldman 2022). Yet members of FFF Kyoto attached a different meaning to their standing protest. For them, standing served not just as a means for sharing their claims and emotions, but also as a means for *reconnection* by which members who were about to fall away from the group gradually regained a sense of togetherness through in-group dialogue and an effort at making their activity fun. By participating in the standing, they confirmed each other's presence and felt a sense of solidarity, which they had failed to achieve over the past five months.

As Christoph Haug (2013) tellingly illustrated, one of the key functions of activist meetings is to create and sustain members' social relationships. The presence of well-functioning meetings within an activist group fosters members' formal as well as informal communications and strengthens their sense of "togetherness." In the case of FFF Kyoto, however, the presence of M and K inevitably reinforced the power relations among members, which prevented other members from establishing social relationships in Haug's sense. Importantly, this was not M and K's fault. As a result of context-responsive development of the movement, certain individuals can inevitably play a core role in order to sustain the movement, and this is not a rare phenomenon (e.g., Gerbaudo 2012; Haug and Rucht 2013). In any case, the regular meeting was not enough for FFF Kyoto's members to maintain solidarity. Members, including M and K, sought opportunities for more social, interactive, and open spaces than their regular meeting, and the standing, where many members come together in person, gradually took over this social role within the movement. One day, T and I had a conversation during the standing, and he explained this social aspect of the standing as follows:

> AUTHOR: What does the standing mean for Fridays?

> T: We are now under the COVID situation. In the standing, someone is coming here physically, not virtually, and we can meet them. This is most important for me. When we can see in person, we can hear their voice, we can know each other. Actually, today I talked with them and know a lot of new things.

> AUTHOR: How is it different from your regular meeting?

> T: Well, the online meeting has a structure. We can of course talk relatively freely, but there is a topic and agenda to be discussed. There is a facilitator. There are minutes. So our talk goes in a particular direction. The standing is different. Our talk in the standing is super casual. We can talk about whatever we want. (fieldnotes, December 10, 2021)

T also said that their meetings were less social than the standing because of the meeting platform (Zoom). On Zoom, everyone's face is on the screen, and it is clear who is the speaker and who is going to speak. From his point of view, there is no opportunity for any kind of chit-chat or a quick, casual conversation between members on Zoom. However, when members' desire for something more social fermented in their meeting, coupled with various dialogue opportunities introduced by M, there was a growing momentum for dialogue among members, leading them to gradually come back to the standing and start talking with each other. Around the end of 2021, some members came to the standing after six months, and others said that they just wanted to talk to members in person and rejoined the standing. The number of members who participated in the standing at that time was still not as many as before the march (approximately 5–7 people). However, this was neither because FFF Kyoto lacked continuity nor because the organizing capacity was insufficient. Some members restarted or continued to engage in the standing because the meaning of their standing had changed from a space for protest to a space for *talking* and *connecting*. In January 2022, T took over the role as a leader from M, and then I undertook the second formal interview with T. In the interview, he obviously recognized how the meaning of the standing had been transformed from "protest" to "reconnection." He said:

> In the middle of the COVID pandemic, our meetings were online-only, as you know. The online meeting forced us to be on online, and it could not take place offline. I think this was a bad aspect of the online meeting, because we could not see each other's faces and feel each other's presence. In the standing, we can always meet in real time and see someone's face at a certain time and place. Even if we do not talk to everyone, we can feel like Friday is here. This does not make a direct and good influence on the social change, you know. But after seeing each other in the standing, the atmosphere of our meeting becomes more friendly and open, and we can gain a sense of belonging. (interview, July 1, 2022)

Some other members even described the standing at that time as "a casual meeting where we exchange information, know each other and confirm our connection" and indicated that "the more someone engages in the standing with a clear-cut protest purpose, the more they withdraw from

FFF Kyoto because there is a gap between what they want to do and what is happening in reality" (fieldnotes, December 26, 2021).

As already noted, FFF Kyoto is almost the only group among the Japanese local FFF groups that has continued to engage in the standing protest every Friday. When seen through the "Greta framing" perspective, this fact can generally be interpreted as follows: Compared to other local groups, FFF Kyoto's members are more concerned and dedicated about climate justice, angrier with their political elites and more anxious about their future, which has jointly fueled their motivation for continuing the standing. Yet viewed in light of the above stories, this interpretation turns out to be misleading. Like other local groups, FFF Kyoto faced a few periods of stagnation in its activities due to the endless challenges of climate change and the pandemic. Nonetheless, group members continued their activities in the public sphere, not because they were emotionally motivated, but because they brought their dialogue culture back to the group and transformed the meaning of the standing in response to the changing situation of COVID-19. The crucial difference between FFF Kyoto and other local groups lay not in the amount of enthusiasm and emotions (e.g., climate grief, climate anxiety) but in the degree to which the dialogue culture and opportunities for connection was shared within the group.

Let us locate this argument within the existing academic field. As one of the recent trends in social movement studies, scholars use the *stage* analogy to interpret the meaning of a movement. In this account, visible and observable protesting activities in the public sphere (e.g., demonstrations, marching, public speeches) are labelled as the *frontstage*, while publicly invisible activities (e.g., meetings, in-group workshops, reading groups) are understood as the *backstage*. The key focal point of empirical study is the interplay between the frontstage and backstage so as to capture the overarching understanding of the meaning of the movement (Haug 2013; della Porta and Rucht 2013a; see also Polletta 2002). According to existing research, in backstage activities, protestors set common objectives, make decisions about how they will protest in the public sphere, and plan how people with different values will work together to achieve their common goals. In this sense, a movement's backstage anchors the quality of its frontstage activity.

These previous studies shed light on power and deliberation within the social movement; and yet the story of FFF Kyoto can further the research in that it alludes to the presence of a third element of the social movement in addition to the frontstage/backstage. At the beginning of my fieldwork, FFF Kyoto's standing had a frontstage function in the sense that it provided members with opportunities to bring their political voices and demands to the fore. Even though they seemingly continued to behave in the same way on the street for a year, they reinterpreted and transformed the purpose and meaning of the standing from a protesting opportunity to a space for communicating together more casually than at their meetings, recognizing one another's presence and bringing their collective identity of FFF Kyoto back to their interpersonal connections. The standing was practiced on the street in a publicly visible way, but it no longer functioned as the frontstage as defined by researchers (Haug 2013; della Porta and Rucht 2013b). In this sense, the standing was transformed into *a boundary-crossing activity* where activists on the front-stage (street) engaged in an extension of backstage activity (e.g., identity formation, group solidarity, in-group communication). Taking the stage analogy, this kind of boundary-crossing activity within the movement shall provisionally be labeled as the *wings of the stage*[19]—the third element of democratic dynamics within a movement. The standing as the wings of the stage was practiced as part of the activists' frontstage activity, while it was also a kind of activity with the aim of bringing members' connection back to their movement. The latter aspect was mostly invisible to the audience.

Note that, however, that the wings of the stage does not mean that FFF Kyoto became less involved in issues about the climate crisis. What changed, especially during the post-march period, was not their attitude toward the climate crisis but the way in which members interpreted the meaning of their movement and (re)defined their collective identity as climate activists. For them, the climate crisis was a long-term challenge, and it was highly unclear when this challenge would be addressed by global society. Such uncertainty, combined with the COVID-19 pandemic, necessitated a rethinking of whether they would accept the status quo or seek to change the nature of their movement. As a result of this reflection process, they redesigned the stage where they acted to continue their political engagement on the issue of climate crisis. In the newly inter-preted stage, they crafted the wings of the stage in the standing protest so that previously almost disconnected members could share a sense of togetherness again and thereby remain as climate activists in the changing public sphere.

Implications for Deliberative Democratic Learning

The classroom is not the only space where learners can experience deliberation. From a systemic perspective of deliberative democracy, acknowledging diverse forms of deliberation is more important than seeking the best possible deliberation. Yet although classrooms often fail to provide students with an opportunity for the best deliberation as part of the curricular activity, this does not mean that democratic education faces defeat. There are varieties of deliberative learning opportunities outside the classroom, and some of them are rarely experienced within the confines of the classroom.

As emphasized in chapter 2, deliberative democratic learning is a systemic practice. As increasingly more children and young people today are politically active in a deliberative system, it is time for democratic education to leave "classroomism." This section will therefore consider how the above story of FFF Kyoto speaks to deliberative democratic learning. More specifically, how is youth climate activists' experience of deliberation similar to and different from students' experience of deliberation in the classroom?

Let us first consider some similarities of classroom deliberation described in part 2 and activists' deliberation. Both include revolutionary, reflective, and collective transformative practices through reexamination and reconstruction of the meaning of existing practice and habit of deliberation, as well as collective implementation of newly interpreted practice. In both the classroom and activist groups, whether each individual becomes knowledgeable and capable of doing something is not a fundamental matter of consideration, because, from the standpoint of Vygotskian psychology, a capacity is something that is not possessed within an individual's mind but mutually shared within the relationship between individuals. Viewed in this light, what is of importance for learners is to become *collectively* capable of crafting the most appropriate democratic environment through collective analysis and reexamination of various conditions under which they deliberate.

Here, a critical and reflective examination about contextualized enabling and inhibiting factors plays an essential role. Through this, learners gain clearer understandings of key conflicts between what prevents their democratic engagement and what plays an essential role in facilitating further deliberation. However, compared to classroom deliberation, social movement is not always bound by deliberative norms. Nor do activist groups usually have rich deliberative conditions such as anteroom deliberation or the presence of an experienced and skilled facilitator who keeps the participants' deliberation on track. Given that, how can youth climate activists grow into deliberative democratic learners?

Ambiguity of the context with which activists have to cope is a possible answer. The cultural, economic, social, and political context that an activist group faces, challenges, and examines is generally broader and more uncertain than those addressed in classroom deliberation. Climate change, symbolically situated at the heart of the FFF movement, is one example of this. The meaning of "solving climate change" can change precariously depending on specific timings (e.g., timing of NDC declaration or specific events such as Global Days for Climate Action).

This does not mean that climate change is an unsolvable problem. As Dryzek (2005) analyzed, varieties of discourses about climate change exist in the field of climate governance, and each discourse is underpinned by different angles of framing the issue, different claim-makers, and different rhetoric, which lead to the coexistence of multiple interpretations of what climate change is and how it should be addressed. Therefore, youth climate activists have to choose one from this diverse mixture of discourses in the climate governance setting to make sense of their activities or sometimes to transform the nature of their actions to adapt to certain discourses.

Furthermore, how to unite members with different sociopolitical interests under the name of climate justice is a contextual question being recurrently examined, especially when, as in FFF Kyoto, for example, a new member who has a stronger interest in subthemes related to climate change (e.g., gender inequality, immigration, poverty, animal rights) is joining the group. Activists also must respond to the global COVID-19 pandemic, a situation that is as uncertain and unpredictable as climate change. Consequently, unlike students in classroom deliberation, youth climate activists inevitably have to deal with various uncertain and changing contextual factors and reinterpret the nature of their actions; otherwise, their movement will soon come to an end.

In face of these unforeseeable broader contextual challenges, activists have to employ varieties of survival strategies such as reframing the scope of the context[20] or adjusting the movement's raison d'être to the changing context. FFF Kyoto took the latter strategy, and their adaptation to the changing context was sometimes quite drastic. As exemplified by the two-person march and the innovation of the wings of the stage in the standing, members of FFF Kyoto tried to survive in an uncertain situation even by reducing the critical and protesting edge that originally characterized the FFF movement. Importantly, however, this collective transformation of the movement and reflective adaptation to the changing context did not come out of nothing. M's leadership is a key to understand how collective transformation and reflective adaptation are possible, although the meaning of "leadership" is different from the conventional one.

When we hear the term "social movement's leader," what comes to mind is a symbolic figure on the frontstage, such as Emma González or Greta Thunberg, who represent their movement's collective identity. As a symbol of the movement, such a leader engages in various contentious actions intended to frame the issue, gather supporters, create social as well as institutional connections, and present the movement's potential to the broader public, thereby continuing and vitalizing the movement. On some occasions, however, the leader confronts unforeseeable challenges (e.g., the COVID-19 pandemic) that force her to adjust or change the movement's framing and purposes. In doing so, the leader has to take a backstage leadership role that is different from the frontstage leadership. That is, the leader has to encourage members to collaboratively redefine "what the movement ought to be," build new collective identities to motivate them and avoid high dropout rates, and then stimulate the movement to go forward in response to the changing situation. In short, the backstage leadership is anchored by the leader's efforts to create and maintain various types of horizontal connectivity (see chapter 6) within the movement. Without such leadership, the movement becomes a group of sheep without a shepherd that sooner or later withdraws from the public sphere.

As Haug (2013, 709) notes, the leader on the frontstage is not always the same as that on the backstage. This applies to FFF Kyoto too, at least when I started this ethnography. As mentioned, until mid-April, M served as an official frontstage leader of FFF Kyoto, while K was a key person who initiated and facilitated their backstage activities such as weekly meetings. However, with the experience of the two-person march, shutdown of their frontstage activities, and K's withdrawal from the group, M had to take on different leadership roles alone, both frontstage and backstage. At the beginning, she found it difficult to distinguish her different roles frontstage and backstage. She sometimes brought her power consolidated on the frontstage onto the backstage and, as a result, widened the gap between her and other members or caused them to feel isolated from the group. However, she gradually shifted the focal point of her leadership toward rebuilding and improving members' sense of connection and made various efforts to create less structured *social* spaces (e.g., the wings of the stage) within the political movement.

Such social space is underpinned by the practice of youth activists' unadulterated and unstructured deliberation happening on an everyday basis, or what Anna Tanasoca calls *naturalized* deliberation. According to Tanasoca (2020, ch. 4), naturalized deliberation is a form of networked deliberation, or a discursive chain, in which opinions, information, and reasons provided by each individual citizen are linked together in a sequential and unorganized manner through social and institutionalized networks of people. Within this discursive chain, people can, whether directly or indirectly, know each other's ways of thinking and sometimes find new connections with others and the wider public sphere.

In FFF Kyoto, members formed a discursive chain through various (in)formal practices of communication such as pre-march meetings, the two-person march, conversations between M and K, and philosophical or dialogue workshops. The standing then became one symbolic space where these different forms of communication were associated. The chains of communicative practices loosely formulated the common ground of FFF Kyoto and became a source of their collective interpretation of what FFF Kyoto ought to look like. Within the discursive chain, not all members deliberated together at the same time. Rather, each member communicated in a different setting within the chain. Yet as far as they engaged in the chain of communication, they indirectly became part of the process of creation of their common ground.

Due to their engagement in this naturalized deliberation, they crafted the wings of the stage in their movement, connected with one another, maintained their identity as FFF Kyoto, and continued to act as youth climate activists in the public sphere—which was not achieved by most other local groups of Japanese FFFs. FFF Kyoto's naturalized delibera-tion was different from a designed (meta-)deliberation in the classroom: nonetheless, they allowed new culture and habits of communication to take root in the heart of their activity through continued participation in naturalized deliberation for six months. As a result, they transformed the nature of their movement collectively and presented new ways of surviving in the changing situation as youth climate activists.

The key to understanding M's leadership in FFF Kyoto lies in the fact of the creation of a facilitative environment for naturalized deliberation. M exerted her leadership not by actively becoming involved in members' communication (like the involved facilitator in chapter 5), because she knew that her direct involvement could run the risk of reinforcing her power and putting unnecessary pressure on other members. Instead, she redesigned the structure of the group's regular practice (e.g., the standing, philosophical dialogue workshop) in a way that intentionally reduced its protesting edge and instead brought its social aspect to the fore, thereby facilitating members' naturalized deliberation in an indirect manner.

Viewed in this light, naturalized deliberation does not happen naturally, at least in the context of an activist group. In order to generate a climate for naturalized deliberation within the movement, neither charismatic leadership on the frontstage nor involved facilitative leadership on the backstage is sufficient: what is more important is a facilitative task-sharer (see chapter 5) who is skilled at enrooting habits of naturalized deliberation within the movement by stepping back from members' interactions and collaborating with other members to transform the nature of the movement in response to the changing contextual requirements as a shared task, thereby encouraging the movement's self-transformative capacity. Put differently, what makes a social movement's self-transformation possible is not leadership for contentious action but leadership for connectivity building. Without a connective leader at the center of the movement, activists may fail to grow into deliberative and revolutionary activists.

Conclusion

This chapter has discussed somewhat of a neglected aspect of activist groups—that is, the activist group as a space for practicing and learning about deliberative democracy. The fact that the activist group has neither a deliberative curriculum nor designated facilitators encourages its members to design, (re)interpret, and implement their own democratic practice, thereby learning how to practice democracy. In responding to changing contextual requirements and challenges, the movement's shared goal, the nature of its regular activity, and its strategy for surviving in the larger deliberative system have been continuously reexamined and transformed through meta-deliberations among its members. To consider this point in a more concrete manner, this chapter drew on my ethnographic study with FFF Kyoto to show how the nature and meaning of the group's main activity (standing protests) has been transformed through shared deliberative inquiry. Members' continuous meta-deliberation within the group shifted the original meaning of the standing protest as a space for contestation toward that of a space for gathering, deliberating, and (re)connecting. This chapter has argued that such meaning-making practice is itself a trigger for facilitating participants' deliberative democratic learning.

In order for meta-deliberation within the movement to work, it is necessary to reconsider the meaning of leadership. Scholars often highlight the role of strong leadership in a social movement, assuming that charismatic leaders are the key agents of the movement's success. By classifying elements of an activist group into a publicly visible frontstage activity (e.g., standing, marching) and publicly invisible backstage that gives shape to its frontstage activity (e.g., group meetings), this chapter has revealed that strong leadership on the frontstage is not necessarily equally effective backstage. On the contrary, overly assertive leadership backstage may run the risk of generating new power relations in group deliberation, and even lead to the movement's implosion. As demonstrated by the story of K and M, having different leaders for the frontstage and backstage who can share power effectively is key for the group to function as a healthy deliberative space. Alternatively, as M's efforts after K left the group to study abroad shows, it is important for the leader in the frontstage to be a task-sharer backstage so as to naturalize deliberation in the group. When these conditions were in place, FFF Kyoto functioned as a space for deliberative democratic learning, insofar as its members could engage in revolutionary, context-responsive, and collective meaning-making and learn what is not yet there.

Conclusion

Given that children have democratic agency, what should democratic education be and what forms can it take? This book has been primarily geared toward addressing this question. For a long time, the view that children have democratic agency has not been taken into account or even criticized due to the widespread assumptions of children's biological immaturity and their lack of knowledge and experience. Whether implicitly or explicitly, scholars in the democratic education camp have fallen into ablism and elitism, assuming that democracy is not open for "amateurs"—in other words, assuming that only knowledgeable, capable and mature citizens can and should legitimately contribute to democracy. In addition, with a Piagetian-inspired evolutionary view of human development, people believe that citizenship is something to be gained after the successful completion of predetermined learning steps. Taken together, these viewpoints have ensured that children are seen as *future citizens* who have to wait until they become more capable and complete all the required steps to participate in democratic processes. Democratic education has been designed and theorized accordingly.

As the deliberative turn becomes dominant in democratic theory, however, such traditional explanations of children and democracy are found to be less persuasive than before, precisely because deliberative democracy is open for all. Deliberative democracy should not be the concern only of educated and capable individuals; it is rather a macrocosm of verbal as well as nonverbal democratic communications by diverse individuals across diverse sociopolitical settings, each of whom has different capacities and makes unique contributions. As demonstrated in chapter 1, the supposed fact of children's biological immaturity no longer justifies the view that their contributions to deliberative democracy are inferior to adults, because children are *already* actively contributing to deliberative democracy's ideal, albeit in different ways and in different spaces from adults. The exclusion of children from the scope of deliberative democracy on the ground of their immaturity or lack of competence is, normatively speaking, a form of injustice and, practically speaking, a great epistemic loss for our democracy. It is time to reframe democratic education's guiding question, moving away from considerations of "what children cannot do," toward considerations of "what they can do." Only once this shift has taken place can we begin to truly democratize democratic education.

Having said that, some may object to my suggestion by indicating that democratic education research has long explored ways of situating children's agency at its heart. Of course, I fully acknowledge that existing empirical findings about practical applications of deliberative theory to educational settings show that well-designed deliberative practices develop children's deliberative capacities, agency, and knowledge, thereby helping them to become effective deliberators. Nonetheless, I would caution that the terms "effective deliberators," "deliberative capacities," and "deliberative agency" as defined by the existing studies are unilaterally theorized, framed, and defined by adults (more specifically, researchers, teachers, and parents).

Children's deliberative engagement and learning are significantly bounded by the adult gaze, and we adults usually say that "our educational practice is successful" within the scope of our own definition and framework. However, is it still *democratic* education if children have no right to define what democracy ought to be and to practice deliberation accordingly? Given that children are agents of deliberative democracy, why do they occupy a subordinate position to adults in democratic education? If democratic education is more than just a preparation for or means of adapting to what adults expect, what can children do and how should adults facilitate children's activities?

To respond to these questions, chapter 2 reconsidered the meaning of development in democratic education. I pointed out that democratic education, especially education for deliberative democracy, is implicitly based on a Piagetian-inspired psychological paradigm with respect to the meaning of development and competency, which, I also argued, has reinforced and reproduced ideas of the "creation of deliberative all-rounders as a goal of democratic education" and seeing "adults as mature citizens and children as immature future citizens." Using Vygotsky-inspired sociocultural psychology and deliberative systems theory to countertheorize democratic education, chapter 2 demonstrated that (1) guiding children to a predetermined path and thereby creating deliberative all-rounders are not the central aims of democratic education, (2) children should not be treated as mere recipients and reproducers of what adults create, because children have sufficient agency to form and refine their own norms and practices from within their sociocultural context, and (3) children can, under the appropriate learning conditions, nurture their agency differently in different spaces and in different ways. Taken together, I theorized the idea of deliberative democratic learning that is *revolutionary* (the aim of deliberative democratic learning is to enable children's agency of meaning-making) and includes elements of *reflection* and *contextuality* (deliberation and its competence should be understood as a socioculturally embedded tool that is open for reflective reinterpretation), *collective transformation* (the unit of analysis is a transformation of a process of collective engagement in meaning-making), and *systemic* practice (deliberative democratic learning occurs both in and beyond the classroom). Deliberative democratic learning is in opposition to traditional pedagogical approaches, where educators define "ideal citizens" and "necessary competencies" without reference to context and prior to the beginning of educational practice, and then expect children to behave accordingly.

We can design deliberative processes in a way that encourages children to engage in deliberation in the classroom in accordance with teacher expectations. But while such educational practice can produce good "classroom citizens" who behave democratically within the classroom and under the supervision of their teacher, it runs the risk of reinforcing their dependency on the teacher. This ultimately leads to reinforcing and justifying the existing asymmetrical relationship between children and adults in democracy. In contrast, deliberative democratic learning does not expect children to be mere consumers of the teacher's democratic norms. The revolutionary feature of deliberative democratic learning lies in an iterative process where children reflectively examine "what already exists" (e.g., existing deliberative norms, their own deliberative habits) and innovate and implement "what is not yet there" (Engeström 2016). In other words, the most important feature of deliberative democratic learning is to provide students with the opportunity to make their own meaning out of "what democracy ought to be" and decide how one's own norms of democracy should be translated into practice.

If this is right, then practical questions immediately present themselves: How can we design deliberative democratic learning in real contexts? What should deliberative democratic learning look like? In responding to such questions, what I wanted to avoid in the process of theorization was the irresponsible one-sided presentation and imposition of a scholar's ideal theory of education onto the educational field without taking its current realities into account. It is always possible to transform ideal theory into practice if there is sufficient money, human resources, and time. However, in real educational settings, ideal situations are rarely found. If one's educational theory can be achieved only in educational conditions with plenty of resources, democratic education becomes an ideal that only elites can hope to realize. A normative theory of democratic education that bypasses actual educational contexts may meet with responses like, "Well, it's theoretically gorgeous, but . . . ," and be seen as little more than stillborn theory.

For this reason, this book's value lies not only in its theoretical impetus for rethinking democratic education, but also in empirical data collected from the field. The data was gained mainly as a result of asking, "If this theory were to be put into practice, what form would it take and what would be its normative implications?" In the course of responding to this question, fieldwork was conducted with a variety of different aims, different research subjects, and in different settings, which necessitated different ways of doing qualitative research. Sometimes, I took on the role of an action researcher studying and practicing deliberation in the classroom with students of various age groups. At other times, I became an ethnographic observer who immersed myself in the field to see the underlying logic of people's behavior or the processes of meaning-making from the inside. As readers might have already noticed, my fieldwork covered a small number of cases that provided minor implications in terms of generalizability. However, an active participation in and deep observation of each case through immersion helped me discern the systemic implications of observed facts (see King, Keohane, and Verba 1994), or the conditions under which the observed phenomenon occurs. This ultimately provided me with normative implications for my study of children's democratic agency and learning.

In addition to providing these normative implications, my fieldwork also fills a theoretical research gap. Theory is an abstraction and simplification of reality, which is analogous to putting a ball inside a square box. When skillfully chosen, the ball occupies most of the box, but even a near-perfect fit will inevitably leave gaps. In the course of writing this book, it was my fieldwork that provided clues to fill such gaps and provide a more concrete perspective. For instance, this book purposefully separated the classroom from the school, which I was not able to see the ramifications of before undertaking the fieldwork. Another example is the importance of meta-deliberation. The role of meta-deliberation and its various forms and applications would not have been clear without fieldwork, but it is obviously key to generating revolutionary action in the democratic education process.

By going back and forth between theory and the field, I finally developed a comprehensive and innovative theory of deliberative democratic learning. As indicated in the introductory chapter and chapter 2, my arguments in chapters 3–7 are not the application of a ready-made theory of deliberative democratic learning. It is the other way around. The theorization of deliberative democratic learning is a result of combinations of insights from the field.

Chapter 3 and chapter 4 attempted to clarify what it means for children to take ownership of the meaning-making process in democratic education by focusing on the practice of reason-giving and listening in the classroom. Reason-giving and listening are subjects of investigation not only because they are two important components of deliberation, but also because democratic education has tended to underestimate the significance of how children internalize predetermined norms of reason-giving and listening at the expense of children's lived experience and lifeworld. These chapters then made a case for the significance of meta-deliberation as a way of avoiding excessive intervention from adults and, at the same time, encouraging children's meaning-making activities. Unlike deliberation about a specific topic (which is already conducted in many educational settings), meta-deliberation is deliberation about deliberation, wherein children deconstruct and reconstruct norms of deliberation through a critical and collaborative examination of their habits, experiences, perspectives, values, and beliefs.

Note that, however, giving such ownership of meta-deliberative meaning-making to children is different from simply adopting a laissez-faire attitude. Deliberative democratic learning cannot be achieved by simply leaving everything to children and letting them do whatever they wish. In chapter 5, I illustrated that there are at least three different ways for theorizing the ethical role that adults/facilitators can play in enabling children's deliberative democratic learning. Drawing on my experience as a facilitator of classroom deliberation with Australian students, I first examined two major facilitative ideals (involved and passive facilitation) and concluded that the ethical facilitator is neither an individual who expects children to deliberate in accordance with deliberative norms and intervenes in children's deliberative practices in a paternalistic fashion, nor an individual who puts complete trust in students' autonomous agency and listens to their deliberation from afar. Learning from John Dewey's theory of community of inquiry and the role of task-sharer, I unpacked the idea that an ethical facilitator is primarily responsible for making an intervention in the deliberative environment in which children are embedded so as to design optimal conditions for students to engage in meta-deliberative sessions, as well as be sensitive to meta-deliberative moments.

While the book dedicates half of its contents to deliberations happening in the classroom, as many democratic education scholars do, it also cautions that we should avoid "classroomism." Given that, as theorized in chapter 1, children are constantly deliberating in various spaces and in various forms across deliberative systems, there is no reason to limit their opportunity for democratic learning within the classroom. Even if some children find it difficult to deliberate in the classroom for various reasons (e.g., testimonial injustice), they can be and often are effective deliberators outside the classroom (e.g., social movements). Some children even experience and learn deliberation by bypassing classroom deliberation entirely, as there are a variety of pathways through which they may learn how to exercise their deliberative agency. The classroom is, of course, one such pathway. However, other out-of-classroom pathways also provide unique deliberative experiences for children.

In part 3 of this book, I contended that democratic education should not ignore this point; otherwise, we overlook different forms of children's deliberative agency in a deliberative system and its pedagogical implications. As part of this discussion, chapter 6 examined the deliberative democratic role that schools can play. Although people often use the term "classroom" and "school" interchangeably, I contended that children's experience in the classroom and school is conceptually as well as qualitatively distinct. As the case of the democratic school Byrd Community Academy showed, democratic schools provide children not only with learning opportunities in the classroom but also with political and social experiences. Democratic schools can coordinate their educational, political, and social functions so as to be a hub for children's various deliberative engagements across deliberative system. This is what I called the democratic school's mediating function. Drawing on the insights gained from my fieldwork in Japanese schools, I demonstrated that, even when children cannot fully enjoy deliberative opportunities inside their school, the school can nonetheless provide them with opportunities to engage in revolutionary, collective, and reflective meaning-making practices if its mediating function develops its vertical and horizontal connectivity with out-of-school human and institutional agents.

Shifting our attention away from traditional learning settings (i.e., classrooms and schools), chapter 7 showed that, under certain conditions, even an activist group can serve as a space for deliberative democratic learning. On the basis of my ethnographic research with youth climate activists in Kyoto, I described FFF Kyoto's publicly invisible deliberative meaning-making practice and its interplay with their publicly visible practices (e.g., standing protests) in order to consider how youth climate activists collectively enhance the self-transformative capacity of their group. In responding to changing situations, youth climate activists who regularly engaged in meta-deliberative practices developed shared norms, the raison d'être of the movement, and their identity as climate activists. Unlike deliberation in the classroom, FFF Kyoto did not have facilitating adults present. Nonetheless, the idea of dividing the labor of leadership to suit the needs of the group's frontstage and backstage activities respectively, as well as encouraging facilitative task-sharing in the backstage, enhanced the internal solidarity of the group and encouraged further meta-deliberation among its members. As a result, this helped the movement transform in a context-responsive fashion. During this process, the movement intentionally reduced its protesting edge and instead brought its social aspect to the forefront. Normally, this is interpreted as a "failure" of the movement; however, from the perspective of deliberative democratic learning, this is the collectively reconstructed meaning of activism that youth activists have crafted through shared inquiry.

Through these discussions, I have proposed a theory of deliberative democratic learning in which children engage in the (re)construction of democratic education itself. This is a series of theoretical restructurings resulting from a change of perspective from "children as future citizens" to "children as deliberators," thereby providing a novel way of connecting children, democracy, and education. I know that trusting in children's agency is not easy. It usually takes time. Its consequences are usually unforeseeable. Yet if we educators oppress children's agency just for the sake of self-protection, democratic education immediately becomes tokenistic. If children are told to behave as if they were a copy of adults, or asked to do something uncritically in accordance with adults' expectations, it may satisfy us, but it does not cure the illnesses that democracy faces in our time. If anyone feels afraid of situating children's agency at the heart of the learning process, it would be worth remembering that democracy underscores the value of including previously marginalized individuals and asking oneself, "As an educator of *democratic* education, am I ready to welcome children as collaborators in the task of updating our democracy together?"

Appendix

Notes for the Ethics of Studying *with* Children

In the past eight years, I have worked with children of different age groups, teachers, activists, and adults in civil societies and performed varieties of fieldwork in different countries (mainly Japan and Australia), different spatial contexts (classrooms, schools, and activist groups), all of which were geared toward giving shape to the idea of deliberative democratic learning. Classrooms, schools, and activist groups can be defined as "field" locations (as opposed to a laboratory setting) in that they accommodate various cultures of children and are noncontrolled physical locations.

My fieldwork has profoundly benefited from sociology, anthropology, and pedagogy. They may be derived from different fieldwork traditions, but they all value immersion. This is a strategy to see the logic of people's behavior or the process of meaning-making from the inside, which can be likened more to "using a microscope than a magnifying glass" (Longo and Zacka 2019, 1068). The question would then point to the manner in which inside (or microscope) benefits our understanding of democratic education. On the one hand, it facilitates a higher quality of logical inferences for contemplating democratic education.

Ethics always accompanied my study. The fact that my research subjects were mainly children necessitated a thorough ethical consideration regarding the fieldwork process. Research with children requires more than the "usual" ethical regard (e.g., gaining informed consent), because the unequally distributed power between me (researcher) and the children could lead to various ethical troubles (see Punch 2002; Hill 2005; Nishiyama 2018). Some readers might think that such ethical consideration, to be illustrated below, is tantamount to "overthinking." However, if one cannot justify the legitimacy of the data collection process in the field-work without discussing the ethical dimensions of the process, nothing is wrong with overthinking ethical factors. Ethical troubles may disrupt a healthy relationship with these children, easily diminishing the validity and trustworthiness of my research. As Timothy Pachirat's (2009) field-work in a slaughterhouse tellingly shows, fieldwork offers deep insights into politics, but at the same time, the presence of the fieldworker per se is also political.

Researching children is not easy. Samantha Punch indicated that children "may actually prefer an adult researcher not to invade their child's space" (Punch 2002, 328). Even though a researcher successfully enters the children's space, they can feel uneasy because a researcher is usually older and more powerful than them. Whether consciously or unconsciously, children develop a range of resistive strategies against the nonethical researcher. For instance, children are often accustomed to "please adults and thus to give socially desirable or confirmatory responses" (Due, Riggs, and Augoustinos 2014, 218) if rapport is not fully established. As Malcom Hill (2005) rightly suggested, making children perform according to the expectations of an adult researcher risks putting them on guard and thus places a great burden on them, which fundamentally prevents the researcher from approaching their lived experience.

Scholars working with children have, to date, made considerable ethical efforts, with a view to addressing or minimizing the issue of power within the research process. In longitudinal research, the significance of building rapport is continuously emphasized, and various methods to ensure this have been suggested (Corsaro and Molinari 2008). Drawing on ethnographic research involving migrant and refugee children, Due, Riggs and Augostinos (2014, 217–18) argued that a researcher must acknowledge the importance of spending time with children through regular visits so that they trust the researcher. Similarly, Davis, Watson, and Cunningham-Burley (2008) contended that the role of the researcher should be as nonauthoritative and friendly as possible for children to recognize the researcher as a "mate." The ethical considerations of my own fieldwork were primarily informed by and designed based on such wisdom.

Specifically, the most important ethical point I adhered to through-out my fieldwork was *reciprocity*. As many textbooks emphasize, the participatory research process should not be a grab-and-run, in which a researcher takes information without providing any benefits. Otherwise, it "will have you shown to the door in very quick time" (Madden 2010,

67). During the fieldwork, I worked not only as a data collector but also as a collaborator, helping school children and young activists in various ways. Sometimes, a teacher would invite me as a guest speaker to discuss with students my study experience overseas. I would also serve as an advisor who would brainstorm with children about how to make their regular dialogue activity more effective. Other times I worked as a photographer taking group photos of the climate activists. On certain occasions I was an older friend who would listen to their daily concerns (e.g., relationships with parents). Sometimes the activists would visit my office, and we would have many conversations on different topics not limited to the climate crisis.

As Herzog and Zacka (2017) pointed out, it is impossible for a researcher to gain "access to an invisibility position that allows them to collect data 'uncontaminated' by observer-observed interactions" (778). In other words, no matter how significant a researcher's efforts to minimize their power, it is impossible to eliminate power altogether. Nonetheless, this should not mean that a researcher does not need to make any efforts to mitigate their power. Some efforts may be minuscule but sometimes quite essential. For instance, I made sure that I never took fieldnotes while working with the climate activists or observing the children's deliberations in the classroom. Instead, I mostly used my "headnotes" or "jotting" and then typed up fieldnotes at my home or workplace. Some may wonder why I did such a complicated practice of fieldnote writing, but my priority was fostering a trusting relationship with the research subjects. Field researchers are "very sensitive to the way in which the stance and act of writing are very visible to and can influence the quality of their relationship with those studied" (Emerson, Fretz, and Shaw 2011, 23). Regarding activist ethnography, moreover, I spent the first couple of months building rapport rather than collecting data. Every Friday, I just stood next to the activists and engaged in many conversations with them to know about them. Although I had a lecture at my workplace on Friday afternoon, I wore a T-shirt instead of a suit and changed my hairstyle to create a relaxed atmosphere. In addition, while I was quite aware of how important the activists' regular meetings were for deepening my understanding of their deliberative learning within their group, I did not ask to participate unless they invited me. This is because my presence itself could put some pressure on teenager-only meetings and prevent free and relaxed conversations if I forced myself to attend them without any invitation. This may easily produce a structure where children are consumed by adults. For interpretive researchers, data collection is an absolute must for successful research, yet for those who study children in a deeper and interactive fashion, ethical considerations are as important (or even more so).

Interviews were another topic of consideration. When I carried out my first fieldwork in schools (as a fieldwork beginner), I made one ethical mistake. I invited a 13-year-old female student who agreed to have an interview with me. I was not so self-reflective about how I proceeded with the preparations for the interview. I wore a suit, the interview was undertaken behind closed doors, and I was older than her. As result, there was a quite limited room for enabling her to tell her own story freely with no pressure. Indeed, she was silent for almost 40 percent of the interview, and a few months later, she told me that she felt I preached. With this failure in mind, I then developed a new form of interview method called "the deliberative interview" or "the community of inquiry" (Nishiyama 2018), which is based on a practical application of deliberative theory to interviews. This interview method was used throughout my fieldwork.

Despite these ethical considerations, I do not think that I was completely accepted by the children. Nor did the above argument mean I was able to see things exactly the same way as children did. The purpose of fieldwork is neither to be identical to others nor to act in the same way as them. Fieldwork is also not something that the researcher immerses themselves in to the point of no turning back. Rather, the key purpose of fieldwork is to "study with others, not to make study of them" by "paying attention to them, watching what they do and listening to what they say" (Ingold 2018, 6) so that we can take others seriously. Thus, ethical sensitivity was an integral part of my research process itself and, at the same time, the process of empowering children. Ethical sensitivity helps ensure that power, hierarchy, and other elements that adults bring into a child's world can be minimized and naturalized as much as possible, creating a research environment where children exercise their potential and agency, which then allows the researcher to access their lived experience.

Notes

Introduction

1. Typical examples can include the following: "Future citizens need to develop some imaginative sympathy" (Callan 1997, 8), ". . . those forms of education necessary to prepare children for future citizenship . . ." (Gutmann 1999, 45), "If we wish to prepare our future citizens to participate in our current democratic systems, then we can continue with the kind of civic education that they now receive" (Crittenden 2002, 85), and "Scholarship on civic education strives to understand how we ought to prepare students for effective social and political participation" (Camicia and Knowles 2021, 7).

2. "A child means every human being below the age of eighteen years unless under the law applicable to the child, majority is attained earlier" (UNICEF 1989).

3. This social aspect of children and their right to participate is clearly recognized in UNCRC article 12, which calls for ensuring children's right to participate in all matters affecting them.

4. Historically, children's purity has been used in a political process for a strategic purpose. During elections in some medieval European countries, for example, children served as soothsayers who called out the names of the winning candidate or drew lots instead of adults, which contributed to symbolically enhance the innocence and neutrality of the electoral process (Sintomer 2020).

5. As demanded by the situation and context, the book will use the terms *children*, *teenagers*, and *students* interchangeably, but these terms will be used within the scope of this definition. Again, the purpose of my definitional engagement is to briefly clarify what I mean by "children" and not to provide its universal account.

6. Note that this does not mean that political democracy and social democracy are mutually exclusive. Rather, Dewey and Deweyan philosophers have emphasized the intertwined relationship between these democracies, arguing that political institutions, systems, and processes should be a foundation for enabling citizens' free social inquiry (Dewey 1927; Reed 1996; Bohman 2004).

7. This claim resonates with Gilbert Burgh and Simone Thornton's (2022) conceptual distinction between *education for democracy* and *democratic education*. According to their account, "whereas *education for democracy* focuses on the acquisition of knowledge and skills to improve the capacity of future citizens to participate effectively in civic life and contribute to the social, political and economic future of their communities and the political system, *democratic education* recognizes the social role of schooling as that of reconstruction and that children and adolescents have an integral role to play in shaping democracy" (59; original emphasis).

8. Chapter 2 will illustrate what I mean by Piagetian Geist in more detail. To put it simply, there are many education theories and practices that do not directly refer to Piaget's series of work on children's psychological development and nonetheless are significantly influenced by the Piagetian ways of thinking. I do not call it *Piaget's* Geist but a *Piagetian* one because these theories and practices tend to ground themselves in the Piagetian psychologist's interpretation of Piaget, including its overemphasized or oversimplified version.

9. The term "Vygotsky's left-wing" was first used by Fred Newman and Lois Holzman (1993, 67–69). The Vygotsky's left-wing, according to their account, centers on the dialectic unity of learning and development through a revolutionary practice (or what Newman and Holzman call the "practical-critical activity of everyday life" [68]). In such practice, a well-designed learning leads to further learning and, in this sense, has no endpoint. They did not define what Vygotsky's right-wing is, but perhaps their argument implies that right-wing's core question may be how Vygotsky's developmental theory is applied to a learning process in which children effectively respond to adults' expectation of development.

10. It should be made clear that the book does not aim to propose an optimistic view that deliberative democratic learning is always possible under a deliberative curriculum, that schools always have an optimal environment to support and encourage children's participation, or that social movement always offers a perfect learning environment. Rather, the book is geared toward unpacking the black box of deliberative democratic learning in these spaces with some key questions, such as "What kind of learning design do we need to enable deliberative democratic learning in the classroom?" "What is the role of adults for enabling deliberative democratic learning?" and "To what extent is the idea of deliberative democratic learning meaningful in out-of-classroom settings?"

Chapter 1

1. See Dryzek (2000). From a philosophical point of view, the roots of deliberative democracy can be traced back to Socrates (Chambers 2018).

2. This authentic principle of deliberation has, however, been contested by a number of early critics. The most notable and well-known criticism is that the authenticity requirement is often grounded in hyperrationalism. According to

difference politics thinkers, such as Young (2000), the idea of authentic deliberation suggested by Rawlsian and Habermasian theorists often focuses too much on speech acts that privilege dispassionate, logical, and public-spirited argumentation, which in turn marginalizes disadvantaged groups whose speech culture is different from the rationalist one. See also chapter 3 of this book.

3. Sass and Dryzek (2014) also argue the significant role of the cultural dimension of deliberation. Even if one form of reason-giving in one culture is seen as nondeliberative with respect to normative ideals of deliberation, it sometimes allows people to participate in a political communication process in another culture. Thus, an inclusive theory of deliberative democracy should be something that takes diverse cultural context into account. See also chapter 3 of this book.

4. Chambers (2004) also argues that deliberative democracy studies often ignore the power of mass publics by paying specific attention to deliberative minipublics.

5. See also Kuyper (2017, 17) for the conceptual evolvement of deliberative systems.

6. While this "new generation" forges a new standard against which we understand deliberative democracy, some scholars view deliberative systems theory skeptically on the grounds that this idea loses sight of the normative foundation of deliberative democracy (Owen and Smith 2015). The most common response to this kind of criticism can be summarized by stating that "every democratic forum that affects the public should be *as deliberative as possible* unless there are good systemic reasons why it should or could deviate from deliberative norms" (Bächtiger et al. 2018, 15; emphasis added). Insofar as deliberative democracy's normative core (authenticity and inclusiveness) is anchored across a system, concept stretching can be justified. It is important to keep our eyes open for various ways the authenticity and inclusiveness principles are implemented within different contexts in which the system itself is embedded.

7. González currently uses her new personal name, X González.

8. "Scott Morrison Tells Students Striking over Climate Change to Be 'Less Activist,'" *Guardian*, November 26, 2018.

9. Jungkunz illustrates this happening through a story of a female student at school. During the class, the student says nothing to teachers or her classmates. When a teacher calls upon her repeatedly, she remains silent. Although her silence and nonparticipation in classroom activities seem odd from a teacher's point of view, her silent engagement turns out to be her protest against the harassment of her LGBT classmates. Thus, Jungkuntz argues, "her silence acts as a valuable protest and teaching lessons, as it exposes how the absence of a given voice really matters, thereby demonstrating how much we stand to lose due to exclusionary practices" (Jungkuntz 2012, 127–28). Silence per se is neither a speech act nor an explicit form of reason-giving, but it serves as a key strategy for the student to express herself in the classroom, thereby helping other students and teachers to take the LGBT students more seriously. We will return to this point in chapter 3.

10. See also the essays written by Greta's parents (Ernman et al. 2018).

11. See also Wahlström, et al. (2019) for the European case.

12. Examples: Wahlström et al. (2019); Bowman (2019); Boulianne, Lalancette, and Ilkiw (2020); Nishiyama (2020); Catanzaro and Collin (2021).

13. Mattheis (2020) also illustrates some potential legal risks that school strikers can take, though Mattheis is critical about penalizing school strikes.

14. Viral engagement is a form of democratic engagement producing "a political message or campaign that spreads quickly, reaches large audiences and calls for action" (Fung and Shakabatur 2015, 155) through low-cost activities, such as clicking the like or dislike button, signing a petition, or sharing clips, memes, or images. See also Ernman et al. (2018) for Greta Thunberg's effective use of social media for circulating her critical claims to wider audiences.

15. See, Mansbridge (1999, 2007) and Tamura (2014) for exceptions.

16. In chapter 7, however, I caution that understanding the FFF movement only through the lens of what Thunberg says and does (which is so-called "Greta framing" [Neas, Ward, and Bowman 2022]) runs the risk of neglecting various and rich grassroots efforts of youth climate activists.

17. Some of her famous speeches made in the past several years are available at FFF's official website (https://fridaysforfuture.org/what-we-do/activist-speeches/). I use the same source for the quotations from speeches that will be coming up.

18. Example: "According to the IPCC report we are about 11 years away from being in a position where we set off an irreversible chain reaction beyond human control. To avoid unprecedented changes in all aspects of society, actions need to have taken place within this coming decade, including a reduction of our $CO2$ emissions by at least 50% by the year 2030" (Speech in the European Economic and Social Committee, February 21, 2019).

19. Example: "You lied to us. You gave us false hope. You told us that the future was something to look forward to. And the saddest thing is that most children are not even aware of the fate that await us" (Speech in the London Assembly, April 23, 2019).

20. Examples: "I shouldn't be up here. I should be back in school on the other side of the ocean. Yet you all come to us young people for hope. How dare you!" (Speech in the United Nations, September 23, 2019). "I don't want your hope. I don't want you to be hopeful. I want you to panic" (Speech in the World Economic Forum, January 25, 2019).

21. Hendriks (2016) problematizes the term "transmission," as it focuses solely on input/output relations of different sites and suggests using the term "coupling" instead to approach communication dynamics in a deliberative system.

22. For example, on Twitter (December 12, 2019), the former US president Donald Trump contended that "Greta must work on her Anger Management program then go to a good old fashioned movie with a friend!" For another example, in the Conservative Political Action Conference, 19-year-old female "climate realist" Naomi Seibt criticized FFF as just "hysteria."

Chapter 2

1. Examples include, ". . . the development of 'deliberative' or what I shall interchangeably call 'democratic' character" (Gutmann 1999, 52); "in a problem-solving discussion, they [learners] can practice making decisions using dialogue. This might be beneficial for the development of the various skills, attitudes, and values that are necessary to participate in democratic deliberation" (Samuelsson 2016, 5); "any citizenship curriculum should seek to develop young people's understanding of democracy, government and the rights and responsibilities of citizens" (Pontes, Henn, and Griffiths 2019, 5); "liberal notions of citizenship emphasize individual development of capabilities to meet the needs of a diverse contemporary life" (Camicia and Knowles 2021, 30).

2. See Griffin (2011) and Moshman (2020) as exceptions.

3. Bidell (1992, 307) acknowledges that "Piaget's stage theory of development tacitly reflects the ideology of individualism"; but he also points out the ambiguity in Piaget's own position because his theory of knowledge development resonates with social constructivism and in this sense rejects the individualist, or Cartesian, interpretation of development. See also, Cole and Wertsch (1996), Matusov and Hayes (2000), Lourenço (2012), and Aslanian (2018).

4. Piaget's emphasis on individual development is widely criticized on the grounds that Piaget ignored the significance of the social process in the course of human development. However, scholars in defence of Piaget have contended that Piaget actually had a good understanding of the dialectical dynamics of the individual and society; therefore, situating Piaget's theory in the individual-social antinomy is an overinterpretation (Cole and Wertsch 1996; Lourenço 2012). When compared with Vygotsky's positioning, Piaget might prioritize biological and autonomous processes of development over social process. Again, what is important at least for this chapter is not to inquire what the genuine interpretation of Piaget is, but how the Piagetian Geist's universalism gives shape to democratic education.

5. Englund called such ideal deliberators "educated deliberative citizens" who are "to be open for thinking anew and to be open for the possibility of changing [their] preferences and views in light of argumentation, to be self-critical and to listen to other's arguments and to respect the concrete Other, in sum to embrace pluralism" (Englund 2022, 3).

6. Recent empirical findings also show that the gap of people's different (linguistic) competencies can be remedied by a structural design of a deliberative process or by what Gerber et al. (2016) call "supportive conditions." Usually, most deliberative minipublics provide citizens with various supportive conditions, including instruction on deliberative norms, opportunities to talk with and question experts, and the presence of trained facilitators, and evidence show that these conditions enable citizens to engage in a high quality of deliberation while avoiding some deliberative pitfalls (e.g., group polarization, domination) (Bäch-

tiger and Parkinson 2019, ch. 3; see also Fishkin 2009; Strandberg, Himmelroos, and Grönlund 2019).

7. Stetsenko summarizes Vygotsky and Vygotskian psychologist's use of the term "culture" as "a *quality of human life*, something that people constantly and continuously *enact*—a unique quality of the way in which people *collaboratively* engage their world through *collective* efforts to make things happen" (Stetsenko 2017, 278; original emphasis). Viewed in this light, culture is an artifact produced as a result of an individual's active participation in collaborative and collective practice. Cole (2017) also indicates that such an artifact should not be understood in a purely materialist fashion, as artifacts can be simultaneously conceptual (e.g., symbol, sign) and material (e.g., physical tool) and have been mutually developed and modified.

8. It should be made clear again that both Piaget and Vygotsky understood the significance of the individual-social dynamics in the process of development of thinking, and in this sense, I do not intend to argue that Piaget had no awareness of the social. What is important here is rather their thoughts on the origin of human development (psychogenesis or sociogenesis) and the degree to which they emphasize the individual and the social. See also Cole and Wertsch (1996).

9. To understand Bronfenbrenner's theory of development in a more concrete manner, consider Malala Yousafzai's story. When seen through the lens of the Piagetian Geist, her bravery and critical attitude toward the right to education and women's rights may at first be explained through a biological lens in that she must have developed and internalized a sense of bravery prior to her participation in activism. However, Bronfenbrenner's bioecological framework enables us to read and interpret her biographical essay differently. For instance, as she clearly mentioned, she nurtured her political interest during a discussion with her friend in the school (microsystem) and a political conversation with her father (Ziauddin Yousafzai) and his friend at her home (mesosystem) where she "sat on [her] father's knee listening to everything he and his friends discussed" (Yousafzai with Lamb 2013, 47). Her interest in education of women was also inspired in an indirect but significant manner by her father, an educational activist who encouraged girls to go to school (exosystem). Such an interest in education rights and women's rights was also anchored in the traditional culture of Pakistan, which is quite oppressive and discriminatory to women in general (macrosystem), and by the fact that such culture has not changed and has instead become worse over time (chronosystem). As a result of all these influences, she nurtured her bravery and critical mind.

10. See also the introduction of Engeström (2015), entitled "Learning by expanding: Origins, applications, and challenges," newly inserted into the second edition of his book *Learning by Expanding*. The introduction offers a quite relevant and well-written overview of Engeström's activity theory.

11. See Holzman (2009) and Newman and Holzman (2014) for a more detailed explanation of the significance of play in Vygotsky.

12. Much knowledge contributes to Engeström's establishment of the theory of expansive learning, but Engeström himself notes that the theory benefits significantly from Aleksei Leont'ev, Evald Il'enkov, Vasily Davydov (all known as activity theorists) as well as Gregory Bateson and Mikhail Bakhtin. See Engeström and Sannino (2017, 105–8) on the theoretical roots of expansive learning.

Chapter 3

1. Harbermas argued that his theory of communicative action is often misunderstood in deliberative studies (Habermas 2018, 872–73). What Habermas attempted to pursue was not the realization of an ideal situation in the real world where there are absolutely no "irrational" communicative acts such as manipulation, suppression, or deception. Instead, his inquiry focused on how people, despite a situation where political dispute includes several "irrational" acts, can collaboratively adopt the correct solution to the problems in question. Habermas believed that the argument can be corrected toward a better direction only when the discourse participants presuppose the unforced force of the better argument as a norm of argumentation (Habermas 1996).

2. Dryzek also depicted Dr. Martin Luther King, Jr., as a "brilliant rhetorician" (Dryzek 2010, 71) on the ground that his rhetoric reframed civil rights issues from a matter surrounding black liberation to one about human rights, thus avoiding unnecessary conflicts between black and white people and instead facilitating their collaboration and reflection.

3. Landemore did not intend to use the term "truth" in a (neo-)Kantian manner (i.e., truth as a single transcendental goal) but rather in a more pragmatic way (i.e., truth as a fallibilistic meaning of "betterment" with a procedure-independent value) (Landemore 2013).

4. I must clarify that I do not condone hate speech or harassment at all. What I am highlighting here is the need for the meaning and scope of an anti-deliberative practice to be defined more carefully from a normative as well as a contextual perspective, because some people can stigmatize certain types of critical comment and opinion as "anti-deliberative" hate speech.

5. Drawing on the case of interviews with children, I showed how an interviewer's series of "logical" questionings runs the risk of frightening and silencing an interviewee (Nishiyama 2018).

6. The democratic role of humor has been widely discussed in the field of social movements, a good example of which is Erdem Çolak's (2014) study on protest art and humor at the Gezi Park protests in Turkey.

7. Some deliberative system theorists have formulated the idea of meta-deliberation. So far, they have focused their attention on a site where meta-deliberation can or should take place. Claudia Landwehr (2015), for example, called for an institutionalized meta-deliberation in a deliberative system to formally guarantee the system's reflective capacity. By contrast, Holdo offered a more relaxed understanding of meta-deliberation that occurs "when someone raises a problem that does not concern . . . substantive topics but rather the way such topics are being discussed" (Holdo 2020, 111). Rather than focusing solely on the formalized and institutionalized form of meta-deliberation, Holdo drew the example of feminist activists' T-shirts that helped facilitate the public's deeper understanding of how misogyny is deeply rooted in the current political discourse and revealed how people's everyday deeds create a meta-deliberative moment in a deliberative system.

8. Chapter 5 discusses details about my facilitator experience.

9. Guided by a learning-by-doing methodology informed by action research (Stringer 2014), the research focused on the interactive cycles of planning, acting, and reflecting, which integrates the study of the phenomenon with an intervention and a further study of the results. In the "planning" phase, our team reviewed key literature on deliberative pedagogy, deliberation in the classroom, and democratic education to start designing our deliberative intervention. We drew on this review and on our own practical experiences and expertise as a deliberation practitioner in schools (Nishiyama), a deliberative practitioner and facilitator (Russell), and a teacher (Chalaye) in a series of regular research meetings to write a proposal and construct an initial version of our deliberative curriculum. We then organized project meetings with key actors (teachers, school principal, research colleagues) to refine our design in response to curriculum and learning needs and develop a collaborative relationship with the teachers before implementing our project in each school. In the "action" phase, our team conducted five deliberative sessions followed by one follow-up session working with teachers. To augment our own reflections on our practice experience, we asked volunteers to act as observers (and timekeepers). Before and during the deliberative practice, we occasionally changed our curriculum design flexibly in response to students' situations, advice from teachers and observers, and other issues that emerged. In the "reflection" phase, we organized a debriefing immediately after each session to listen to feedback from observers and teachers; share stories from our observations and experiences, including things that had excited, surprised, or concerned us; and discuss problems, barriers, and challenges found in our practice. Based on this project meeting, we redesigned our deliberative curriculum for the next session by adding new activities (or omitting some of them) in response to both content and process issues. Each researcher took notes for reflection before, during, and after the practice, which we then uploaded to our shared Dropbox folder. The field descriptions illustrated below were mainly informed by our collaborative fieldnotes.

Chapter 4

1. I use the term "listening" rather than "hearing" for the etymological reason. As Lipari (2014, 50) describes, the latter is a perceptive and receptive action, while the original meaning of the former emphasizes attentive and provisional nature of human action. Although they frequently overlap in our daily lives, I chose to use the term "listening" because the focus of this chapter's discussion is on how students listen in the first sense.

2. To be fair, this does not mean that all deliberative democrats have never taken listening into account seriously. For instance, Dryzek questioned the deliberative theory's lack of attention to listening, arguing that "the most effective insidious way to silence others in politics is a refusal to listen" (Dryzek 2000, 149).

3. Examples of different procedural designs can be observed in Fishkin's (2009) projects. In the European-wide Deliberative Poll "Tomorrow's Europe," free simultaneous translation service was provided in order to develop an environment where all participants could speak in their mother language and listen to the opinion of people who spoke other languages.

4. A Brazilian education activist, Paulo Freire, framed this type of over-prioritization of talk as "narration sickness" (Freire 1970, 71).

5. Some scholars employ Fricker's argument to explain the fact of testimonial injustice in educational settings. According to Murris (2013) and Kotzee (2017), prejudices held by teachers toward children face the danger of resulting in racial unfairness in the classroom and at school. Hookway develops Fricker's argument and examines epistemic injustice that does not entail testimonial exchange. For example, shy students frequently miss the ideal opportunity to participate in a class topic where chatty students control the general process of conversation. When such a situation continues, some participants gradually share a prejudicial assumption (e.g., shy students cannot do discussion, they do not listen, they have no opinion). The outcome can be that no one believes that shy students are relevant knowers or thereby talks to the students. Despite the absence of testimony, Hookway says that this is a sort of epistemic injustice since it is a "refusal to take seriously the ability of the agent to provide information that is relevant in the current context" (Hookway 2010, 158).

6. One day, police officers arrested a rapist who had a picture of Marie. Then they realized that Marie did not tell a lie.

7. Scudder placed the speaker's satisfaction only at the end, but this does not imply that she undervalues its importance. She contends that "the speaker's satisfaction would enhance the overall listening score," and yet "the absence would not detract from other indicators of listening, including a substantive response" (Scudder 2022, 122).

8. *Kosen* is a higher educational institution for future engineers. Typically, prospective engineers are admitted into Kosen after graduating from a junior high school (aged 15).

9. Examples include "too much nodding," "no smile," "using a smart phone while listening," "a response that begins with 'but . . . ;'" and so forth.

10. English translation of figure 4.1:

> Step 0: (a) Become furious and commit violence, (b) Develop an atmosphere of turnoff, (c) Blink an extreme number of times.
>
> Step 1: (a) Talk and response are not engaged meaningfully, (b) Listen with scary look, (c) Making causal response.
>
> Step 2: (a) Look at eyes of a speaker, (b) Stare at a speaker, (c) Not obviously out of line of sight, (d) Not looking intensively at one's smart phone.
>
> Step 3: (a) Ask to repeat one's talk, (b) Express sympathy, (c) Do not nod without listening properly, (d) Look at a speaker as if you want to respond to him/her, (e) Prevent a response with monotone, (f) Avoid doing the same type of causal response again and again.
>
> Step 4: (a) Natural response, (b) Look at a speaker naturally.

11. Scudder (2020) also raised the limitation and danger of one-sided sympathy.

12. Scudder specifically recognizes the challenge of quantifying nonverbal behaviors. She notes, "LQI is still a relatively voice-centric measure of listening, insofar as it concentrates on listening *to* speech acts. In other words, in its current form, LQI cannot easily capture listening to non-verbal or embodied expression, nor to what is not said" (Scudder 2022, 124).

Chapter 5

1. This would range from the school system (assessment system, timetables, and architectural structure of classroom) to sociocultural environments of the students (locality, family environment, linguistic diversity, and prejudice against certain identities shared in a particular community).

2. Rancière is rather critical of Socrates on the ground that Socrates feigned ignorance. From Rancière's point of view, Socrates was not ignorant, because he knew at least one thing: he is the wisest person in Athens). As is sometimes indicated, what Socrates always did was to speak with others and then "make clear to his interlocutors that they do not know what Socrates already knows" (Kohan, Santi, and Wozniak 2017, 256), thereby placing the interlocutors in a lower status than Socrates. For this reason, Rancière argues that the Socratic method is "a perfected form of stultification" (Rancière 1991, 29).

3. We can find a contemporary version of Jacotot in a wide range of research fields not only within primary and secondary education (Kohan, Santi,

and Wozniak 2017) but also in higher and lifelong education (Engels-Schwarzpaul 2015).

Chapter 6

1. Details of the protest were reported in the *Guardian* (January 20, 2015).

2. To be fair, some researchers and practitioners undertook theoretical and empirical study with an appropriate use of the term "school," taking a whole-school approach to deliberative civic learning. Examples can be found in the discussions of the Democracy Day program (Davis, Gray, and Stephens 1998) and Pasek et al.'s (2008) long-term study of the Student Voices program in Philadelphia public high schools, as well as that of Youniss (2011) on the democratic role of American schools. In addition, as the title of Hess's seminal book *Controversies in the Classroom* (2009) and that of Molnar-Main's practical investigation *Deliberation in the Classroom* (2017) clearly show, their focus is intentionally narrowed to students' curriculum-based activities within the classroom.

3. In *Spectacular Things Happen along the Way*, Schultz (2018) used a pseudonym (William D. Carr Community Academy, or Carr Community Academy) for ethical reasons. However, I consider that using the real name of the school (Richard E. Byrd Community Academy, dubbed Byrd Community Academy) would not contradict research ethics, for the following four reasons. Firstly, in *Democratic Schools*, edited by Apple and Beane (2007), Schultz's chapter disclosed the real name of the school. Second, the real name of the school is referred to in Schultz's CV, which is publicly available on his webpage. Third, the literature discussing Schultz's democratic practices tends to use the real name of the school (Hughes 2007). Finally, the case of Byrd Community Academy has received some media attention, and many media reports (e.g., news article, blogs, radio reports) used the real name of the school (e.g., Zorn 2004).

4. The Byrd Community Academy closed in 2004.

5. Dewey and Dewey ([1915] 2002) conceptualized the school as a social center: "Using the school plant as a social center is recognition of the need for social change and of the community's responsibility to help effect it" (227).

6. A similar view, albeit in a more contemporary version, is suggested by Senge, who contended that we should consider the complex social location of today's school. Senge (2012, 23) pointed to various examples of social connections to the contemporary school, including the family, private businesses, hospitals, churches, police, local and international media, publishers, universities, professional groups, state and national government, the internet, and so forth.

7. The term "mediating space" was coined for this use, but similar concepts exist elsewhere, under the names of "mediating structures" (Berger 1976) and "mediating institutions" (Wolbrecht 2005; Flanagan 2013). Those concepts

were introduced in different academic disciplines, and their shared claim is that a mediating space/institution/structure is a type of space that stands "between the individual in his private space and the large institution of public space" (Berger 1976, 401).

8. In accordance with the research ethics guidelines of my university, all information that could identify individuals (e.g., the name of school and interviewees) was omitted to ensure anonymity.

9. For the purposes of transparency, what follows provides some key information regarding fieldwork and analysis. The fieldwork had two parts. During the first part, I spent 49 days in total in the K School and observed 39 deliberative practices with 397 students. The 20 students (students A to T) who finally agreed to the interview were officially invited. The interview lasted around 40 to 50 minutes per student, and all interviews were conducted at K School. The interviews were semi-structured, focusing mainly on (1) students' oral history of their experience of deliberation in and outside the school and (2) their self-understanding of the contribution that the school made to their activities. To observe students' experiences from multiple angles, the author also conducted interviews with three teachers. The recorded interview data were transcribed to ensure familiarity with the data and, more importantly, to prepare for the next analysis step. The transcript was analyzed based on the insights gained from the thematic analysis (Braun and Clarke 2006). The analysis consisted of open coding (grouping the most basic segment of the raw data), second coding (identification of subthemes by grouping different initial codes), and theme identification and naming (identification of key theme of the topic). The initial analysis was conducted in 2017 with the use of Excel spreadsheet. And I reanalyzed the same data in 2020 by importing all text data into the NVivo software (QSR International) intended to recheck the relevance of my past analysis and engage in more sophisticated coding and interpretation.

10. See also Hayward (2012, 130–31) and Nishiyama (2020, 511), who suggested the idea of vertical and horizontal connectivity to explain networks in which schools are embedded. See also Senge (2012, ch. 1) for the related argument.

11. A similar point was made by Engeström, who calls this issue "encapsulation of school learning from experience and cognition outside the school" (Engeström 2008, 90).

Chapter 7

1. Sidney Tarrow (1998) then continues, "They [movements] build organizations, elaborate ideologies, and socialize and mobilize constituencies, and their members engage in self-development and the construction of collective identities."

2. Navne and Skovdal (2021) is one interesting exception. The first author is a high school student and climate activist who attempts to bridge between his own experience as a climate activist and academic language with support from the second author (an academic researcher) and to describe the first-person experience of what FFF means.

3. Haug and Rucht (2013) caution that the term "structurelessness" may run the risk of misleading our understanding of the reality of the contemporary social movement.

4. During my fieldwork, I acknowledged the significance of observing activist meetings but decided to attend FFF Kyoto's regular meetings only when I was invited by core members. I tried to be as sensitive as possible about my power as a university instructor at a well-known university in Kyoto that inevitably created a power imbalance between myself and young members. Even though I felt that we established a good relationship during the ethnographic study, I thought that my presence at their regular meetings would run the risk of pre-venting members from talking and discussing matters in a less pressured way. I also did not want them to feel unnecessary anxiety that I might be monitoring their meetings even though I had no such intention. As della Porta and Rucht point out, "many social movement groups do not welcome detached observers within their meetings" (della Porta and Rucht 2013b, 3). Yet, due to my regular participation and continuous support of FFF Kyoto's activities, members gradu-ally expressed their trust in me. As a result of this, M (the official leader of FFF Kyoto in 2021) sometimes shared the minutes of their regular meetings with me. The minutes allowed me to see the outline and process of their meetings without direct observation, which means that they served as a key source of knowledge that enabled me to overcome both ethical and methodological barriers at the same time and to an acceptable degree.

5. For me, Ashley Mears's (2020) ethnography in the global party cir-cuit is a treasure box that offers much guidance concerning an ethnographer's positionality and behaviour when the ethnographer is located on the borderline between insider and outsider.

6. I use the term "sort out," but its meaning is different from cherry-picking. Whereas the latter is to select only desirable and useful information from a dataset, "sorting out," at least in ethnography, comes with a critical and reflective confession from which perspective the ethnographer attempts to view the phenomenon. Whether from anthropology-origin or sociology-origin, eth-nography is not a research method for writing observed phenomenon objectively and comprehensively. Any attempts at objective or comprehensive description are strongly condemned by postmodern ethnographers, as best exemplified by *Writ-ing Cultures*, edited by Clifford and Marcus (1986). For them, the ethnographer's primary job is a *translation* of the insider's perspective gained from firsthand

experience into the outsider's one, or academic language. Pratt argues that this translation process is neither objective nor comprehensive, because "to convert fieldwork, via field notes, into formal ethnography requires a tremendously difficult shift from the latter discursive position (face to face with the other) to the former" and therefore "much must be left behind in the process" (Pratt 1986, 32–33). Clifford (1986) calls such translation activity "writing *partial* truth." Even though their description is partial and selective, ethnographers are normatively required to be sensitive about and aware of what they have chosen and what they have discarded. By disclosing it honestly, they create a guidepost for what their writings represent and how their writing should be read.

7. M was also my first-contact person. I sent a direct message via Twitter (FFF Kyoto's official account), and she responded to me immediately.

8. A quick history of the development of FFF in the Japanese context is as follows. Some high school and university students first organized FFF Tokyo around early 2019 and started a regular protesting action in front of the office of the Ministry of Economy, Trade, and Industry and the House of Parliament. Soon after that (around 1–2 months later), FFF Kyoto was established as the second local group of FFF. Other local FFF groups (e.g., FFF Sendai, FFF Osaka, FFF Saitama) were also established one after another within a year. Many youth climate activists gradually saw a need for strong solidarity among local groups, and this idea was strengthened amid the COVID-19 pandemic. Then some core members of each local group decided to establish FFF Japan as a hub group, the purpose of which is to foster communication between local groups and address their common problems (climate crisis) collaboratively.

9. Another member, R, who joined FFF Kyoto after M also described FFF Kyoto's bad atmosphere at that time. During the interview, she said, "Oh man, yes, it was such a hard time. Everyone was so smart. Everyone was logical, everyone could speak whatever they wanted. I . . . yes, I respected them. But for me, they were a bit scary" (interview, April 15, 2021).

10. One example is what they called "check-in." This is a kind of icebreaker practiced at the beginning of their regular meeting in which all members briefly share some stories about a casual topic (e.g., What was your good news today? Where did you go last weekend?). For members, particularly newcomers, check-in is important, because "I can speak something at least once and so I can feel less pressured during the main meeting" (interview, April 21, 2021). No matter how urgent the issue they had to discuss, they never skipped the check-in.

11. Of course, climate change results in causing these issues in the form of, for instance, biodiversity loss, animal extinction, gender inequality of global south caused by climate change, climate refugees, and so forth.

12. Benjamin Bowman (2019, 298) cautioned that a traditional top-down framework for explaining the FFF movement tended to impose what he called

"negative" emotions (e.g., sadness or anger) in disregard of the places and roles of joy, dancing, excitement, and positivity.

13. The existing reduction goal at that time was 26 percent, so a 62 percent reduction goal would have represented a significant acceleration, at least from the Japanese government's standpoint. Former prime minister Yoshihide Suga attended the summit.

14. In Japan, a group of police must walk with protestors in officially approved protest marches for security purposes.

15. A few months later, I found out that he was a member of Kikou Network (an environmental NGO).

16. When I attended the meeting on August 14, 2021, I developed a more concrete understanding of M and K's concern about power. The relevant excerpt from my fieldnotes is as follows: "These days M often complains that the regular meeting is less lively. Today, I got a sense of what M was saying. Yes, it was true. Many members were passive and quiet with no laughter. They shared their thoughts only when M or K asked for an opinion. M and K were the dominant speakers during the whole meeting, and there were even members who turned their screens off. We knew they were listening behind the screen, but I was not sure whether we could feel that we were talking *together*. . . . In the middle of the meeting, we divided the members into several breakout rooms on Zoom. My group had four members including M, G, S, and myself. G suggested one opinion, but it was almost a repeat of what M had just said. S seemed to hesitate to share her opinion with us, but she finally spoke her thoughts in the last minute. Of course, we had no time to deepen our understanding of what she had said" (fieldnotes, August 14, 2021).

17. When she decided to hand over her position as a leader to one of the members (T) in November 2021, M recalled her experience over the past six months and said, "It was really hard job. Nobody has helped me in the last six months. I know I did not laugh at all. I am about to cry now" (fieldnotes, November 6, 2021).

18. Philosophy for Children (P4C) is one of the practical applications of philosophical dialogue in educational settings. See Gregory, Haynes, and Murris (2017). See also chapter 6 of this book.

19. In Erving Goffman's classic work *The Presentation of Self in Everyday Life* (1959), he introduced the *stage* analogy to explain the everyday logic of people's social interaction in a public space. He defined the frontstage as a space where people play a certain role in accordance with social expectations and the backstage as a space where they are emancipated from the expected social role. Goffman also proposed the idea of "outside," a more routine activity that is classified as neither frontstage nor backstage. Some readers might think that his idea of outside resonates with my idea of the wings of the stage, but I believe it does

not. FFF Kyoto's standing is not "outside" in Goffman's sense, because its core feature is that, while what members do during the standing is almost similar to what activists in general do backstage, the way in which members present their activity to others pro forma takes the frontstage form. In my view, therefore, a simple application Goffman's idea of outside would run the risk of masking the boundary-crossing feature of the standing. Put differently, the standing itself is practiced in a frontstage form, but nonetheless its connective feature has a backstage function that is unobservable at least for outsiders. To emphasize this boundary-crossing feature, I decided to use the term "wings of the stage" rather than Goffman's idea of outside. On a real stage, the wings are part of the front-stage, but they are unobservable to the audience: and in many cases, the wings are an important place where performers create and share their own culture.

20. Activists construct a specific phenomenon into a "social problem" through what David Snow et al. (1986) call "framing" intended to give people a new framework for interpreting the phenomenon and to mobilize them effectively for collective action. When the original framing set by activists is less fruitful than they expect, they extend or transform it in a way that alters the scope of the problem or uses a different phrase to define the situation. By doing so, activists try to locate themselves within the changing situation and continue their movement.

Works Cited

Abendschön, Simone, ed. 2014. *Growing into Politics: Contexts and Timing of Political Socialisation.* Colchester, UK: ECPER Press.

Alanen, Leena. 1988. "Rethinking Childhood." *Acta Sociologica* 31 (1): 53–67.

Allen, Jay. 2020. "'Logical Harassment': The Latest Curse of the Japanese Workplace?" *Unseen Japan*, October 13. https://unseenjapan.com/logical-harassment-japan/.

Apple, Michael, and Beane James, eds. 2007. *Democratic Schools: Lessons in Powerful Education.* 2nd ed. Portsmouth, NH: Heinemann.

Arendt, Hannah. 1958. *The Human Condition.* Chicago: University of Chicago Press.

Ariés, Philippe. 1996. *Centuries of Childhood.* Translated by Robert Baldick. London: Pimlico.

Aristotle. 1985. *Nicomachean Ethics.* Translated by Irwin Terence. Indianapolis: Hackett.

Aslanian, Teresa. 2018. "Recycling Piaget: Posthumanism and Making Children's Knowledge Matter." *Educational Philosophy and Theory* 50 (4): 417–27.

Bächtiger, André, John Dryzek, Jane Mansbridge, and Mark Warren, eds. 2018. *The Oxford Handbook of Deliberative Democracy.* Oxford: Oxford University Press.

Bächtiger, André, and John Parkinson. 2019. *Mapping and Measuring Deliberation: Toward a New Deliberative Quality.* Oxford: Oxford University Press.

Barvosa, Edwina. 2018. *Deliberative Democracy Now: LGBT Equality and the Emergence of Large-Scale Deliberative Systems.* Cambridge: Cambridge University Press.

Beauvais, Edana. 2020. "Deliberation and Non-deliberative Communication." *Journal of Deliberative Democracy* 16 (1): 4–13.

Bell, Daniel. 1997. "Democratic Deliberation: The Problem of Implementation." In *Deliberative Politics: Essays on Democracy and Disagreement*, edited by Stephen Macedo, 71–78. New York: Oxford University Press.

Benhabib, Seyla. 1996. "Toward a Deliberative Model of Democratic Legitimacy." In *Democracy and Difference*, edited by Seyla Benhabib, 67–94. Princeton, NJ: Princeton University Press.

Benneckenstein, Heidi. 2019. *Ein deutsches Mädchen: Mein Leben in einer Neonazifamilie*. Stuttgart: Tropen.

Berger, Peter. 1976. "In Praise of Particularity: The Concept of Mediating Structures." *Review of Politics* 38 (2): 399–410.

Bickford, Susan. 1996. *The Dissonance of Democracy: Listening, Conflict and Citizenship*. Ithaca, NY: Cornell University Press.

Bidell, Thomas. 1992. "Beyond Interactionism in Contextualist Models of Development." *Human Development* 35:306–15.

Biesta, Gert. 2017. "Don't Be Fooled by Ignorant Schoolmasters: On the Role of the Teacher in Emancipatory Education." *Policy Futures in Education* 15 (1): 52–73.

Bingham, Charles, and Gert Biesta. 2010. *Jacques Rancière: Education, Truth, Emancipation*. London: Continuum.

Blundell, David. 2016. *Rethinking Children's Spaces and Places*. London: Bloomsbury.

Bohman, James. 1996. *Public Deliberation: Pluralism, Complexity, and Democracy*. Cambridge, MA: MIT Press.

———. 1998. "Survey Article: The Coming of Age of Deliberative Democracy." *Journal of Political Philosophy* 6 (4): 400–425.

———. 2004. "Realizing Deliberative Democracy as a Mode of Inquiry: Pragmatism, Social Facts and Normative Theory." *Journal of Speculative Philosophy* 18 (1): 23–43.

———. 2012. "Representation in the Deliberative System." In *Deliberative Systems*, edited by John Parkinson and Jane Mansbridge, 72–94. Cambridge: Cambridge University Press.

Bottrell, Dorothy, and Susan Goodwin. 2011. *Schools, Communities and Social inclusion*. South Yarra, Australia: Palgrave Macmillan.

Boulianne, Shelley, Mireille Lalancette, and David Ilkiw. 2020. "School Strike 4 Climate: Social Media and the International Youth Protest on Climate Change." *Media and Communication* 8 (2): 208–18.

Bowman, Benjamin. 2019. "Imagining Future Worlds alongside Young Climate Activists: A New Framework for Research." *Fennia* 197 (2): 295–305.

Braun, Virginia, and Victoria Clarke. 2006. "Using Thematic Analysis in Psychology." *Qualitative Research in Psychology* 3 (2): 77–101.

Brennen, Samantha, and Robert Noggle. 2000. "Rawls's Neglected Childhood: Reflections on the Original Position, Stability and the Child's Sense of Justice." In *The Idea of a Political Liberalism: Essays on Rawls*, edited by Victoria Davion and Clark Wolf, 46–82. Lanham, MD: Rowman and Littlefield.

Bronfenbrenner, Urie. 1979. *The Ecology of Human Development: Experiments by Nature and Design*. Cambridge, MA: Harvard University Press.

Bulling, Denise, Lyn Carson, Mark DeKraai, Alexis Garcia, and Harri Raisio. 2013. *Deliberation Models Featuring Youth Participation*. Publication of the University of Nebraska Public Policy Center 136.

Burbules, Nicolas. 2000. "The Limits of Dialogue as a Critical Pedagogy." In *Revolutionary Pedagogies: Cultural Politics, Instituting Education and the Discourse of Theory*, edited by Trifonas Peter Pericles, 251–73. New York: RoutledgeFalmer.

Burgh, Gilbert, and Simone Thornton. 2022. *Teaching Democracy in an Age of Uncertainty: Place-Responsive Learning.* London: Routledge.

Cairns, Ed. 1996. *Children and Political Violence.* Oxford, UK: Blackwell.

Callan, Eamonn. 1997. *Creating Citizens: Political Education and Liberal Democracy.* Oxford: Oxford University Press.

Cameron, Sara. 2000. "The Role of Children as Peace-Makers in Columbia." *Development* 43 (1): 40–45.

Camicia, Steven, and Ryan Knowles. 2021. *Education for Democracy: A Renewed Approach to Civic Inquiries for Social Justice.* Charlotte, NC: Information Age.

Catanzaro, Michelle, and Philippa Collin. 2021. "Kids Communicating Climate Change: Learning from the Visual Language of the SchoolStrike4Climate Protests." *Educational Review* 75 (1): 9–32.

Chambers, Simone. 2004. "Behind Closed Doors: Publicity, Secrecy, and the Quality of Deliberation." *Journal of Political Philosophy* 12 (4): 389–410.

———. 2009. "Rhetoric and the Public Sphere: Has Deliberative Democracy Abandoned Mass Democracy?" *Political Theory* 37 (3): 323–50.

———. 2018. "The Philosophic Origins of Deliberative Ideals." In *The Oxford Handbook of Deliberative Democracy*, edited by André Bächtiger, John Dryzek, Jane Mansbridge, and Mark Warren, 55–69. Oxford: Oxford University Press.

Chetty, Daren, and Judith Suissa. 2017. " 'No Go Areas': Racism and Discomfort in the Community of Inquiry." In *Routledge International Handbook of Philosophy for Children*, edited by Maughn Gregory, Joanna Haynes, and Karrin Murris, 11–18. Abingdon, UK: Routledge.

Christiano, Thomas. 2001. "Knowledge and Power in the Justification of Democracy." *Australian Journal of Philosophy* 79 (2): 197–215.

Clifford, James. 1986. "Introduction: Partial Truths." In *Writing Culture: The Poetics and Politics of Ethnography*, edited by James Clifford and George Marcus, 1–26. Berkeley: University of California Press.

Clifford, James, and George Marcus. 1986. *Writing Culture: The Poetics and Politics of Ethnography.* Berkeley: University of California Press.

Cohen, Joshua. 1989. "Deliberation and Democratic Legitimacy." In *The Good Polity: Normative Analysis of the State*, edited by Alan Mamlin and Philip Pettit, 17–34. Oxford, UK: Blackwell.

Çolak, Erdem. 2014. "Art in Street: The Significant Role of Using the Art, Literature, and Humour in the Gezi Resistance." *International Journal of Arts and Sciences* 7 (4): 463–76.

Cole, Michael. 2017. "Putting Culture in the Middle." In *Introduction to Vygotsky*, 3rd ed., edited by Harry Daniels, 73–99. London: Routledge.

Cole, Michael, and James Wertsch. 1996. "Beyond the Individual-Social Antinomy in Discussions of Piaget and Vygotsky." *Human development* 39 (5): 250–56.

Corsaro, William, and Luisa Molinari. 2008. "Entering and Observing in Children's Worlds: A Reflection on a Longitudinal Ethnography of Early Education in Italy." In *Research with Children: Perspective and Practices*, 2nd ed., edited by Pia Christensen and Allison James, 239–59. New York: Routledge.

Crittenden, Jack. 2002. *Democracy's Midwife: An Education in Deliberation*. Lanham, MD: Lexington Books.

Crocco, Margaret, Avner Segall, Anne Halvorsen, and Rebecca Jacobsen. 2018. "Deliberating Public Policy Issues with Adolescents: Classroom Dynamics and Sociocultural Considerations." *Democracy and Education* 26 (1): 1–10.

Curato, Nicole. 2019. *Democracy in a Time of Misery: From Spectacular Tragedy to Deliberative Action*. Oxford: Oxford University Press.

Curato, Nicole, John Dryzek, Selen Ercan, Carolyn Hendriks, and Simon Niemeyer. 2017. "Twelve Key Findings in Deliberative Democracy Research." *Daedalus* 146 (3): 28–38.

Davis, Ian, George Gray, and Paul Stephens. 1998. "Education for Citizenship: A Case Study of 'Democracy Day' at a Comprehensive School." *Educational Review* 50 (1): 15–27.

Davis, John, Nick Watson, and Sarah Cunningham-Burley. 2008. "Disabled Children, Ethnography and Unspoken Understandings: The Collaborative Construction of Diverse Identities." In *Research with Children: Perspective and Practices*, 2nd ed., edited by Pia Christensen and Allison James, 220–38. New York: Routledge.

della Porta, Donatella, and Dieter Rucht. 2013a. *Meeting Democracy: Power and Deliberation in Global Justice Movements*. Cambridge: Cambridge University Press.

———. 2013b. "Power and Democracy in Social Movements: An introduction." In *Meeting Democracy: Power and Deliberation in Global Justice Movements*, edited by Donatella della Porta and Dieter Rucht, 1–22. Cambridge: Cambridge University Press.

Dewey, John. (1915) 2001. *The School and Society and The Child and the Curriculum*. Mineola, NY: Dover.

———. (1916) 2004. *Democracy and Education: An Introduction to the Philosophy of Education*. Garden City, NY: Dover.

———. 1927. *The Public and its Problems: An Essay in Political Inquiry*. University Park: Pennsylvania State University Press.

———. 1938. *Logic: The Theory of Inquiry*. New York: Holt.

Dewey, John, and Evelyn Dewey. (1915) 2002. *Schools of To-morrow*. Bristol, UK: Thoemmes.

Dillard, Kara. 2013. "Envisioning the Role of Facilitation in Public Deliberation." *Journal of Applied Communication Research* 41 (3): 217–35.

Dobson, Andrew. 2014. *Listening for Democracy: Recognition, Representation, Reconciliation.* Oxford: Oxford University Press.

Donaldson, Sue, and Will Kymlicka. 2016. "Rethinking Membership and Participation in an Inclusive Democracy: Cognitive Disability, Children and Animals." In *Disability and Political Theory*, edited by Barbara Arneil and Nancy Hirschmann, 168–97. Cambridge: Cambridge University Press.

Dryzek, John. 2000. *Deliberative Democracy and Beyond: Liberals, Critics, Contestations.* Oxford: Oxford University Press.

———. 2005. *The Politics of the Earth: Environmental Discourses.* 2nd ed. Oxford: Oxford University Press.

———. 2010. *Foundations and Frontiers of Deliberative Governance.* Oxford: Oxford University Press.

Dryzek, John, and Jonathan Pickering. 2018. *The Politics of the Anthropocene.* Oxford: Oxford University Press.

Due, Clemence, Damien Riggs, and Martha Augoustinos. 2014. "Research with Children of Migrant and Refugee Backgrounds: A Review of Child-Centred Research Methods." *Child Indicators Research* 7 (1), 209–27.

Dzur, Albert. 2018. *Rebuilding Public Institutions Together: Processionals and Citizens in a Participatory Democracy.* Ithaca, NY: Cornell University Press.

Elstub, Stephen, Selen Ercan, and Ricardo Mendonça. 2016. "The Fourth Generation of Deliberative Democracy." *Critical Policy Studies* 10 (2): 139–51.

Emerson, Robert, Rachel Fretz, and Linda Shaw. 2011. *Writing Ethnographic Fieldnotes.* 2nd ed. Chicago: University of Chicago Press.

Engels-Schwarzpaul, A.-Chr. 2015. "The Ignorant Supervisor: About Common Worlds, Epistemological Modesty and Distributed Knowledge." *Educational Philosophy and Theory* 47 (12): 1250–64.

Engeström, Yrjö. 1999. "Activity Theory and Individual and Social Transformation." In *Perspectives on Activity Theory*, edited by Yrjö Engeström, Reijo Miettinen, and Raija-Leena Punamäki, 19–38. Cambridge: Cambridge University Press.

———. 2008. *From Teams to Knots: Activity-Theoretical Studies of Collaboration and Learning at Work.* Cambridge: Cambridge University Press.

———. 2015. *Learning by Expanding: An Activity-Theoretical Approach to Developmental Research.* 2nd ed. Cambridge: Cambridge University Press.

———. 2016. *Studies in Expansive Learning: Learning What Is Not Yet There.* New York: Cambridge University Press.

Engeström, Yrjö, and Annalisa Sannino. 2017. "Studies of Expansive Learning: Foundations, Findings and Future Challenges. In *Introduction to Vygotsky*, 3rd ed., edited by Harry Daniels, 100–146. London: Routledge.

Englund, Tomas. 2000. "Rethinking Democracy and Education: Toward an Education of Deliberative Citizens." *Journal of Curriculum Studies* 32 (2): 305–13.

———. 2022. The Educated, Deliberative Citizen: Constituents for a Normative Model. *Nordic Journal of Studies in Educational Policy* 8 (2): 149–55.

Ercan, Selen, and Jean-Paul Gagnon. 2014. "The Crisis of Democracy: Which Crisis? Which Democracy?" *Democratic Theory* 1 (2): 1–10.

Ercan, Selen, Carolyn Hendriks, and John Dryzek. 2019. "Public Deliberation in an Era of Communicative Plenty." *Policy and Politics* 47 (1): 19–35.

Ernman, Beata, Malena Ernman, Greta Thunberg, and Svante Thunberg. 2019. *Greta tatta Hitorino Strike* [Scener ur Hjärtat; Scenes from the Heart], translated by Hane Yukari. Tokyo: Umi to Tsuki Sha.

Escobar, Oliver. 2019. "Facilitators: The Micropolitics of Public Participation and Deliberation." In *Handbook of Democratic Innovation and Governance*, edited by Oliver Escobar and Stephen Elstub, 178–95. Northampton, MA: Edward Elgar.

Eveland, William, Jr., Kathryn Coduto Osei Appiah, and Olivia Bullock. 2020. "Listening during Political Conversations: Traits and Situations." *Political Communication* 37 (5): 656–77.

Fishkin, James. 2009. *When the People Speak: Deliberative Democracy and Public Consultation*. Oxford: Oxford University Press.

Fiumara, Gemma Corriadi. 1990. *The Other Side of Language: A Philosophy of Listening*. London: Routledge.

Flanagan, Constance. 2013. *Teenage Citizens: The Political Theories of the Young*. Cambridge, MA: Harvard University Press.

Fraser, Nancy. 1990. "Rethinking the Public Sphere: A Contribution to the Critique of Actually Existing Democracy." *Social Text*, no. 25/26, 56–80.

Freire, Paulo. 1970. *The Pedagogy of the Oppressed*. Translated by Ramos Myra Bergman. New York: Herder and Herder.

———. (1974) 2005. *Education for Critical Consciousness*. New York: Continuum.

Fricker, Miranda. 2007. *Epistemic Injustice: Power and the Ethics of Knowing*. Oxford: Oxford University Press.

Fung, Archon, and Jennifer Shakabatur. 2015. "Viral Engagement: First, Cheap and Broad but Good for Democracy?" In *From Voice to Influence: Understanding Citizenship in a Digital Age*, edited by Danielle Allen and Jennifer Light, 155–77. Chicago: University of Chicago Press.

Gastil, John, and Peter Levine, eds. 2005. *The Deliberative Democracy Handbook: Strategies for Effective Civic Engagement in the Twenty-First Century*. San Francisco: Jossey-Bass.

Gerbaudo, Paolo. 2012. *Tweets and the Streets: Social Media and Contemporary Activism*. London: Pluto.

Gerber, Marlène, André Bächtiger, Susumu Shikano, Simon Reber, and Smuel Rohr. 2016. "Deliberative Abilities and Influence in a Transnational Deliberative Poll (Europolis)." *British Journal of Political Science* 48 (4): 1093–1118.

Goffman, Erving. 1959. *The Presentation of Self in Everyday Life*. Garden City, NY: Doubleday Anchor.

Goldman, Linda. 2022. *Climate Change and Youth: Turning Grief and Anxiety into Activism*. New York: Routledge.

Goodin, Robert. 2003. *Reflective Democracy*. Oxford: Oxford University Press.

———. 2018. "If Deliberation Is Everything, Maybe It's Nothing." In *The Oxford Handbook of Deliberative Democracy*, edited by André Bächtiger, John Dryzek, Jane Mansbridge, and Mark Warren, 883–99. Oxford: Oxford University Press.

Grant-Smith, Deanna, and Peter Edwards. 2011. "It Takes More than Good Intentions: Institutional and Attitudinal Impediments to Engaging Young People in Participatory Planning." *Journal of Public Deliberation* 7 (1): 1–19.

Gregory, Maughn, Joanna Haynes, and Karin Murris, eds. 2016. *The Routledge International Handbook of Philosophy for Children*. Abingdon, UK: Routledge.

Griffin, Martyn. 2011. "Developing Deliberative Minds: Piaget, Vygotsky, and the Deliberative Democratic Citizen." *Journal of Public Deliberation* 7 (1): 1–28.

Gutmann, Amy. 1999. *Democratic Education*. Princeton, NJ: Princeton University Press.

Gutmann, Amy, and Dennis Thompson. 1996. *Democracy and Disagreement*. Cambridge, MA: Belknap Press of Harvard University Press.

———. 2004. *Why Deliberative Democracy?* Princeton, NJ: Princeton University Press.

———. 2018. "Reflections on Deliberative Democracy: When Theory Meets Practice." In *The Oxford Handbook of Deliberative Democracy*, edited by André Bächtiger, John Dryzek, Jane Mansbridge, and Mark Warren, 900–912. Oxford: Oxford University Press.

Habermas, Jürgen. 1996. *Between Facts and Norms: Contradictions to a Discourse Theory of Law and Democracy*. Translated by William Rehg. Cambridge, MA: MIT Press.

———. 2018. "Interview with Jürgen Habermas." In *The Oxford Handbook of Deliberative Democracy*, edited by André Bächtiger, John Dryzek, Jane Mansbridge, and Mark Warren, 872–81. Oxford: Oxford University Press.

Hart, Roger. 1997. *Children's Participation*. New York: UNICEF.

Hartung, Catherine. 2017a. "Civics and Citizenship Education: Defender or Divider of Democracy?" In *Young People, Citizenship and Political Participation: Combating Civic Deficit?*, edited by Mark Chou, Jean-Paul Gagnon, Catherine Hartung, and Lesley Pruitt, 55–75. London: Rowman and Littlefield.

———. 2017b. *Conditional Citizens: Rethinking Children and Young People's Participation*. Singapore: Springer.

Haug, Christoph. 2013. "Organizing Spaces: Meeting Arenas as a Social Movement Infrastructure between Organization, Network and Institution." *Organization Studies* 34 (5–6): 705–32.

Haug, Christoph, and Dieter Rucht. 2013. "Structurelessness: An Evil or an Asset? A Case Study." In *Meeting Democracy: Power and Deliberation in Global*

Justice Movements, edited by Donatella della Porta and Dieter Rucht, 179–213. Cambridge: Cambridge University Press.

Haugestad, Christian, Anja Duun Skauge, Jonas Kunst, and Séamus Power. 2021. "Why Do Youth Participate in Climate Activism? A Mixed-Methods Investigation of the #FridaysForFuture Climate Protests." *Journal of Environmental Psychology* 76:101647.

Hauver, Jennifer. 2019. *Young People's Civic Mindedness: Democratic Living and Learning in an Unequal World.* New York: Routledge.

Hayes, Nóirín, Leah O'Toole, and Ann Marie Halpenny. 2017. *Introducing Bronfenbrenner: A Guide for Practitioners and Students in Early Years Education.* London: Routledge.

Hayward, Bronwyn. 2012. *Children, Citizenship and Environment: Nurturing a Democratic Imagination in a Changing World.* New York: Routledge.

———. 2021. *Children, Citizenship and Environment: Nurturing a Democratic Imagination in a Changing World.* #SchoolStrike ed. Abingdon, UK: Routledge.

Hendriks, Carolyn. 2005. "Lay Citizen Deliberations: Consensus Conferences and Planning Cells." In *The Deliberative Democracy Handbook: Strategies for Effective Civic Engagement in the Twenty-First Century*, edited by John Gastil and Peter Levine, 80–110. San Francisco: Jossey-Bass.

———. 2016. "Coupling Citizens and Elites in Deliberative Systems: The Role of Institutional Design." *European Journal of Political Research* 55 (1): 43–60.

Hendriks, Carolyn, Selen Ercan, and John Boswell. 2020. *Mending Democracy: Democratic Repair in Disconnected Times.* Oxford: Oxford University Press.

Hendriks, Carolyn, Selen Ercan, and Sonya Duss. 2019. "Listening in Polarised Controversies: A Study of Listening Practices in the Public Sphere." *Policy Sciences* 52:137–51.

Herzog, Lisa, and Bernardo Zacka. 2017. "Fieldwork in Political Theory: Five Arguments for an Ethnographic Sensibility." *British Journal of Political Science* 49: 753–84.

Hess, Diana. 2009. *Controversy in the Classroom: The Democratic Power of Discussion.* New York: Routledge.

Hess, Diana, and Paula McAvoy. 2015. *The Political Classroom: Evidence and Ethics in Democratic Education.* New York: Routledge.

Hill, Malcom. 2005. "Ethical Considerations in Researching Children's Experiences." In *Researching Children's Experience: Approaches and Methods*, edited by Shelia Greene and Diane Hogan, 61–86. London: Sage.

Hogan, Michael, Jessica Kurr, Michael Bergmaier, and Jeremy Johnson. 2017. *Speech and Debate as Civic Education.* University Park: Pennsylvania State University Press.

Holdo, Markus. 2020. "Meta-deliberation: Everyday Acts of Critical Reflection in Deliberative Systems." *Politics* 40 (1): 106–19.

Holmberg, Arita, and Aida Alvinius. 2020. "Children's Protest in Relation to the Climate Emergency: A Qualitative Study on a New Form of Resistance Promoting Political and Social Change." *Childhood* 27 (1): 78–92.
Holzman, Lois. 2009. *Vygotsky at Work and Play*. Abingdon, UK: Routledge.
hooks, bell. 1994. *Teaching to Transgress: Education as the Practice of Freedom*. New York: Routledge.
Hookway, Christopher. 2010. "Some Varieties of Epistemic Injustice: Reflections on Fricker." *Episteme* 7 (2): 151–63.
Hughes, Sherick. 2007. "Toward a Critical Race Pedagogy of Hope: A Rejoinder to Brian Schultz." *Journal of Educational Controversy* 2 (1): 1–7.
Ingold, Tim. 2018. *Anthropology: Why It Matters*. Cambridge, UK: Polity.
Invernizzi, Antonella, and Jane Williams, eds. 2008. *Children and Citizenship*. London: Sage.
Jacobs, Lawrence, Fay Lomax Cook, and Michael Delli Carpini. 2009. *Talking Together: Public Deliberation and Political Participation in America*. Chicago: University of Chicago Press.
Jacquet, Vincent. 2017. "Explaining Non-participation in Deliberative Mini-publics." *European Journal of Political Research* 56 (3): 640–59.
Jans, Marc. 2004. "Children as Citizens: Toward a Contemporary Notion of Child Participation." *Childhood* 11 (1): 27–44.
Journell, Wayne. 2017. *Teaching Politics in Secondary Education: Engaging with Contentious Issues*. Albany: State University of New York Press.
Jungkuntz, Vincent. 2012. "The Promise of Democratic Silence." *New Political Science* 34 (2): 127–50.
Kanra, Bora. 2012. "Binary Deliberation: The Role of Social Learning in Divided Societies." *Journal of Public Deliberation* 8 (1): 1–24.
Karpowitz, Christopher, and Tali Mendelberg. 2014. *The Silent Sex: Gender, Deliberation and Institutions*. Princeton, NJ: Princeton University Press.
Kettunen, Marika. 2020. "We Need to Make Our Voices Heard: Claiming Space for Young People's Everyday Environmental Politics in Northern Finland." *NGP Yearbook* 2020:32–48.
King, Gary, Robert Keohane, and Sidney Verba. 1994. *Designing Social Inquiry: Scientific Inference in Qualitative Research*. Princeton, NJ: Princeton University Press.
Kittay, Eva. 1999. *Love's Labour: Essays on Women, Equality, and Dependency*. New York: Routledge.
Kjørholt, Anne. 2007. "Childhood as a Symbolic Space: Searching for Authentic Voices in the Era of Globalisation." *Children's Geographies* 5 (1/2): 29–42.
Kohan, Walter, Marina Santi, and Jason Wozniak. 2017. "Philosophy for Teachers: Between Ignorance, Invention, and Improvisation." In *Routledge International Handbook of Philosophy for Children*, edited by Maughn Gregory, Joanna Haynes, and Karrin Murris, 253–59. Abingdon, UK: Routledge.

Kohlberg, Laurence. 1984. *The Psychology of Moral Development: The Nature and Validity of Moral Stages*. San Francisco: Harper and Row.

Kotzee, Ben. 2017. "Education and Epistemic Injustice." In *Routledge Handbook of Epistemic Injustice*, edited by Ian James Kidd, José Medina, and Gaile Pohlhaus, Jr., 324–35. London: Routledge.

Krause, Sharon. 2008. *Civil Passions: Moral Sentiment and Democratic Deliberation*. Princeton, NJ: Princeton University Press.

Kuyper, Jonathan. 2017. "The Instrumental Value of Deliberative Democracy, or Do We Have Good Reason to Be Deliberative Democrats?" *Journal of Public Deliberation* 14 (1): 1–35.

Kymlicka, Will. 2002. *Contemporary Political Philosophy: An Introduction*. 2nd ed. Oxford: Oxford University Press.

Laguarta, Ramírez José. 2020. "A More Colorful Picture of My Own Vision: Expansive Learning in Puerto Rico's Student Anti-austerity Movement." *Social Movement Studies* 19 (3): 325–41.

Landemore, Hélène. 2013. *Democratic Reason: Politics, Collective Intelligence, and the Rule of the Many*. Princeton, NJ: Princeton University Press.

———. 2017. "Beyond the Fact of Disagreement? The Epistemic Turn in Deliberative Democracy." *Social Epistemology* 31 (3): 227–95.

Landwehr, Claudia. 2015. "Democratic Meta-deliberation: Toward Reflective Institutional Design." *Political Studies* 63 (1): 38–54.

Lee, Francis. 2015. "Social Movement as Civic Education: Communication Activities and Understanding of Civil Disobedience in the Umbrella Movement." *Chinese Journal of Communication* 8 (4): 393–411.

Lipari, Lisbeth. 2014. *Listening, Thinking, Being: Toward an Ethics of Attunement*. University Park: Pennsylvania State University Press.

Lipman, Matthew. 2003. *Thinking in Education*. 2nd ed. New York: Cambridge University Press.

Longo, Matthew, and Bernardo Zacka. 2019. "Political Theory in an Ethnographic Key." *American Political Science Review* 113 (4): 1066–70.

Lourenço, Orlando. 2012. "Piaget and Vygotsky: Many Resemblances, and a Crucial Difference." *New Ideas in Psychology* 30 (3): 281–95.

Luskin, Robert, James Fishkin, Neil Malhotra, and Alice Siu. 2007. *Deliberation in the Schools: A Way of Enhancing Civic Engagement?* Paper presented at the Biennial General Conference of the European Consortium for Political Research, Pisa.

Lyons, Benjamin. 2017. "From Code to Discourse: Social Media and Linkage Mechanisms in Deliberative Systems." *Journal of Public Deliberation* 13 (1): 1–35.

Madden, Raymond. 2010. *Being Ethnographic: A Guide to the Theory and Practice of Ethnography*. London: Sage.

Maia, Rousiley C. M., and Gabriella Huber. 2020. "The Emotional Dimensions of Reason-Giving in Deliberative Forums." *Policy Sciences* 53:33–59.

Mansbridge, Jane. 1999. "Everyday Talk in the Deliberative System." In *Deliberative Politics: Essays on Democracy and Disagreement*, edited by Stephen Macedo, 211–39. New York: Oxford University Press.

———. 2007. "Deliberative Democracy or Democratic Deliberation?" In *Deliberation, Participation and Democracy: Can the People Govern?*, edited by Shawn Rosenberg, 251–271. London: Palgrave Macmillan.

Mansbridge, Jane, James Bohman, Simone Chambers, Thomas Christiano, Archon Fung, John Parkinson, Dennis Thompson, and Mark Warren. 2012. "A Systemic Approach to Deliberative Democracy." In *Deliberative Systems: Deliberative Democracy at the Large Scale*, edited by John Parkinson and Jane Mansbridge, 1–26. Cambridge: Cambridge University Press.

Mansbridge, Jane, James Bohman, Simone Chambers, David Estlund, Andreas Føllesdal, Archon Fung, Cristina Lafont, Bernard Manin, and José Luis Martí. 2010. "The Place of Self-interest and the Role of Power in Deliberative Democracy." *Journal of Political Philosophy* 18 (1): 64–100.

Martí, Eduard. 2013. "Mechanisms of Internalisation of Knowledge in Piaget's and Vygotsky's Theories." In *Piaget-Vygotsky: The Social Genesis of Thought*, edited by Anastasia Typhon and Jacques Vonèche, 57–84. East Sussex, UK: Psychology Press.

Martiskainen, Mari, Stephen Axon, Benjamin Sovacool, Siddharth Sareen, Dylan Furszyfer Del Rio, and Kayleigh Axon. 2020. "Contextualizing Climate Justice Activism: Knowledge, Emotions, Motivations, and Actions among Climate Strikers in Six Cities." *Global Environmental Change* 65:1–18.

Mattheis, Nikolas. 2020. "Unruly Kids? Conceptualizing and Defending Youth Disobedience." *European Journal of Political Theory* 21 (3): 466–90.

Matusov, Eugene, and Renee Hayes. 2000. "Sociocultural Critique of Piaget and Vygotsky." *New Ideas in Psychology* 18 (2–3): 215–39.

McAvoy, Paula, and Diana Hess. 2013. "Classroom Deliberation in an Era of Political Polarization." *Curriculum Inquiry* 43 (1): 14–47.

Mears, Ashley. 2020. *Very Important People: Status and Beauty in the Global Party Circuit*. Princeton, NJ: Princeton University Press.

Medearis, John. 2005. "Social Movements and Deliberative Democratic Theory." *British Journal of Political Science* 35 (1): 53–75.

Mehltretter Drury, Sara, Rebecca Kuehl, and Jenn Anderson. 2017. "Deliberation as Civic Education: Incorporating Public Deliberation into the Communication Studies Curriculum." In *Speech and Debate as Civic Education*, edited by Michael Hogan, Jessica Kurr, Michael Bergmaier, and Jeremy Johnson, 191–204. University Park: Pennsylvania State University Press.

Melucci, Alberto. 1989. *Nomads of the Present: Social Movements and Individual Needs in Contemporary Society*. Philadelphia: Temple University Press.

Molnar-Main, Stacie. 2017. *Deliberation in the Classroom: Fostering Critical Thinking, Community and Citizenship in Schools*. Dayton, OH: Kettering Foundation Press.

Morrell, Michael. 2010. *Empathy and Democracy: Feeling, Thinking and Deliberation*. University Park: Pennsylvania State University Press.

———. 2018. "Listening and Deliberation." In *The Oxford Handbook of Deliberative Democracy*, edited by André Bächtiger, John Dryzek, Jane Mansbridge, and Mark Warren, 237–50. Oxford: Oxford University Press.

Moshman, David. 2020. *Reasoning, Argumentation, and Deliberative Democracy*. New York: Routledge.

Mouffe, Chantal. 2000. *The Democratic Paradox*. London: Verso.

Murris, Karin. 2013. "The Epistemic Challenge of Hearing Child's Voice." *Studies in Philosophy and Education* 32 (3): 245–59.

Mutz, Diana. 2008. "Is Deliberative Democracy a Falsifiable Theory?" *Annual Review of Political Science* 11:521–38.

Navne, Daniel Emdal, and Morten Skovdal. 2021. "Small Steps and Small Wins in Young People's Everyday Climate Crisis Activism." *Children's Geographies* 19 (3): 309–16.

Neas, Sally, Ann Ward, and Benjamin Bowman. 2022. "Young People's Climate Activism: A Review of the Literature." *Frontiers in Political Science* 4:1–13.

Newman, Fred, and Lois Holzman. 2014. *Lev Vygotsky: Revolutionary Scientist*. Classic ed. London: Routledge.

Niemeyer, Simion, and John Dryzek. 2007. "The Ends of Deliberation: Meta-consensus and Intersubjective Rationality as Ideal Outcomes." *Swiss Political Science Review* 13 (4): 497–526.

Nishiyama, Kei. 2017. "Deliberators, not Future Citizens: Children in Democracy." *Journal of Public Deliberation* 13 (1): 1–24.

———. 2018. "Using the Community of Inquiry for Interviewing Children: Theory and Practice." *International Journal of Social Research Methodology* 21 (5): 553–64.

———. 2019. "Enabling Children's Deliberation in Deliberative Systems: Schools as a Mediating Space." *Journal of Youth Studies* 22 (4): 437–48.

———. 2020. "Between Protection and Participation: Rethinking Children's Rights to Participate in Protest on Streets, Online Space, and Schools." *Journal of Human Rights* 19 (4): 501–17.

———. 2021. "Democratic Education in the Fourth Generation of Deliberative Democracy." *Theory and Research in Education* 19 (2): 109–26.

———. 2023. "Deliberation in Citizens' Assemblies with Children." In *De Gruyter Handbook of Citizens' Assemblies*, edited by Min Reuchamps, Julien Vrydagh, and Yanina Welp, 169–81. Berlin: De Gruyter.

Nishiyama, Kei, Wendy Russell, Pierrick Chalaye, and Tom Greenwell. 2023. "Deliberative Facilitation in the Classroom: The Interplay of Facilitative Technique and Design to Make Space for Democracy." *Democracy and Education* 31 (1): 1–11.

Noddings, Nel. 2013. *Education and Democracy in the 21st Century*. New York: Teachers College Press.

Nussbaum, Martha. 2012. *Not for Profit*. Princeton, NJ: Princeton University Press.

OECD. 2020. *Innovative Citizen Participation and New Democratic Institutions: Catching the Deliberative Wave*. Paris: OECD. https://www.oecd.org/gov/innovative-citizen-participation-and-new-democratic-institutions-339306 da-en.htm.

O'Flynn, Ian. 2021. *Deliberative Democracy*. Cambridge, UK: Polity.

Owen, David, and Graham Smith. 2015. "Survey Article: Deliberation, Democracy, and the Systemic Turn." *Journal of Political Philosophy* 23 (2): 213–34.

Pachirat, Timothy. 2009. "The Political in Political Ethnography: Dispatches from the Kill Floor." In *Political Ethnography: What Immersion Contributes to the Study of Power*, edited by Edward Schatz, 143–61. Chicago: University of Chicago Press.

Parker, Walter. 2010. "Listening to Strangers: Classroom Discussion in Democratic Education." *Teachers College Record* 112 (11): 2815–32.

Parry, Lucy. 2017. "Don't Put All Your Speech-Acts in One Basket: Situating Animal Activism in the Deliberative System." *Environmental Values* 26 (4): 437–55.

Pasek, Josh, Lauren Feldman, Daniel Romer, and Kathleen Jamieson. 2008. "Schools as Incubators of Democratic Participation: Building Long-Term Efficacy with Civic Education." *Applied Development Science* 12 (1): 26–37.

Pateman, Carole. 2012. "Participatory Democracy Revisited." *Perspective on Politics* 19 (1): 7–19.

Percy-Smith, Berry, and Nigel Thomas, eds. 2010. *A Handbook of Children and Young People's Participation: Perspective from Theory and Practice*. Abingdon, UK: Routledge.

Piaget, Jean. 1952. *The Origins of Intelligence in Children*. New York: International Universities Press.

———. 1962. "The Stages of the Intellectual Development of the Child." *Bulletin of the Menninger Clinic* 26 (3): 120–28.

Piaget, Jean, and Bärbel Inhelder. 1969. *The Psychology of the Child*. New York: Basic Books.

Polletta, Francesca. 2002. *Freedom Is an Endless Meeting: Democracy in American Social Movements*. Chicago: University of Chicago Press.

Pontes, Ana, Matt Henn, and Mark Griffiths. 2019. "Youth Political (Dis)engagement and the Need for Citizenship Education: Encouraging Young People's Civic and Political Participation through the Curriculum." *Education, Citizenship and Social Justice* 14 (1): 3–21.

Posey, Kamili. 2021. *Centering Epistemic Injustice: Epistemic Labor, Willful Ignorance and Knowing across Hermeneutical Divides*. Lanham, MD: Lexington Books.

Pratt, Mary Louise. 1986. "Fieldwork in Common Places." In *Writing Culture: The Poetics and Politics of Ethnography*, edited by James Clifford and George Marcus, 27–50. Berkeley: University of California Press.

Prout, Alan, and Allison James. 2015. "A New Paradigm for the Sociology of Childhood? Provenance, Promise, and Problems." In *Constructing and Reconstructing Childhood: Contemporary Issues in the Sociological Study of Childhood*, 3rd ed., edited by Allison James and Alan Prout, 6–28. Abingdon, UK: Routledge.

Punch, Samantha. 2002. "Research with Children: The Same or Different from Research with Adults?" *Childhood* 9 (3): 321–41.

Rancière, Jacques. 1991. *The Ignorant Schoolmaster: Five Lessons in Intellectual Emancipation*. Translated by Kristin Ross. Stanford, CA: Stanford University Press.

———. 2010. "On Ignorant Schoolmasters." In *Jacques Rancière: Education, Truth, Emancipation*, edited by Charles Bingham and Gert Biesta, 1–24. London: Continuum.

Rawls, John. 2001. *Justice as Fairness: A Restatement*. Cambridge, MA: Belknap Press of Harvard University Press.

Reed, Edward. 1996. *The Necessity of Experience*. New Haven, CT: Yale University Press.

Reimer, Joseph, Diana Pritchard Paolitto, and Richard Hersh.1990. *Promoting Moral Growth: From Piaget to Kohlberg*. 2nd ed. Prospect Heights, IL: Waveland.

Reuchamps, Min, Julien Vrydagh, and Yanina Welp, eds. 2023. *De Gruyter Handbook of Citizens' Assemblies*. Berlin: De Gruyter.

Rietmulder, Jim. 2019. *When Kids Rule the School: The Power and Promise of Democratic Education*. Gabriola Island, BC: New Society.

Rodgers, Diane. 2005. "Children as Social Movement Participants." *Sociological Studies of Children and Youth* 11:239–59.

Rollo, Tobby. 2017. "Everyday Deeds: Enactive Protest, Exit and Silence in Deliberative Systems." *Political Theory* 45 (5): 587–609.

Rosenberg, Shawn. 2014. "Citizen Competence and the Psychology of Deliberation." In *Deliberative Democracy: Issues and Cases*, edited by Stephen Elstub and Peter McLaverty, 98–117. Edinburgh: Edinburgh University Press.

Rostbøll, Christian. 2011. "Freedom of Expression, Deliberation, Autonomy, and Respect." *European Journal of Political Theory* 10 (1): 5–21.

Sabherwal, Anandita, Matthew Ballew, Sander van der Linden, Abel Gustafson, Matthew Goldberg, Edward Maibach, John Kotcher, Janet K. Swim, Seth A. Rosenthal, and Anthony Leiserowitz. 2021. "The Greta Thunberg Effect: Familiarity with Greta Thunberg Predicts Intentions to Engage in Climate Activism in the United States." *Journal of Applied Social Psychology* 51 (4): 321–33.

Samuelsson, Martin. 2016. "Education for Deliberative Democracy: A Typology of Classroom Discussions." *Democracy and Education* 24 (1): 1–9.

Sass, Jensen, and John Dryzek. 2014. "Deliberative Cultures." *Political Theory* 42 (1): 3–25.

Schaffer, Timothy, Nicholas Longo, Idit Manosevitch, and Maxine Thomas. 2017. *Deliberative Pedagogy: Teaching and Learning for Democratic Engagement*. East Lansing: Michigan State University Press.

Schultz, Brian. 2007. "'Feelin' What They Feelin'': Democracy and Curriculum in Cabrini Green." In *Democratic Schools: Lessons in Powerful Education*, 2nd ed., edited by Michael Apple and James Beane, 62–82. Portsmouth, NH: Heinemann.

———. 2018. *Spectacular Things Happen Along the Way: Lessons from an Urban Classroom*. 2nd ed. New York: Teachers College Press.

Scudder, Mary. 2020. *Beyond Empathy and Inclusion: The Challenge of Listening in Democratic Deliberation*. New York: Oxford University Press.

———. 2021. "Measuring Democratic Listening: A Listening Quality Index." *Political Research Quarterly* 75 (1): 175–87.

———. 2022. "Listening Quality Index." In *Research Methods in Deliberative Democracy*, edited by Selen Ercan, Hans Asenbaum, Nicole Curato, and Ricardo Mendonça, 115–28. Oxford: Oxford University Press.

Senge, Peter. 2012. *Schools That Learn: A Fifth Discipline Fieldbook for Educators, Parents and Everyone Who Cares about Education*. Rev. ed. New York: Crown Business.

Sintomer, Yves. 2020. "A Child Drawing Lots: The 'Pathos Formula' of Political Sortition?" In *Sortition and Democracy: History, Tools, Theories*, edited by Liliane Lopez-Rabatel and Yves Sintomer, 467–503. Exeter, UK: Imprint Academic.

Smith, William. 2016. "The Boundaries of a Deliberative System: The Case of Disruptive Protest." *Critical Policy Studies* 10 (2): 152–70.

Snow, David, Burke Rochford, Jr., Steven Worden, and Robert Benford. 1986. "Frame Alignment Processes, Micromobilization, and Movement Participation." *American Sociological Review* 51 (4): 464–81.

Sorial, Sarah, and Andrew Peterson. 2019. "Australian Schools as Deliberative Spaces: Framing the Goal of Active and Informed Citizenship." *Curriculum Journal* 30 (1): 24–39.

Steiner, Jürg. 2012. *The Foundations of Deliberative Democracy: Empirical Research and Normative Implications*. Cambridge: Cambridge University Press.

Steiner, Jürg, and Maria Clara Jaramillo. 2019. "How to Arrive at Peace in Deeply Divided Societies? Using Deliberation to Refine Consociational Theory." *Journal of Public Deliberation* 15 (3): 1–18.

Stetsenko, Anna. 2017. "Teaching-Learning and Development as Activist Projects of Historical Becoming: Expanding Vygotsky's Approach to Pedagogy." In

Introduction to Vygotsky, 3rd ed., edited by Harry Daniels, 275–86. London: Routledge.

Stevenson, Hayley, and John Dryzek. 2014. *Democratising Global Climate Governance*. Cambridge: Cambridge University Press.

Stitzlein, Sarah. 2014. *Teaching for Dissent: Citizenship Education and Political Activism*. Boulder, CO: Paradigm.

Strandberg, Kim, Staffan Himmelroos, and Kimmo Grönlund. 2019. "Do Discussions in Like-Minded Groups Necessarily Lead to More Extreme Opinions? Deliberative Democracy and Group Polarization." *International Political Science Review* 40 (1): 41–57.

Stringer, Ernest. 2014. *Action Research*. 4th ed. Sage.

Sunstein, Cass. 2000. "Deliberative Trouble? Why Groups Go to Extremes." *Yale Law Journal* 110:71–119.

Tamura, Tetsuki. 2014. "Rethinking Grassroots Participation in Nested Deliberative Systems." *Japanese Political Science Review* 2:63–87.

Tanasoca, Ana. 2020. *Deliberation Naturalized: Improving Real Existing Deliberative Democracy*. Oxford: Oxford University Press.

Tarrow, Sidney. 1998. *Power in Movement: Social Movement and Contentious Politics*. 2nd ed. Cambridge: Cambridge University Press.

Thomas, Mary. 2009. "The Identity Politics of School Life: Territoriality and the Racial Subjectivity of Teen Girls in LA." *Children's Geographies* 7 (1): 7–19.

Thomas, Nancy. 2010. Editor's notes. In *Educating for Deliberative Democracy*, edited by Nancy Thomas, 1–9. San Francisco: Jossey-Bass.

Thompson, Dennis. 2008. "Deliberative Democratic Theory and Empirical Political Science." *Annual Review of Political Science* 11:497–520.

Thornberg, Robert, and Helene Elvstrand. 2012. "Children's Experiences of Democracy, Participation, and Trust in School." *International Journal of Educational Research* 53:44–54.

UNICEF. 1989. United Nations Convention on the Rights of the Child. https:// www.unicef.org.uk/what-we-do/un-convention-child-rights/.

Vygotsky, Lev. 1978. *Mind in Society: The Development of Higher Psychological Process*. Cambridge, MA: Harvard University Press.

———. 2006. *Vygotsky Collection: Development and Education of Children with Disabilities*. Translated by Shibata Yoshimatsu and Miyasaka Yuko. Tokyo: Shindokusho-Sha.

———. 2012. *Thought and Language*. Rev. and expanded ed. Edited and translated by Eugenia Hanfmann, Gertrude Vakar, and Alex Kozulin. Cambridge, MA: MIT Press.

Wahlström, Mattias, Kocyba Piotr, Michiel De Vydt, and Joost de Moor. 2019. *Protest for a Future: Comparison, Mobilisation, and Motives of the Participants in Fridays for Future Climate Protests on 15 March 2019 in 13 European Cities*. ResearchGate.

Wall, John. 2019. "From Childhood Studies to Childism: Reconstructing the Scholarly and Social Imaginations." *Children's Geographies* 20 (3): 257–70.

Wolbrecht, Christina. 2005. "Mediating Institution." In *The Politics of Democratic Inclusion*, edited by Christina Wolbrecht and Rodney Hero, 103–7. Philadelphia: Temple University Press.

Young Iris. 1997. "Difference as a Resource for Democratic Communication." In *Deliberative Democracy: Essays on Reason and Politics*, edited by James Bohman and William Rehg, 383–406. Cambridge, MA: MIT Press.

———. 2000. *Inclusion and Democracy.* Oxford: Oxford University Press.

Youniss, James. 2011. "Civic Education: What Schools Can Do to Encourage Civic Identity and Action." *Applied Development Science* 15 (2): 98–103.

Yousafzai, Malala, with Christina Lamb. 2013. *I am Malala: The Girl Who Stood Up for Education and Was Shot by the Taliban.* London: Weidenfeld and Nicolson.

Zorn, Eric. 2004. "Despite School's Closing, Pupils' Battle a Success." *Chicago Tribune*, June 8, 2004.

Index

accountability, 46–47
action research, 107–108, 113, 131
activist meeting, 213, 247n4
Arendt, Hannah, 182
Aristotle, 1, 119
Ari to Pla, 178–180, 184–185, 189
authenticity, 53, 236–237n2; authentic
communication, 27

Bächtiger, André, 27, 63, 96
banking concept of education,
146–147. *See also* Freire Paulo
Barvosa, Edwina, 32
Bell, Daniel, 54
Bickford, Susan, 119, 122–123
Biesta, Gert, 105
Bohman, James, 25, 65, 95, 106
Bowman, Benjamin, 248–249n12
Bronfenbrenner, Urie, 70, 74, 83–84,
240n9
Byrd Community Academy, 170–173,
175–176, 183–184, 187–188, 245n3,
245n4

Chambers, Simone, 95, 237n4
children: as agents of transmission,
34–35, 45–46; as future citizens, 1,
11, 18, 67, 235n1; as deliberators, 5,
36–39, 48, 229; childhood, 38, 59;
definition of, 6–8; in empowered
space, 34, 43–45; in public space,
34, 41–42; in private space, 34, 43
Christiano, Thomas, 29
Clifford, James, 247–248n6
climate: activism, 41, 194–198;
change, 40–41, 191, 202, 218,
248n11; crisis, 42, 191, 216;
governance, 40–42, 46, 218;
justice, 210, 214, 218; march,
204–207; strike, 46; United Nations
Framework Convention on Climate
Change (UNFCCC), 41
Cohen, Joshua, 91, 94
collective transformation, 52, 219, 225
competency, 5–6, 24, 53–55, 62–64,
67–68, 71–72, 184, 224–225, 239n6;
lack of, 38, 67, 224; sociocultural
nature of, 71; comprehensiveness
of, 71–72
connectivity, 183–188, 219, 221,
246n10; horizontal, 183–185;
vertical, 183–185
consensus, 35, 81; rationally
motivated, 4, 35
contextuality, 14, 52, 82, 225
contradiction, 78–79, 81–83
COVID-19, 47, 191, 198, 200, 202,
204, 215–216, 218, 248n8

Crittenden, Jack, 61, 64
Curato, Nicole, 28
curriculum, 177–178, 187–188;
  deliberative, 187–188, 236n10,
  242n9

decision-making, 4, 34, 211
deliberation: anti-, 47, 97–98, 100–
  103, 241n4; all-rounder, 14, 63–66;
  naturalized form of, 220–221; non-,
  32–33, 47, 97–98, 99, 103, 237n3.
  See also deliberative democracy
deliberative democracy: deliberative
  turn, 26–28, 223; deliberative wave,
  27; generation of, 29–30, 237n6;
  minipublics, 28–30, 237n4, 239–
  240n6; systemic turn of, 28–31.
  See also deliberation, deliberative
  system
deliberative democratic learning,
  11–17, 52, 84, 217, 225, 236n10
deliberative system, 16, 30,
  37–39, 46–47, 65–68, 167, 175,
  237n6, 242n7; agents of, 31–33;
  consequence of, 35–37; spaces of,
  33–35, systemic critique, 65–68
deliberator model, 37–39, 48, 67
democracy, 8–10; crisis of, 26–27. See
  also deliberative democracy
democratic education, 3–4, 10, 11–17,
  56–57, 80–82, 120, 169, 189,
  224–230, 236n7
democratic school, 166–167; 187–188,
  189; as a mediating space, 174–176,
  186–187, 245–246n7; functions of,
  169–173
development, 7, 11–15, 51–52, 58–60,
  62, 68–71, 73–74, 76, 78, 80, 223–
  224, 236n8, 236n9, 239n1, 239n2,
  239n3, 240n8; developmental stage,
  69; developmental psychology, 6,
  18, 58

Dewey, John, 8–10, 33, 153–155, 168,
  174, 187, 235n6, 245n5
disagreement, 35, 123, 142–143,
  148, 152, 157–159; intentional
  avoidance of, 143, 161; deliberative
  disagreement exercise, 157–159
disruptive expression, 100–103
Dobson, Andrew, 119
Dryzek, John, 32, 41, 46, 106, 218,
  237n3, 241n2, 243n2
Dzur, Albert, 154

education for deliberative democracy,
  11–18, 52, 57, 61, 63, 68, 72–73, 84,
  173, 224
Engeström, Yrjö, 74, 76–78, 80, 105,
  241n12, 246n11
entrepreneur, 32, 186
evolutionism, 59, 61, 67
expansive learning, 74, 241n12
experiment, 9–10

facilitation, 57, 139–140; as task-
  sharing, 153–155; by design, 155,
  157, 160; by technique, 155, 161;
  facilitator, 130, 139–140, 160–161,
  227–228; involved, 146–147;
  passive, 149–151
fieldwork, 167, 177, 226–227, 231–
  234, 246n9; ethnographic, 196–197,
  233, 247n4, 247n5, 247n6
Fishkin, James, 28; Deliberative Poll,
  28, 55, 91, 169, 243n3
formative agent, 32
Freire, Paulo, 146–147, 243n4. See
  also banking concept of education
Fricker, Miranda, 121–122, 144
Fridays for Future (FFF), 39–43,
  45–47, 67; Fridays for Future Japan
  (FFF Japan), 248n8; Fridays for
  Future Kyoto (FFF Kyoto), 192–193,
  197–198, 248n8

Gerber, Marlène, 54–55, 65, 239n6
Goldman, Linda, 195
González, Emma, 32, 99, 219, 237n7
Goodin, Robert, 67, 82
Griffin, Martyn, 58–59, 62–63
Gutmann, Amy, 12, 56, 61, 95–96

Habermas, Jürgen, 94–95, 237n2, 241n1
habit, 10, 14, 105–106, 116, 129–130, 180; deliberative habit, 106–107
Hart, Roger, 2
Haug, Christoph, 213, 219, 247n3
Hess, Diana, 120, 139, 147, 172, 245n2. See also McAvoy Paula
Holdo, Marcus, 93, 107, 242n7
Holzman, Lois, 13, 73, 81, 236n9. See also Newman Fred

immaturity, 1, 7, 11–12, 33, 37, 61, 66, 223–224
inclusiveness, 27–29, 54, 82, 101, 237n6
injustice: epistemic, 121–122, 243n5; testimonial, 121–123, 126, 143–145, 148, 152, 159, 243n5
inquiry, 153–154; community of, 154, 161, 228, 234; social, 235n6; shared, 9, 229

Jungkunz, Vincent, 237n9

Kanra, Bora, 36
Kotzee, Ben, 153, 243n5
Krause, Sharon, 56
Kuyper, Jonathan, 35, 237n5

Landemore, Hélène, 96, 241n3
leadership, 200, 219–222
listening, 117–118, 119–124, 142, 243n1, 243n2; assessment of, 120–124; Listening Quality Index (LQI), 124–129, 137, 244n12; listening quality index (lqi), 130–131, 137
logical argumentation, 98–99
Luskin, Robert, 63, 169

Mansbridge, Jane, 30, 34, 101
March for Our Lives, 33, 47
Mattheis, Nikolas, 2, 8, 38, 47, 238n13
McAvoy, Paula, 120, 139, 147, 172. See also Hess Diana
meaning-making, 15, 52, 73, 76–77, 80, 82–83, 137–138, 161, 221–222, 225–227, 229
Melucci, Alberto, 193
meta-deliberation, 18, 93, 105–107, 116, 129–130, 134, 137, 143, 156, 221–222, 227–228, 242n7; anteroom deliberation, 113–114, 141, 160; meta-deliberative moment, 110–112; meta-deliberative session, 108–110, 148, 156
Molnar-Main, Stacie, 61–62, 245n2
Morrell, Michael, 56, 117
Morrison, Scott, 38, 101–102, 237n8
Moshman, David, 60, 62, 67, 98
Mutz, Diana, 17

Newman, Fred, 73, 236n9. See also Holzman Lois
Noddings, Nel, 189

Occupy Playground, 165–166
O'Flynn, Ian, 54

Piaget, Jean, 6, 58–60, 62–63, 68–69, 239n3, 239n4, 240n8; Piagetian Geist, 58–61, 63, 67, 70, 236n8, 239n4
Parker, Walter, 56
Parkinson, John, 27, 63, 96
Parry, Lucy, 36

Philosophy for Children (P4C), 177–178, 181–183, 249n18; philosophical dialogue, 210–211
Pickering, Jonathan, 32
political socialization, 60
politics: contemporary 27; political democracy, 9–10; talk about, 43, 201, 203
Posey, Kamili, 123–124
power imbalance, 100, 140–141, 147–148, 151–152, 155–157
pragmatism, 9–10, 153–154
protective mechanism, 46–47
Rancière, Jacques, 149–150, 152, 244n2
Rawls, John, 1, 94

reason-giving, 91–92, 93–97, 103–104, 227; anti-deliberative, 98; nondeliberative, 98; the fact of the plurality of, 96, 102
reflection, 12–13, 52–53, 79, 81–82, 106–107, 189, 217; self-, 47, 106, 144, 184, 216
revolutionarity, 11–12, 52, 71, 80–81, 137, 217, 225, 229
rhetoric, 45–46, 95–96, 105, 241n2
Rosenberg, Shawn, 54, 67–68
Rostbøll, Christian, 100–102

Scotland's Climate Assembly, 31
Scudder, Mary, 118, 123–124, 135, 243n7, 224n11, 224n12. See also listening
Senge, Peter, 169, 245n6, 246n10
silence, 99–100, 103, 237n9
social media, 35, 202, 211; hashtag, 46, 202; viral engagement, 238n14
social movement, 193, 196–197; frontstage and backstage of, 215–216, 219, 222, 229, 249–250n19; self-transformation of, 193, 221,

247n3; wings of the stage of, 216, 220, 249–250n19
sociocultural critique, 68–73; socioculturally mediated action, 75; sociocultural theory of development, 71, 83
Socrates, 99, 236n1, 244n2
speech, 44–46; 237n2; hate, 241n4; inner, 69–70
standing (protest), 191–193, 199, 202–203, 209, 212–216, 220
Steiner, Jürg, 55, 63
storytelling, 45, 96, 195
Sunstein, Cass, 54

Tarrow, Sidney, 196, 246n1
teacher, 57, 104, 113–114, 126, 141, 146–148, 150, 155, 186. See also facilitation
The Future Talk (TFT), 181–183
Thompson, Dennis, 56, 61, 93, 95–96
Thunberg, Greta, 32, 40, 43, 45, 96, 194–195; Greta framing, 195–197, 201, 215, 238n16; Greta Thunberg effect, 194–195
tool and result methodology, 73
transmission, 34–35, 45–46, 238n21
truth, 153–154, 241n3; partial, 248n6

United Nations Convention on the Rights of the Child (UNCRC), 2, 7, 34; Article 1, 235n2; Article 12, 205n3
universalism, 62–64, 74, 104

Vygotsky, Lev Semenovich, 15, 58, 69–71, 73–75, 240n7, 240n8; mediation, 74–75; Vygotsky's left-wing, 73, 236n9

Young, Iris, 28, 95, 237n2
Yousafzai, Malala, 46, 240n9

www.ingramcontent.com/pod-product-compliance
Lightning Source LLC
Chambersburg PA
CBHW031412270326
41929CB00010BA/1431